here's one for
you

they were a
jewish feminist
who enjoyed
any diatribe.
go on a target
today for them

for alex
12/1/90 - 3/7/24

DREAMS OF AN INSOMNIAC
JEWISH FEMINIST ESSAYS, SPEECHES AND DIATRIBES

Dreams of an Insomniac

Jewish Feminist Essays, Speeches and Diatribes

IRENA KLEPFISZ

THE EIGHTH MOUNTAIN PRESS
PORTLAND · OREGON · 1990

Copyright © 1977, 1982, 1985, 1986, 1989,1990 by Irena Klepfisz
Introduction Copyright © 1990 by Evelyn Torton Beck
All rights reserved
No part of this book may be reproduced, stored in a retrieval system or transmitted in any form, by any means, including mechanical, electronic, photocopying, recording or otherwise, without prior permission of the publisher.

"Women Without Children/Women Without Families/Women Alone" was first published in *Conditions*. It was reprinted in *Why Children?* (The Women's Press, London; Harcourt Brace, New York) and *Politics of the Heart* (Firebrand Books, Ithaca).

"The Distances Between Us: Feminism, Consciousness and the Girls at the Office" was first published in *Sinister Wisdom*. It was reprinted in *Out the Other Side: Feminist Prose* (Virago Press, London; The Crossing Press, Freedom, CA).

"Anti-Semitism in the Lesbian/Feminist Movement" was first published in *Womanews*. It was reprinted in *Nice Jewish Girls: A Lesbian Anthology* (Beacon Press, Boston).

"Resisting and Surviving in America" was first published in *Nice Jewish Girls: A Lesbian Anthology*.

Excerpts from *"Yom Hashoah, Yom Yerushalayim*: A Meditation" originally appeared in *Genesis 2*. The entire essay was published in the second edition of *Nice Jewish Girls: A Lesbian Anthology*.

"Secular Jewish Identity: *Yidishkayt* in America" was first published in *The Tribe of Dina: A Jewish Women's Anthology* (Beacon Press, Boston).

"Jewish Progressives and the Jewish Community" was first published in *Tikkun*.

Library of Congress Cataloging-in-Publication Data
Klepfisz, Irena 1941 -
    Dreams of an insomniac : Jewish feminist essays, speeches, and diatribes / by Irena Klepfisz ; introduction by Evelyn Torton Beck.
    —1st ed.
        p.   cm.
      ISBN 0-933377-08-8 (acid-free paper) : $22.95. — ISBN 0-933377-05-3 (pbk. : acid-free paper) : $11.95
      1. Women, Jewish—United States. 2. Feminism—United States. 3. Lesbianism—United States. I. Title.
HQ1172.K54   1990
305.48'696—dc20   90-3694
                                                           CIP

Cover by Marcia Barrentine
Book design by Ruth Gundle

Manufactured in the United States of America
This book is printed on acid-free paper.
First Edition 1990   10 9 8 7 6 5 4 3 2 1

Published by The Eighth Mountain Press
624 Southeast Twenty-ninth Avenue
Portland, Oregon 97214

tsu der bavegung
to the movement and
the lesbian/feminists who made this work possible

Preface ix

Introduction xvii

I
Women without Children/Women without Families/
   Women Alone 3

The Distances Between Us: Feminism, Consciousness and the
   Girls at the Office 15

II
Anti-Semitism in the Lesbian/Feminist Movement 53

Resisting and Surviving America 61

Jewish Lesbians, the Jewish Community, Jewish Survival 71

III
Oyf keyver oves: Poland, 1983 85

Yom Hashoah, Yom Yerushalayim: A Meditation 115

IV
Secular Jewish Identity: *Yidishkayt* in America 143

Forging a Woman's Link in *di goldene keyt:* Some Possibilities
   for Jewish American Poetry 167

The Lamp: A Parable About Art and Class and the Function of
   Kishinev in the Jewish Imagination 175

V
Jewish Progressives and the Jewish Community 181

Khaloymes/Dreams in Progress:
   Culture, Politics, and Jewish Identity 187

Preface

I have always loved examining ideas. More precisely, I have always loved talking about ideas, about politics. Perhaps it is my rabbinic blood, for disputation and argumentation remain one of my greatest pleasures (my father came from a long line of Hassidic rabbis). Nothing is quite as satisfying as sitting with friends around a kitchen table or in a coffee shop and dissecting the *exact* implications of a political position or theory. The push-and-pull in these discussions, the interruptions, the sidetracking, the diversion of an irrelevant joke, the sudden exposure of an assumption or bias and identification of contradictions, the demand to return to the original subject—this free associative, open-ended, unpredictable and always unstructured process makes ideas alive and exciting. It grounds ideas in a common and familiar routine, shapes them according to the rhythms of our lives, smudges them with coffee stains, covers them with the dust of unclipped newspapers, endows them with the urgency emanating from a recent and off-the-wall article ("who would have believed a feminist could write anything *that* outrageous?"). It is in this everyday world where my voice mixes with those of friends and with the noise of clanging radiators and passing trucks that I like to test ideas and their worth. It is in this everyday world that I am certain ideas and theories matter, because with each dirty dish that I wash as I talk and listen, I experience how they affect my life.

I don't always have such certainty when I read articles or essays—others' or my own—and for most of my life I have had some distrust of formal written theory. Philosophy, abstract essays—floating pure in midair—have at times appeared useless, divorced from my life and the lives of women I know, divorced from jobs and bosses, kitchens and laundromats, the streets and subways during rush hour. For example, no *theory* about American Jews has been able to express quite as well the nature and power of Jewish identity as the *moment* when I realized I had passed without a second thought a group of homeless people on a New York City street because I was rushing to a Jewish women's vigil protesting Israeli policies against Palestinians in the Occupied Territories. I saw myself instinctively redefining geography and distance, experiencing how much closer Israel, the West Bank and Gaza felt than the 59th Street stop of the Lexington line. Moments like these, integral parts of our daily lives, simultaneously embody theory and concrete experience and I continue to trust them most.

As a result, I have never aspired to be a theoretician or a devoted essay writer. Prose has always been problematic for me. I am all anxiety at the prospect of having to write an essay about an issue I care about deeply. I dread facing the isolating silence, the empty page which demands that every line reach the right edge of the paper and that I carefully plan in logical order the issue and ideas which it encompasses. Unlike poetry, essays have never felt natural.

These feelings have historical roots. My earliest memories from high school, where I was supposed to master that strange genre called "composition," are mostly painful. During those years I found myself continually failing English. I seemed unable to convey what I thought or felt. I wrote incomplete and run-on sentences. I misplaced adverbs and prepositional phrases. I did not know how to create and then stick to an outline before I understood what it was I was trying to say. And I was stymied by the demand for strict symmetry in both outline and essay: I, A, i, ii, B, i, ii, II, A, etc. (Was it possible that *all* topics could *always* be expressed in the *same* symmetrical form?) Repeatedly my compositions were returned with grammatical and organizational corrections and the same comments: my ideas and paragraphs, according to Miss O'Connor and Miss Smith, were undeveloped, unclear, often incoherent. In fact, my writing deficiencies were deemed so severe that at the end of my junior year, to my total humiliation, Miss Smith recommended that I be removed from honors English—though I was to be continued in all other honor classes. I talked my way back in. Though it's been more than thirty years since these experiences, as I work on this preface I still feel Miss O'Connor and Miss Smith breathing down my neck.

My frustrations with prose continued to plague me in college (where I insisted on majoring in English) and then later in graduate school. I often felt unable to create anything coherent out of the tangled emotions and ideas that rushed through me when I thought about a topic—literary or political—that I cared about. I repeatedly experienced the loss of my voice in the attempt to be organized and logical. When working on a paper, it was not uncommon for me to experience a kind of identity crisis, not knowing how to say what I wanted to say, nor being clear how to formulate concepts, which seemed more a part of my body than my mind: a tension in my chest, the excitement and energy which make me want to dance or call up a friend and talk rather than write. It was a struggle to sit still, to try to make order out of ideas so charged with feeling, so enmeshed with each other they defy separation or coherent organization.

If I thought my problems with prose writing were unique, I became quickly educated when I began teaching. Over the past twenty years, I have seen countless students who are extraordinarily articulate in class or in a conference, who write journals and letters alive with intelligence, details and passion, but who are unable to bring that same level of expression and coherence to their papers about subjects which have close bearing on their lives. For whatever reason, many of our educational institutions have not enabled students to express ideas in writing. Like my students, most of my life I have stayed away from prose, fearing my inability to express adequately what I think, and have instead relied on poetry as a primary form of expression.

From the age of twenty, my ego has been invested in poetry. For me, the prospect of expression through poetry transforms solitary silence and an empty page into sheer pleasure. I feel unafraid, knowing I can break all the rules, invent my own forms. No matter what persona I take on, my voice remains accessible and recognizable. There is no artifice, no pose, no sense that I have to transform myself into someone else. As a poet, I remain comfortably disrespectful. I experiment, take risks which sometimes work and sometimes don't. For years I have had no such courage in essay writing. It has seemed an iron-clad genre that I could neither escape nor fit into.

As this collection attests, I pushed myself to write prose despite all this. Rather, *di bavegung,* "the movement," has pushed, encouraged, and given me space, like it has to many women who lacked confidence in their skills and in the value of their perspectives. Above all, it challenged me to present publicly what I discuss privately, to raise issues that I care about and that are central to my experience as a feminist and lesbian, as a Jew sorting out my identity and my relationship to Jewish history, as an American Jew defining my relationship to events in the Middle East. I have done this with some trepidation and, in looking back, am surprised at how much I have actually written, surprised that I opted so frequently to write prose instead of poetry.

In part this is a result of encouragement from individuals and of my allowing myself to experiment. A few years ago I decided to approach an essay in a different mode by trying to capture the zigzag nature of conversations, free association, and fragmentation. "The Distances Between Us," which I categorized as "An Essay in Fragments," was the result, the form being dictated by circumstances and limited writing time. Wanting to charge the essay with the level of feelings I give to my poetry, I wrote an extended series of short prose sections—journal entries, simple statements, memories—and strung them together. This method provided a release and, for the most part, I felt able to maintain my own voice and identity. Since then (and maybe as a result of that experience) I have become more relaxed with the traditional essay or speech and feel less erased by the demands of the genre. Still, when approaching complicated, multifaceted problems, I find myself returning to the fragmented and nonlinear approach. Perhaps it's all a question of sour grapes. I am aware that the philosophical stances we adopt are often shaped not only by our unconscious biases, but by our own talents and limitations as well. We approve that which we do best. And we do best what we do best and disparage everything else. I admit I'm more comfortable breaking rules than following them. I must also admit that I often don't know how to work any other way.

I present this background because I believe it's important to know why these essays and speeches were written in the form, style and voice in which they appear. At the University of Chicago, where I did my graduate work, the professors continually hammered into us the Chicago-school-of-criticism philosophy: form is content; content form. I would repeat this by rote for many years before I fully understood its implications for my own writing and the writing of others. I began to see the practical applications outside of eighteenth and nineteenth-century literature when I was a member of the *Conditions* collective. Over and over again, we felt stymied about how to categorize material in the table of contents. What is this? a short story? a memoir? a real or fictional journal? It was often hard to tell because women writers were breaking all the rules and overlapping genres. And this, of course, was not limited to literary forms, but to other disciplines as well: history, psychology, philosophy. New forms were being invented to accommodate new visions, new content, new perspectives—and the special circumstances of individual women's lives. Though I instinctively applied this principle to my poetry, it was years before I dared use it in my prose writing.

A. Conclusion One

I see value in retaining the knots we experience in articulating concepts and theories. In the process of creating the "seamless," i.e. orderly, essay, we sometimes smooth over those lumpy intersections which need to be highlighted because they are an integral part of the issues we are examining. In saying this, I am not advocating bad or careless or irresponsible writing, but rather the notion that form and content are determined by our spiritual and material circumstances. By retaining the difficult process by which we reach conclusions (through digressions, free association, interruptions, new beginnings, reiteration) we endow ideas with a three-dimensional reality which makes them accessible and operative in the world. To what degree this is true and the method effective, readers will judge for themselves.

B. Conclusion Two

Two memories: (1) My sophomore year in high school. Though I don't remember the logic or the cause, I apparently decided not to respond to any teacher and, for a number of weeks, refused to answer when called. I would stand, as required, but turn my eyes away. At first the teacher would repeat the question, the other girls would fidget, the room would grow tense. Finally I'd be told to sit down. After a while, they stopped calling on me and a while after that I decided to talk again. Things returned to normal.

(2) My senior year in the honors English class from which I had initially been barred. Mrs. Wessel conducted an anonymous essay contest. Given my problems in writing I don't know why I decided to enter, but I did. When she had finished judging, Mrs. Wessel read us the winning essay. It turned out to be mine. She then questioned the three best English students, each of whom denied having written it. Though from the outset she had guaranteed total anonymity, she could not bear the fact that she hadn't spotted the writer with such good

skills. She announced that she wanted to know the writer's identity. I thought about it for a couple of days and finally declared myself. She was taken aback and, I have a feeling, didn't believe me at first. Then she accepted it. But I never did as well again and everything else I wrote after that came back with the usual comments.

At thirteen I tried silence. At sixteen I tried anonymity. I have since learned these are not the only options.

Acknowledgements

A COLLECTION OF MY ESSAYS AND SPEECHES WAS FIRST SUGGESTED BY JUDY Waterman and I am pleased that she convinced me of its usefulness. Over the past fourteen years, Judy has supported my work in a variety of ways and given me the advantage of daily discussions and rigorous criticism while a number of these essays were first being written.

I am also indebted to Gloria Anzaldúa, Evi Beck, Rita Falbel, Judith Friedlander, Esther Hyneman, Melanie Kaye/Kantrowitz, Clare Kinberg, my mother Rose Perczykow Klepfisz, Lee Knefelkamp, Bernice Mennis, Sandra Shotlander and Rima Shore who at various times taught me and argued and debated many of the subjects and themes presented here. I am particularly grateful to Esther, Clare, Evi, Lee and Judy who provided support, time and attention to selecting, organizing, and editing the final manuscript.

Equally important to me are the women who have written for, edited and published women's and lesbian journals, newspapers and anthologies, run the presses, distributed women's writing through their bookstores, taught courses, organized readings and conferences and have enabled ongoing—sometimes angry, always passionate—discussions. These women have provided the context and the impetus for much of my political writing.

I want to thank Ruth Gundle my publisher for taking on this project and for her care and exactitude in bringing out this collection.

Introduction

THE EXTRAORDINARY POWER OF IRENA KLEPFISZ'S WORK LIES IN THE FORCE OF ITS moral and artistic integrity. These essays interweave and overlap (not only with each other, but also with her poetry) in entirely unexpected ways. Who else but Klepfisz could make us understand so clearly (and always in a framework that is Jewish, lesbian, feminist, and conscious of class) the imperative to speak out against the Israeli occupation of the West Bank and Gaza? Against anti-Semitism and homophobia? Against compulsory motherhood? Against the commercialization of the Holocaust? And to speak as loudly *for* the strengthening and preservation of secular Yiddish culture in the United States? For the demystification of writing? For the celebration and joy of creative work?

At a time of repression, when progressive politics are eroding and hate crimes are on the rise, Klepfisz's essays make plain that the political is personal, and that the personal must continue to be understood as political. Klepfisz's sharp critiques of many movements and communities lead us to take action, which is her way of keeping hope alive.

* * *

Although I have gladly accepted the task of writing the introduction to this volume of essays, it was through her poetry that I first came to know Irena Klepfisz. I can still call up the rush of excited recognition that came over me when, after browsing through the lesbian poetry section of a women's bookstore sometime in 1977, I casually opened *periods of stress* and recognized myself. Here was a woman writing as a child survivor of the Holocaust, as a lesbian, as a feminist, and as a Jew. At the time I knew of no other lesbian/feminist who had also somehow managed *"to escape that fate."*[1] Exhilarated and greatly comforted by the knowledge of her existence, I filed away the information, determined to meet this person "someday." Since I was then living in Madison, Wisconsin and she in Brooklyn, New York I figured it wouldn't be any time soon.

But not many months later, I began the project that became *Nice Jewish Girls: A Lesbian Anthology.*[2] Although by then I felt considerably less isolated because I had come to know the work of several American-born Jewish lesbians who *wrote as Jews*—still a rarity in the late seventies and early eighties—Irena Klepfisz remained the only other Jewish lesbian Holocaust survivor I knew of. It was therefore particularly important to me that she contribute an essay to the volume. Arrogantly perhaps, I assumed she would leap at the opportunity; but when I called her she turned me down, politely but definitely, saying she didn't have anything on hand that explicitly addressed those issues.

Luckily, the anthology was delayed and within a year she changed her mind. Her response took the form of several poems and two essays (both of which are included in this volume): "Anti-Semitism in the Lesbian/Feminist Movement," which had appeared in a special issue of *Womanews* focusing on Jewish women and anti-Semitism, and a letter to me which became "Resisting and Surviving America" in which she articulates the reasons for her initial hesitation:

> I write as much out of a Jewish consciousness as I do out of a lesbian/feminist consciousness. They are both always there, no matter what the topic I might be working on. They are embedded in my writing, totally embedded and enmeshed to the point that they are not necessarily distinguishable as discrete elements. They merge and blend and blur—for in many ways they are the same.... Alienated. Threatened. Un-American. Defiant. *To me they are ever present.* [Emphasis mine.]

Klepfisz was here talking specifically about her poetry, but a similar complexity informs her essays, which in many ways work like poetry in their use of language, image, symbol, and bits of dialogue to tell stories and bring to life glimpses of people who have in one way or another touched Klepfisz's life. These include friends and acquaintances, co-workers and passers-by, as well as members of many different communities in the United States, Israel, and Poland—not only *di lebn geblibene* (those who survived)—but also those who perished, whose bravery and acts of resistance influenced her deeply.

* * *

This volume is appropriately dedicated *tsu der bavegung* (to the movement), a name that calls forth both the progressive Yiddish-speaking Jewish socialist movement in which her Jewish identity was forged and the contemporary lesbian/feminist movement which she helped to create and which gave her voice as a lesbian. These essays are best understood as a series of movements, "attempts," in the original meaning of the word "essay," to articulate problems that are at once particular and general, private and public, issues that "are central to my experience as a feminist and lesbian, as a Jew sorting out my identity and my relationship to Jewish history, as an American Jew defining my relationship to events in the Middle East." ("Preface") These attempts represent a movement toward some temporary resolution that will have to be thought through over and over again. *Experiments,* she calls her essays. *Attempts* at solutions. But Klepfisz has never used the lack of certainty as an excuse to avoid taking action. In addition to her theoretical writings, she has been an organizer in both Jewish and lesbian/feminist communities, lecturing and giving workshops on feminism, Yiddish culture, anti-Semitism, and the Middle East.

* * *

Taking my cue from the author's preface, I have allowed myself to respond to these essays in a nonlinear associative way, which is also my preferred mode of writing. Klepfisz's essays are freeing and engaging because of the honesty she brings to the processes of writing, thinking and rethinking, questioning, reexamining a decision that may seem to be correct today but may prove to be disastrously wrong tomorrow. For example, in *"Yom Hashoah, Yom Yerushalayim"* Klepfisz chronicles the ill-timed letters written by *Di vilde chayes* (a Jewish lesbian/feminist support and study group to which she belonged) in response to anti-Semitism in the women's movement. Present too, in these essays, is the labor and the agony that comes with accepting responsibility, taking a stand. And though she works always from the specificity of her own experiences (she had to learn four different languages in the first decade of her life), she taps into the widespread discomfort with the rules of English grammar shared by immigrants, working-class people, and those who have not had a traditional education. As the lesbian/feminist poet Judy Grahn points out, these rules keep many people (especially women) from writing.[3]

If poetry freed Klepfisz from the shackles of traditional grammar, it was the women's movement that encouraged her to experiment freely with prose, to mix genres and to "create new forms to accommodate new visions," to allow the writing to imitate the "zigzag" nonlinear quality of conversation "where [her] voice mixed with those of friends and the clanging of the radiators and the passing trucks," where ideas are embedded and alive. ("Preface") This is the voice of Klepfisz the essayist—passionate, engaged, fully present, "hurling words" to capture our attention and move us toward action.[4]

These essays break the distance between the genres of poetry and prose. Written in a style that is clear and direct, the accessibility of these essays should not keep us from appreciating the richness of their language which echoes some of the same themes and phrases that give the poetry a haunting quality. Words like *home, hiding, healing, history, distances, wounds, safety, silence* tie the essays to the poems. Although Klepfisz worries that she is abandoning art by her activism (this work more often results in essays than poems) one cannot help but admire the congruity of Klepfisz's projects, which seem to reinforce and strengthen each other.

Klepfisz uses quite different approaches to similar themes. It is interesting to compare the variety of voices that emerge in both the poetry and the prose. For example, *"Yom Hashoah, Yom Yerushalayim*: A Meditation" (on the Holocaust, Israel and the Palestinians) may be paired with the poems "East Jerusalem, 1987: *Bet Shalom* (House of Peace)" and "'67 Remembered"; *"Oyf keyver oves"* with "Warsaw 1983: *Umschlagplatz*" and "Searching for My Father's Body"; "Secular Jewish Identity: *Yidishkayt* in America" and *"Khaloymes*: Dreams in Progress" with the poems *"Etlekhe verter oyf mame-loshn*/A few words in the mother tongue," "*Di rayze aheym*/The journey home" and "Fradel Schtok." Another set of essays and poems focus on the tension that arises from the need to do office work instead of creating art. For example, "The Distances Between Us" can be placed next to "Work Sonnets," "Contexts," and "A Poem for Judy / beginning a new job." "Women Alone/Women without Families/Women without Children" parallels "they are always curious" and "they did not build wings for them" though the mood and tone of these works are quite different.

* * *

Read cumulatively, these essays work together to give the volume a pleasing shape; themes enunciated in early essays reverberate in later ones. Take, for example, "The Distances Between Us," a phrase introduced in the title of an essay placed early in the book, whose complex meanings (now ironic, now serious) reverberate throughout the volume. In that essay, which is subtitled "Feminism, Consciousness, and the Girls at the Office," Klepfisz challenges feminists to consider their participation in perpetuating "distances" among women based on differences in class, education, and opportunity. Yet on another level, the "differences" are somewhat illusory, since women, she suggests, *can* understand each other across apparent differences because so many of our common enemies are the same.

But "distances" also refers to the miles that separate countries (Poland, Israel, and the United States) as well as the distances that separate people (Arabs and Jews; Palestinians and Israelis; one woman from another; one kind of Jew from another). Klepfisz's essays are meant to explore these distances while creating a vision in which peaceful bridging is a real possibility. Her essays move us toward forging coalitions and alliances. They urge us not to be afraid of listening to each other, and to try to imagine ourselves into the feelings of those who oppose our work. "I have to understand their emotions if I ever hope to reach them," she says of those American and Israeli Jews who often violently oppose her politics on the Middle East, which call for a two-state solution and an end to the Israeli occupation of the West Bank and Gaza. ("*Yom Hashoah, Yom Yerushalayim:* A Meditation")

Though Klepfisz insists that differences must be acknowledged and confronted, distances need not be kept. Let me list the myriad distances/differences between us that these essays address, keeping in mind that it is not only the distances themselves, but the "us" that keeps shifting. In one essay Klepfisz speaks as a Jew among lesbians and feminists; in another as a lesbian/feminist among mainstream Jews, or among "progressive" Jews—two different Jewish communities opposed to each other's politics, but almost equally resistant to feminism and gay rights (though progressives pretend to care).

The distances between us are also differences of time and geography and generation. The space between the Jewish Poland of Klepfisz's birth and the "Jew-free" post–World War II Poland marks the path Klepfisz retraces with her mother in 1983, the year marking the fortieth anniversary of the Warsaw Ghetto Uprising. With carefully measured understatement that evokes the raw emotion behind the words, Klepfisz describes the journey in which she and her mother visit her father's grave (actually only a stone erected to his memory) in the Warsaw Jewish cemetery and her aunt's grave in the Christian one.

In *"Oyf keyver oves,"* the journal that grew out of that trip, Klepfisz also introduces us to a wide range of people—Polish Jews and gentiles, many of whom had known her as a child. Especially powerful is a meeting with Marysia, a Catholic who recognizes the child she once knew only by the American cut of her slacks. Marysia, a "Righteous Gentile" who sheltered Jews during the war, had been a very close friend of Klepfisz's Aunt Gina. Though Catholic, Marysia now asks to be buried beside her beloved friend of forty-five years ago, a request that is moving but inevitably leads Klepfisz to feel trapped, since she cannot bring herself to ask the obvious aloud: "Will Marysia want a cross on the grave?" We are left to ponder the complex feelings aroused by this unexpected turn of events. Will this symbolic gesture of love and good will on the part of a Christian finally obliterate the Jew altogether, even in death?

Cemeteries are at the center of *"Oyf keyver oves,"* whose Yiddish title evokes the ancient Jewish custom of visiting ancestors' graves. Klepfisz's impressions of the gravestones—some disintegrating, others overgrown with stones piled on top of one another, without visible Jewish markers, all seeming about to disappear—are powerfully and vividly recorded. These images allow us to re-experience the erasure and desecration of Jewish life in Poland. That Jews have all but disappeared while anti-Semitism has continued to flourish is a stark reality, made even starker by the recent violent desecrations of Jewish graves (and bodies) in France.[5] The emptiness of the Jewish cemeteries in

Poland evokes other emptinesses. "I was utterly unprepared for the size, the seeming endlessness of the cemetery and its totally abandoned condition. Most of it is completely overgrown, not just by grass, but trees, huge trees growing unchecked since 1939. You look down an alley and it is almost completely dark from the overgrowth, the gravestones barely visible." With bitter irony and powerful understatement Irena Klepfisz notes in her journal, "In reviewing the 'Jewish' part of the day I concluded: the major Jewish activity in Warsaw is occurring in the Jewish cemetery and consists of the unchecked sinking of gravestones into the ground. Deeper and deeper."

The journal writer, and we with her, have been prepared for this erasure of Jewish traces in Eastern Europe (even in the concentration camps where stones, rather than any explicitly Jewish symbols, are used in the memorials that honor the Jewish dead). "Jews are not rocks, and rocks are not Jews," she laments. When Klepfisz goes through customs on her arrival in Poland, she is asked to declare any silver or gold objects in her possession. When she points to the Jewish star around her neck, this item is officially recorded (in Polish) as *"one gold chain with pendant."* The meaning of the Jewish star has already disappeared, and with it the continuity of *di goldene keyt*, the golden chain of Jewish culture (a symbol conceptualized by the late nineteenth-century Yiddish writer I. L. Peretz) which was violently ruptured by the Holocaust. By means of her advocacy of a new Jewish secularism, Irena Klepfisz calls to our attention the seriousness of the break and in so doing begins the necessary work of repair.

* * *

But there are still other distances to be traversed—the distances of history. In "Secular Jewish Identity: *Yidishkayt* in America," Klepfisz recognizes that the secular Jewish education that shaped her also created in her a kind of complacency because it never acknowledged some basic contradictions: that "I was learning a Jewish politics which was uprooted...that Jews did not have the right to be anywhere and everywhere...that Yiddish was not my *mame-loshn* (mother tongue)." The Holocaust robbed her not only of her father, who was killed in the Warsaw Ghetto Uprising, but also of Yiddish, her "mother tongue," a language she has been reclaiming in poetry as well as in prose since the early 1980s. And in spite of her wistful acknowledgment that her Yiddish is stiff from disuse, the spirit of Yiddish literature has managed to survive in her work.

In "The Lamp: A Parable about Art and Class and the Function of Kishinev in the Jewish Imagination," different responses to the meaning of Eastern European Jewish experiences are measured in terms of "distances" from that experience. The experience itself is embodied by the lamp whose shade is suggestively yellow—"It looks like a scarecrow that lost its arms and straw during a pogrom. And there it stands, right in my living room." The Jewish writer in whom Jewish history is alive accepts its reality philosophically and with much Jewish irony. "It could be worse. It has been…worse, much worse." To those more "distant" to the suffering which the lamp embodies, the lamp is unacceptable—a hint that those who prefer to "hide the lamp" prefer Jewish assimilation. To the non-Jewish artist the lamp is repulsive, unaesthetic. Jewish history is not "pretty," Jewish suffering not picturesque. To the American Jew, though born poor, the lamp is unacceptable because it "reeks from poverty," and keeps her from coming "together in a unified whole," a very "American" expectation of the world, an option rarely available historically to those Jews who lived in hostile "host" countries. This American Jew is not eager to be reminded of what was, before the Holocaust, the measure of Jewish suffering—the brutal Kishinev pogrom of 1903 that brought Jews flocking to the United States, seeking asylum and *parnose*, livelihood. To the narrator, a Jewish poet, the lamp is part of her history because " it's all more than my grandmother had, more than my grandmother ever hoped for."

This parable is both an embodiment of Jewish experience and a recreation of a short story form created by I. L. Peretz, in which commentary on Jewish experience was often blurred with a surrealistic fictional "reality" that made the meanings both literal and symbolic at the same time. Told from a Jewish feminist perspective, Klepfisz superbly adapts this form and crosses the distances of time and geography to make it come alive in her living room in Brooklyn; rusty and yellowed as the lamp is, the story is fresh and evocative. It begins to forge the sorely needed *woman's* link in Peretz's "golden chain"—without which the chain cannot be whole.

* * *

The need to "set priorities" which the last essay in the book develops is already present in the first. In choosing (as the sole child survivor of her family) not to have a child, the writer has prioritized her own needs against communal pressures. But having made one decision, she discovers, does not free her from the imperative to make others. Having chosen not to bear children, she must still decide to *which* projects she will give priority—art or activism? Poetry, prose, translations or pamphlet writing? Having chosen to give priority to Jewish issues, she is still left with the question of *which* Jewish issues to choose, "how to be an active Jew in the world?"

In the last decade, Klepfisz has become deeply disturbed by a "slow disorientation around [her] Jewish identity" provoked by right-wing Israeli policies, but she is equally alarmed by the rapid dissolution of secular Jewish life in the United States which, she believes, will hasten the process of assimilation. Klepfisz is emphatic that "non-observance," the choice made by the majority of American Jews is not the same as secularism, that consciously chosen pre-Holocaust secularism was always political and cultural, and always associated with a "fierce determination to preserve Jewish identity." She is equally emphatic that "a true commitment to Jewish secularism inevitably means that we must make decisions—just like observant Jews—about how to structure our lives and our relations with Jews and non-Jews—how to incorporate the past.... A true commitment to Jewish secularism inevitably also means a commitment to establishing and supporting secular Jewish institutions that provide us with a sense of community and common purpose." ("*Khaloymes:* Dreams in Progress") Although she begins her final essay torn between the dual pulls (Israel and secularism), her conclusions suggest that forging a secularism—which must include political activism—must be her highest priority. Perhaps it is the necessity to choose that evokes the "dreams of an insomniac" that give this book its title.

* * *

Audre Lorde has said each of us must find the work that is *ours* to do. Irena Klepfisz finds a model in the historical *yidishkayt* that sets

> a fine example for combining culture, politics, Jewish concerns, concern for others. The contemporary secularism I seek will do the same. Its proponents will be willing to use the Arabic word *intifada* and take the next logical and only possible step: public support of Israel and Palestine. Secularists will carry a banner at Gay Pride parades and give public support to gay and lesbian Jews.... Like feminism, lesbian and gay rights will be incorporated into contemporary secularism openly, boldly, without hesitation. So the secularism I advocate does not take us out of the fray, but keeps us active as Jews in both the Jewish and non-Jewish worlds in which we live. (*"Khaloymes:* Dreams in Progress")

This vision invites a celebration of particularity—in this case, secular Jewish culture and the Yiddish language—while at the same time encouraging openness to other heritages. Klepfisz insists on maintaining the integrity of each individual culture as it joins others. This is a vision worth emulating.

* * *

Having acquired as a student and teacher of literature the habit of viewing a body of writing in its totality, I find myself looking at these essays historically, discovering in the process a pattern of movement over time and an underlying structure of development. In these essays, Klepfisz moves from a position of isolation and disconnectedness to a space in which she can have different dreams (*khaloymes*) that, though they keep her awake, allow her to envision a future in which the artist, the Jew, the lesbian, and the survivor will have a place.

While Irena Klepfisz began to publish poetry in 1971 and continues to do so uninterruptedly to the present, her essay writing began in 1978 ("essays never felt natural") and gathered momentum only in 1982, following the publication of *Nice Jewish Girls: A Lesbian Anthology* and the development of a specifically *Jewish* lesbian/feminist movement. As it did for thousands of other gay and lesbian Jews, for Klepfisz too this movement made possible an integration of component parts that had forcibly been kept apart ("I was in two worlds which never overlapped or even touched"—the Yiddish world of YIVO Institute for Jewish Research and the lesbian world of *Conditions* magazine.) The bringing together of these worlds in the 1980s gave her new energy and led her to organize feminist workshops on Jewish identity and anti-Semitism. This experience eventually gave her the determination to stop focusing so heavily on oppression and to begin the work of retrieving and creating Jewish women's culture—a determination that resulted in her co-editing *The Tribe of Dina: A Jewish Women's Anthology.*

This communal work in the public arena helped to heal the nightmare of herself as "bag lady" with her "stained purple bruises" and "barely healed wounds," the incarnation of "isolation and separateness," which induces in others "a fear of contagion." The bag lady is seen by the majority as "a species apart" (the prose equivalent of the caged creatures in "The Monkey House" poems), the embodiment of the Jew, the lesbian, the survivor, who, though feared and rejected, is nonetheless human—"she came from the same world I did, underwent the same life processes: she was born, grew up, lives." ("Women without Children / Women without Families / Women Alone") The bag lady represents the "state of terror" that must be left behind before Klepfisz can move toward the sense of communal purpose that motivates her writings on Israel and the forging of a new Jewish secular identity.

In a 1989 speech at a public event sponsored by the Jewish Women's Committee to End the Occupation of the West Bank and Gaza, Klepfisz articulated what motivates her to action—to organize workshops, co-found the Committee, and travel to Israel to connect with the women's peace movement there:

> We are told that history is made by other people.... We are told this because we are women.... Over and over again the message is monotonously the same: you have no power, you have no power to change anything. But I don't believe this. I believe common, ordinary people are not passive participants in historical events. *How each of us shapes our life, shapes history.*[6]

While the dream as nightmare haunts the first essay of the book, the dream as vision—as possibility, as faith in a future in which one can, as a woman, a lesbian and a Jew, actively participate—fuels the last essay. The hope of the *khaloymes* is muted, but present.

* * *

One of the most striking characteristics of so many of Klepfisz's essays is her ability to develop a bilingual mode of writing, a mode that transplants Yiddish into English, thus preserving *mame-loshn* (the European mothers' tongue), making the language more immediate, less strange. The deep resonances and childhood memories that surfaced when I first read these essays remind me that for Klepfisz, as for me and many other Ashkenazi Jews dispersed throughout the world, Yiddish serves a vital function—it is "the mirror that made me visible to myself." ("Secular Jewish Identity: *Yidishkayt* in America") Klepfisz knows that language is a significant carrier of culture, something that is especially true of Yiddish, which in the context of Jewish history "summons a world beneath the words."[7] Unfortunately, *my* Yiddish, learned in a *folkshule* after I came to the United States and never spoken in my home, is even rustier from disuse than Irena's. And so, to get the full flavor of these essays, you must read them for yourself. Perhaps that is just as well, since an introduction is meant to whet the appetite, *to lead the reader to the work*. As you savor essay after essay and watch the gradual unfolding of Irena Klepfisz's *khaloymes*, from nightmare to vision, you can yourself be building a foundation upon which you can dream your own dreams, envision your own visions.

Evelyn Torton Beck

Notes

1. This phrase is from an untitled poem in Klepfisz's *A Few Words in the Mother Tongue: Poems Selected and New (1971-1990)* (Portland, OR: The Eighth Mountain Press, 1990), which was published as a companion volume to this one.
2. *Nice Jewish Girls: A Lesbian Anthology*, ed. Evelyn Torton Beck (Boston: Beacon Press, 1989).
3. See Grahn's introduction to *True to Life Adventure Stories*, Vol. I, (Freedom, CA: Crossing Press, 1984). Grahn sums up the problem, "Murdering the King's English can be a crime only if you identify with the King."
4. This phrase is taken from the title of Klepfisz's speech "Hurling Words at the Consulate" delivered at a vigil in front of the Israeli Consulate in New York City on January 25, 1989. It is not included in this volume but was published in *Genesis 2: An Independent Voice for Jewish Renewal* (Spring 1988), pp. 18-20.
5. I am referring to the desecration of thirty-four graves in the Carpentras Jewish cemetery, "their tombstones wrenched aside. The body of an elderly woman had been half-dragged from the ground. Sprawled nearby was the cadaver of an 81-year old man buried just two weeks earlier—mutilated and impaled through the rectum with a parasol. The profanation shocked France's 650,000-strong Jewish community and appalled the country.... In nearby Avignon, unknown vandals daubed anti-Semitic signs on build-

ing walls—including several demanding, in German: *JUDE RAUS* (Jew out)." Anti-Semitic graffiti was also found on a war memorial in Aix-en-Provence. *Newsweek*, May 21, 1990, p. 40.

6. Emphasis mine. From "A Jewish Women's Call for Peace—Days of Awe," an unpublished speech.

7. From the introduction to *A Treasury of Yiddish Stories*, edited by Irving Howe and Eliezer Greenberg (New York: Schocken Books, 1973), p. 47. This introduction provides an excellent overview of the complex intersection of Yiddish, Hebrew and the values of the *shtetl* world in which Yiddish literature developed.

I

Women without Children
Women without Families
Women Alone

(1977)

This article has grown out of my need to express some of my feelings and conflicts about being a woman who has chosen to remain childless, as well as to break the silence surrounding the general issue of women without children.

That the silence has persisted despite the presence of the women's movement is both appalling and enigmatic, since the decision not to have a child shapes both a woman's view of herself and society's view of her. I have read a great deal about woman as mother, but virtually nothing about woman as nonmother, as if her choice should be taken for granted and her life were not an issue. And though I have heard strong support of the right of women to have choices and options, I have not seen any exploration of how the decision to remain childless is to be made, how one is to come to terms with it, how one is to learn to live with its consequences. If what follows seems at moments somewhat bleak, it is because I feel very strongly that in celebrating a woman's liberation from compulsory motherhood, we have neither recognized nor dealt with the pain that often accompanies such a decision.

My intent is to be neither objective nor exhaustive. I am aware that this issue evokes many other feelings than those expressed on the following pages, the feelings of women whose lives differ drastically from mine. I hope that they too will break the silence.

1. The Fantasy

At the center of my bleakest fantasy is the shopping-bag lady. I see her sitting on the subway, trudging along the highway, or crouched in a doorway at dusk. Invariably, she clutches her paper shopping bags close to her. From a distance her face looks blank, her skin grey. She is oblivious to the things around her, unresponsive to sounds and movements. She is particularly indifferent to people. Periodically she makes a quick motion, like an animal automatically brushing itself free from an irritation, a tic. Her gesture is loose, flabby, hardly aimed. It is, perhaps, the tremor of a muscle.

I keep my distance from her, though at times in my imagination I venture closer, detecting a faint stale odor, an odor distinctly communicating stagnation. In reality, however, I have moved only close enough to discern the discolored skin, the broken blood vessels on her legs, stained purple bruises, barely healed wounds. I have eyed her socks and stockings, her shoes, her faded dress, the safety pins that hold her coat together. I have studied the surface content of her bags, seen the bits of material (clothing, perhaps), newspapers. I always wanted to know more, to know if the entire bag is filled with rags and papers, or if, deep inside, wrapped neatly and carefully in a clean cloth, lies an object from the past, a memento from a life like mine. But my desire to know has never overcome my real terror of her. So I have never ventured closer.

I have a distinct fear of contagion. But it is not necessarily of disease, though there is that too, the physical fear of being touched by such a creature. My greater fear is that she carries another kind of disease. On a subway, I watch as this creature sits, harmless, self-contained, oblivious to the other people in the car, while an invisible circle seems to form around her. No one will come near her, no one will sit close to her, no one will risk being touched by her. If she has succeeded in excluding us from her world, we must remember that our response to her reflects our equal determination to keep her out of ours. It is almost as if I, as if everyone else in the subway car, were determined to classify her as a species apart, to establish firmly that there is no connection between her and us. By keeping my distance, I affirm that she is not of my world, reassure myself that I could never be like her, that there is nothing she and I have in common—in short, that her disease is not communicable.

It is, I think, the most comfortable way of looking at her, for it deems her irrelevant to my life. Of course, if I were totally convinced, I would lose my fear of contagion. But this is not the case. More and more, I sense my connection to her, allow myself to absorb the fact that her world and mine overlap. More and more I dismiss as romantic the notion that some great, swift calamity, some sudden shock must have overtaken her and reduced her to her present condition. It is far more probable that her separateness, her isolation, resulted not from fire, nor from sudden death, nor from unexpected loss, but rather from a slow erosion, an imperceptible loosening of common connections and relations—a process to which I too am subject. Her disease is one to which I am and will remain vulnerable. She is not an anomaly, nor is her isolation from the rest of us a freak accident. She came from the same world I did, underwent the same life processes: she was born, grew up, lives.

So I remain in a state of terror and keep myself separate from her. I fear that I will not build up the proper immunity to resist the erosion; I am afraid I too will end up alone, disconnected, relating to no one, having no one to care for, being in turn forgotten, unwanted, and insignificant, my life a waste. In the grip of this terror, I can only anticipate a lonely, painful old age, an uncomforted death.

It is difficult to own up to this fantasy. I do so because it is true that I have it, but also because I know I am not unique in having it. I have heard many other women express it, perhaps not always in terms of shopping-bag ladies, but in terms of old age, insecurity. And it is not surprising because among my friends, many in their late thirties and early forties, these issues are becoming increasingly important. It is not surprising because we are living in a depression when everyone is worried about money and jobs, about the possibility of surviving in some decent way. For me, the shopping-bag lady epitomizes these fears, and though I often tell myself that she is an exaggerated example, equally often I think that she is not.

2. The Myths

For a long time I believed (and on some nonrational level still believe) that I could acquire immunity to the shopping-bag lady's disease by having a child. When depressed about the fragility and transiency of friendships, or the inconstancies of lovers, it was the myth of a child, a blood relation and what it could bring me, which seemed to be the only guarantee against loneliness and isolation, the only way of maintaining a connection to the rest of society. And certainly one of the difficulties for me, a woman who now knows that she will never bear children, is to let go of that myth without sinking into total despair.

That the myth is powerful is not surprising, since it is nurtured by everything around us, fostered by the media, by popular literature, by parents, by the questionnaires we fill out for jobs: *Are you married?* No. *Do you have children?* No. *Do you live alone?* Yes. *How many members in your household?* One. It is a myth perpetually reinforced by the assumption that only family and children provide us with a purpose and place, bestow upon us honor, respect, love and comfort. We are taught very early that blood relations, and only blood relations, can be a perpetual, unfluctuating source of affection, can be the foolproof guarantee that we will not be forgotten. This myth, and many others surrounding the traditional family, often make it both frightening and painful for women to think of themselves as remaining childless.

In reality, of course, I know that many shopping-bag ladies are mothers, have families, have children. What is obvious to any mature, rational woman is that children are not a medicine or a vaccine which stamps out loneliness or isolation, but rather that they are people, subject to the same weaknesses as friends and lovers. I have talked to many women whose ties to their families seem to be irrevocably broken. It is common to hear stories of the prodigal daughter going cross-country, returning home after fourteen, fifteen years to parents who are strangers. Expecting a traumatic, painful reunion, the woman returns numbed by the lack of connection, by her indifference to strangers. They are people with no special relation. They follow the accepted and expected rules, in a dire crisis write dutiful checks, and, upon their death, bequeath china to their unmarried daughters. But the emotional pull is not there from either side. There is no exchange of love, of comfort. Blood might indeed be thicker than water, but it, too, is capable of evaporating and drying up.

Yet despite this, despite having read Shakespeare's *King Lear* and Tillie Olsen's *Tell Me a Riddle,* despite having been taught by experience that children often come to love their ideals more than their parents (and vice versa), that children may take different roads, rejecting all ties to the past, despite all this, the myth retains its power and dominates my fantasy life. And there are important reasons why it does.

First, what I have just described is what I would like to believe is an extreme, an exception. There are, after all, many warm, loving relationships between parent and child. In these relationships, one can recognize genuine affection and ties among members of the family, even if often the very same relationships are fraught with tensions and painful encounters.

Once, when talking with a woman about our feelings about being childless, she began to tell me about her relationship with her mother, a relationship which for years had been filled with anger and pain. But I could sense that on some level the woman had a deep attachment, felt genuine concern and responsibility toward her mother, despite the fact that the relationship remained problematic, and many painful conflicts were still unresolved. While she was describing this to me, she suddenly revealed that her mother was on welfare and was receiving $180 a month. When I asked her how her mother could possibly manage on such an absurd amount, the woman laughed and said that, of course, she helped her out financially. We continued talking more generally about the issue, but then the woman suddenly said: "You know, it scares me. Being alone, without family. I think about my mother and what she would be doing now without me. I keep trying to think of her as just a woman, like me, trying to cope with the world. But there is a difference, a major difference between us. She has a daughter."

A second reason for the myth's ability to retain its hold on my fantasy life is that I have found no adequate substitute for it. To discard it is to be left with nothing, to be faced with the void (or so I think in my most depressed moments). I admit this with some hesitancy, because certainly one aim of the lesbian/feminist movement has been to expose the superficiality of the family myth. The movement has consciously struggled to develop new alternatives for women, has, in a certain sense, offered itself as a new and better "home," a source of the support, affection, and security that many of us seek. I think, however, that for women who at one time or another were involved in various movement activities—support groups, collectives, business projects, experimental communes—for those women who, as a result of these activities and groups, experienced the first flush of excitement in their discovery of other women and in the sharing of feelings and goals, for those women who thought that they had indeed found new and permanent homes, alternate families—for them the disappointment has been quite keen. Too often, instead of providing a new and supportive home, the collective experiments ended in frustration, bitter anger, a hard silence that severed what everyone had hoped would be permanent ties. That this occurred, is repeatedly occurring, is not surprising. Because expectations were so high, because we wanted these groups to fulfill so many divergent needs, they were destined to disappoint. For me and for many other women it was a sobering experience, to say the least.

I do not mean to imply that nothing has worked or that we are standing in the midst of ruins. What I wish to emphasize is rather the sense of disillusionment and disappointment experienced by me and by many women with whom I have spoken, a sense which has contributed to a feeling of insecurity and, to some degree, pessimism. It is when these feelings become acute that I am most vulnerable, that my fantasy returns again to the concept of family and children. The old images resurface. But the difference between envisioning them now and envisioning them years ago is that now they hold no solace, they remain empty. Their uselessness in my life creates further pain, for I am without the alternatives which a few years ago, when I first became involved in the lesbian/feminist movement, I thought I had. I find the community's present and future only vaguely delineated; whatever community exists is still very young and rather shaky. The emptiness of the past, the vagueness of the future, leave me fearful, hesitant about my decision not to have a child.

Many women have had to face a similar issue on a more personal and more immediate level. They have had to face the fact that lesbian relationships are not instantly more stable, more secure, more permanent, than heterosexual ones. And because of this, the myth of motherhood takes on added power. A woman who thought she was about to break up with her lover told me: "For the first time in a really long time, I thought about having a child. I won't do it of course. But I did think about it." She was clearly expressing the idea that somehow a child would guarantee her a permanent relationship.

The emphasis is, of course, on *guarantee* and on *permanent*. If the parent is good, so the logic of the fantasy goes, then the relationship with the child will withstand shock, change, growth, poverty, differences in temperament and ideals—in short, anything and everything. The woman who dreams this way may acknowledge that such a relationship has yet to be realized, but she may be quick to add that she has learned a great deal from her own experience as a daughter, that with *her* child, she will avoid all the mistakes that her parents made with her. By learning from their errors, the woman now fantasizes, she will establish a far more perfect, loving, supportive relationship with her child and thereby guarantee for herself a permanent connection during her lifetime.

My fantasy of being a mother and my desire to have a child have been with me for a long time. It has taken me years to realize, however, that both the fantasy and the desire were to a great degree expressions of my dissatisfaction with my relationship with my own mother. It seems clear to me now that by becoming the calm, loving, patient, supportive mother I have so often envisioned, I have hoped to annihilate the impatient, critical voice within myself, the voice that has kept me insecure and dissatisfied. Thus my desire to become the perfect mother, to act out that fantasy, has in reality nothing to do with having a child, but rather with my desire to experience something I wish I had experienced. It is not a child I wish to mother, it is myself.

In my fantasy, of course, the understanding, the patience, the support are always outwardly directed, because the myth of motherhood demands that they be so. According to the myth, if I do not have a child I will never experience that caring, that uncritical peace, that completely understanding sensibility. Only the role of mother will allow me that. This is clearly a wrong reason for having a child—one which can be ultimately disastrous.

This kind of thinking, however, points up another aspect of the myth about having children: that certain qualities can only be expressed through a relationship with a child. I am not saying that a relationship with a child is not unique. It is. But some of the qualities which we attribute to it are not limited to child-parent relationships. I would like to discuss just one of these qualities. Women expressing a desire to have a child often explain that they want their values and beliefs to be passed on. They feel that by having a child they can have some measure of control, some input into the future. A child, after all, can be molded and influenced; to a child can be passed on a whole way of life. That parents have tremendous influence over their children is, of course, self-evident. But the myth excludes the fact that they do not have total influence over their children, that they can never exert total control. As a woman once said to me about her child who was going to a day-care center: "Oh yes, I have great influence. I send her off in the morning looking like a human being, and she comes back in the evening wearing green nail polish because green nail polish is some teacher's idea of femininity."

There is something extraordinary in the idea of being able to participate so immediately in the shaping of another life, no matter how much other factors attempt to undermine that influence. Nevertheless, it is not only through a growing child that a woman can influence the world around her, though in the interest of the traditional family, women are taught to believe that it is the most direct and most meaningful way for them. Obviously, a woman taught to think this way will think that her life, her work, are totally useless and ineffectual if she does not have a child, an heir to her ideals and values. This is another real impasse for many women who decide to remain childless. I was interested in a conversation I had with a woman who told me she was considering adopting a child. One of her main reasons was the one I have just discussed. Later in the conversation, she told me about a talk she had had with a friend. Sometime after the talk, her friend told her that she had had a tremendous impact on her, that the talk had helped her in making certain basic decisions about her life. The woman told me, "I was really stunned. I always consider conversations with friends just talk. It never occurs to me that anyone really listens to me, or that what I say has any effect on anyone."

This is not to say that for every aspect of a relationship with a child we can find a substitute, and women who decide not to have children can somehow "make up for it" by looking elsewhere. I believe a relationship with a child is as unique as a relationship with a friend or lover. Each has its own special qualities. But myths about having children do prevent women from seeing just what it is they want from having a child and from participating in such an intimate way in another life. It is something which needs closer examination, so that when a woman decides not to have children she knows what she is giving up—both the negative and positive aspects of being a mother—knows it in a real, concrete way, and not in the foggy, idealized, sticky-sentimentalized version with which we are all so familiar.

3. The Consequences

Myths and private fantasies are not the only obstacles in the way of women coming to terms with their childlessness. There are also the very real, often harsh, circumstances of living in a society where a woman who does not marry and, above all, does not have a child, is stigmatized, characterized as cold, as unwomanly and unfeminine, as unnatural in some essential way. I wince when I recall how throughout my twenties, when I was certain that I was destined to marry and to have children, I would assume with total confidence that a married woman who did not have children must either have physical problems or deep psychological ones. And I remember with some shame the freedom with which I would mouth these opinions.

Today many of us know better. But although we may understand that a woman has a right to choose to remain childless, the society in which we live still does not, and most of the time it is extremely difficult to be a woman who is deliberately not a mother. On the most immediate level, a childless woman must deal with the painful confrontations and equally painful silences between her family and herself. Let me use myself as an example. I am an only child, a survivor of World War II. My father was killed during the war, as was his whole family; my mother is the only family I have. Most of her friends are, like us, surviving members of families which were wiped out. It was an unstated aim of the individuals of this circle to regenerate the traditional family, thereby making themselves "whole." And over the years, most of them were quite successful. Some remarried; those who did not had the satisfaction of watching their children grow up and of knowing that they would take the "normal" route. Soon there were in-laws, then grandchildren. The nuclear family seemed to reassert itself.

It has been extremely difficult as well as painful for me to live with the knowledge that I deliberately never produced the child who could have continued "my father's line"; that I never provided my mother with the new family and the grandchildren she was sure would appear, which she thought were her right to expect. I know that other women, coming out of different circumstances, have experienced similar difficulties and pain—women who were raised as only children, who were given the burden of providing their parents with the stereotypical props of old age. These women have complained bitterly about how their parents' disappointment in them (as if they had failed at something) has affected them. The "you're-the-last-of-the-line" argument always makes the woman who chooses not to have children appear perverse, stubborn, ungiving, selfish. Equally painful can be the excitement of parents when they inform the childless daughter of the birth of a friend's grandchild. I have heard this kind of excitement in my mother's voice, and have often resented the fact that nothing that I could achieve could elicit that tone of voice, that kind of lasting, enduring satisfaction. Her envy of her friend is clear; and underneath it, I know, lies a silent, unstated criticism of me: I have held back.

A woman who is not an only child is often relieved of this kind of burden and pressure when one of her siblings marries and gives birth. But this, too, creates its own problems; often the childless woman feels resentment and jealousy because the parents seem so pleased with the other sibling for making them grandparents. A woman once told me how her sister, who had recently given birth, said to her that she was glad she had been able to provide their mother with the pleasure of seeing her first grandchild. The mother was dying. The woman felt deeply hurt, not only because of her sister's insensitivity to her feelings, but also because she felt she had nothing comparable to offer her mother.

At moments like these, women often yearn for the perfect excuse which will relieve them of the burden of having chosen to remain childless, which will convert them back into "warm, loving women." The choice seems too great a responsibility, seems too much against the values of our society. I remember a few years ago, when I had to have surgery on my uterus, how frightened I was at the prospect of having a hysterectomy. I told the doctor that, if at all possible, I wanted to keep my ability to have children. What I did not express to anyone, and barely to myself, was that a part of me wished that in fact a hysterectomy would be necessary. By becoming sterile, I would be relieved of having to make an agonizing decision. Remaining childless would no longer be a result of my "perverseness." I would be childless because I could not bear children. What could anyone possibly say to me after I had had my hysterectomy? I have heard other women reluctantly confess similar secret thoughts, women with raised, feminist consciousness, who nevertheless find it difficult to make the decision not to have children, and also to take full responsibility for it without feeling defensive and to some degree unjustified.

In the end, I did not have a hysterectomy, and my childlessness is a result of my own decision. The process by which that decision was made is in large measure difficult for me to reconstruct. To a certain degree, I think I made it over a long period of years, during many of which, on the surface at least, I was not consciously thinking about the issue. Certainly, for a long time I thought there was no decision to be made; I was sure that I would marry and have a family. Furthermore, I never doubted my intense desire to have a large family, never stopped to question whether I really wanted this, or whether it was something I thought I should want. Looking back, I find that often, in order to appear normal to myself, I adopted attitudes and values which were clearly not my own. In this particular case the unconscious argument went as follows: A normal woman wants children; I am a normal woman; I want children. This kind of short-circuiting of real feelings is quite common with many women, women who cling to fantasies created by others. These fantasies, many women think, will keep them in the mainstream, will prevent them from appearing different or conspicuous.

I fantasized about my future family for a long, long time, though in my actual life there was nothing to indicate that I was moving in that direction, that the fantasy would become a reality. I never married, never became pregnant. Yet I continued to assume that it was simply a question of time, that of course *it* would happen. *It* did not.

At the age of thirty, I was finally able to admit to myself that I did not want to marry. That realization, however, did not resolve the question of whether or not I should have children, and so I began to think about the issue in more real, more concrete terms. Two years later I became involved with a woman, and a year later I had to have my operation. At that point I was already thirty-three, was beginning to realize that I had to make a clear decision. And I made it by doing nothing about it. I thought a good deal about children, my need for them, my intense longing for them, my fears about being without them. But I did nothing.

The long years during which I was making my decision were extremely difficult. Most of the time I felt inadequate and incomplete. I was conscious that many people around me thought it was peculiar that I was not being swept away by "a normal woman's instinct" to bear and rear children, an instinct which should have overridden any of my qualms about marriage. The message communicated to me was that I—a woman alone, without a partner, without children—was enigmatic at best, superfluous at worst. In those years, I was unable to articulate to myself or to others that I was following other instincts. The best defense that I could muster was to say, "I'm too *selfish* for that life." Nevertheless, I evolved my decision and stuck to it.

4. Conclusion

This past April I became thirty-six and I think it is not accidental that it was about that time I began thinking about writing this article. Though most of the time I really do not know what to make of my age, it is around the issue of having a child that my age becomes real to me. For if I do not feel thirty-six (whatever feeling that is supposed to be), I certainly know that biologically my body is thirty-six, that the time for bearing children is almost over for me, and that once I pass a certain point, the decision not to bear a child is irrevocable. That the decision has already been made is very clear to me, though I cannot pinpoint the exact moment when I made it. No matter what my age, the issue is closed.

Often, of course, I wish I had done *it*, done it in those unconscious years when so many women I knew were doing it. They are now mothers whose children are almost adults—eight, ten, twelve years of age. Frequently I find myself envying those mothers for having gotten it over with in those early years. That certainly seems to be the perfect solution: have the child in the past, so you can have it now. Fantasizing in this way, I can easily skip over all the hardships and frustrations that many of these women have experienced in the past ten or twelve years of raising their children under extremely difficult circumstances, hardships which they continue to experience, and which I can only partly understand.

Still, there are moments when I can actually assert a certain amount of pride in the way I have chosen to lead my life, when I can feel extremely good about the fact that I did not succumb and did not keep myself in line. I am pleased that I withstood the pressures, that I kept my independence, that I did not give in to the myths which surrounded me. I know, of course, that there are various reasons why I did not and others did, which include conditions over which none of us had very much control. Nevertheless, I do experience momentary delight in the fact that I escaped and did what I wanted to do (even when that was somewhat unclear), that I did not give in to the temptation to please my mother, did not give in to the pleas of my father's ghost to keep him alive, did not conform with the rest of my friends, but instead kept myself apart and independent in some essential way. In moments like these, I can easily take responsibility for my life and say it is the life that I have chosen.

None of this is ever very simple. There are pleasures that one gives up when one decides not to have children. But as I keep telling myself: you can't have everything. Choices have to be made, and consequences have to be lived with. The act of choosing inevitably brings loss. It is a difficult lesson to understand and accept. I keep trying to relearn it.

While writing this article I visited my mother who had just discovered, stuck away somewhere in a closet, my favorite doll. I was surprised by my instant sadness at seeing and then holding it. The sweetness of the face, the smallness of the head against the palm of my hand. I felt as if I wanted to cry. But in touching it, it was not a baby I envisioned, but rather myself, five or six years old, cradling the doll in her arms and rocking it gently to sleep.

The Distances Between Us:
Feminism, Consciousness and the Girls at the Office
An Essay in Fragments

(1985)

*for Melanie Kaye/Kantrowitz,
who insisted I write it*

This essay is based on my experience doing office work, something I have done on and off for the past 25 years, supporting myself through college and graduate school as a typist, receptionist, medical transcriber, and librarian's assistant (file clerk). This was not unusual. In the late '50s and through the '60s most students at CCNY and most graduate students at the University of Chicago worked (stipends and government loans never sufficed; men usually got added income from wives).[1] During this period, office work seemed to me necessary and tolerable because I assumed it was temporary. While I was sensitive to many of the inequities, I did not really focus on them. I assumed they would not be my problems. I was looking forward to a teaching career. I received my Ph.D. in 1970.

Between 1969 and 1973, I had a full-time teaching job as an assistant professor of English in New York City. When enrollment dropped, the teaching market was already glutted and I, along with non-tenured faculty across the country, was laid off. While I have done some adjunct teaching since then, I have never held another full-time teaching position.

After a year collecting unemployment I fell back on my office skills. For the past 10 years, with breaks for adjunct teaching and editorial work, I have held what seems an infinite number of jobs—frequently two or three part-time jobs at once. These were usually higher level office positions such as legal secretary, proofreader, copyeditor. In addition, I taught Yiddish for a while, tried my hand at Yiddish translation, and taught creative writing workshops at home.

These essays and speeches were written over a period of thirteen years in a variety of contexts and the current collection reflects the styles and voices which I originally adopted for different audiences. I have also retained my personal form for emphasizing statistics, historical periods and economic realities which, I am aware, may not always conform to standard literary style.

But always sandwiched in was simple office work: typing, answering the phone, xeroxing, filing, and, more recently, word processing. My income has never been steady, always uncertain. I remain constantly worried about where the next job will materialize.

In the mid-'70s it was still possible to survive by working part time, but by the end of the decade I had to return to full-time secretarial work—first in a law office, later in a school for disturbed boys, finally and more recently in a posh psychiatric hospital. During this 4-year period, which ended in November 1983, I managed to carve out one block of uninterrupted time—8 months unencumbered by a job—that allowed me to write. I had saved some money and received support from my mother and then from a grant. One thread: my livelihood.

The second thread: my writing. Since I began to publish in the early '70s, my writing itself has brought me virtually no income. I have self-published or have been published, have accumulated a substantial number of credits. But as for money, in 11 years I have earned a total of $695 from contributions to anthologies.[2] As an editor of Conditions I received $1200 for 4 1/2 years of work.[3]

Where the threads converge: Keeper of Accounts was the collection I worked on during my eight-month "break" in 1981-82. Though I have so far made no money from it, the positive response to that collection has freed me, at least for now, from office work. Keeper has made me better known as a writer, thereby qualifying me for a number of creative writing jobs and for a writer-in-residence grant.[4] Since November 1983 I have lived on income from these as well as from adjunct teaching in two different colleges. It has been a relief.

I offer these details about my work history, my career as a writer and a teacher, and my economic situation because I want to be clear that I am not writing from the perspective of an office worker who has only done office work and has never had other kinds of opportunities. Clearly, for a long time my life had all the markings of upward mobility, and the Ph.D. was intended to place me solidly in the middle class. It was a course I had chosen and which I was not ashamed of. It was only the economic situation that checked these plans.

My history is not unique in this sense; I believe there is a far greater mixture and mix-up of education, class, and economic insecurity among women than feminists recognize. Some of the reasons for this I discuss in this essay. Melanie Kaye/Kantrowitz, in one of our numerous dialogues, pointed out that on the whole our movement has too often equated the issues of class and race, thereby obscuring the need for a separate analysis of each. One result has been an erasure of the white working-class experience. A white woman—and especially a Jew like myself—is usually assumed to be middle class, while a woman of color—especially Black, Hispanic or Native American—is usually assumed to be working-class or poor, which is often, but not inevitably, true.

My own experience in the movement substantiates Melanie's analysis. Much of the impetus for this article has stemmed from my frustration and anger at what I have observed: distortion and erasure of the lives of women I have worked with at various jobs; the ignoring, misunderstanding, and romanticizing of my own experience. The resistance to clarity, has, predictably, been greatest from middle-class and downwardly mobile women who have never felt and thus simply do not understand economic traps and limitations.

Because the office experience is not my life's work either, because I expect that the next 10 years will be like the last (with office work comprising only part of my working life), because I expect to continue benefiting from my writing and my training as a teacher, I too cannot completely convey what it means to remain for 25 or 35 years typing at a desk and never have any other options. And while I have frequently been broke and am constantly in debt, I have never been the poorest of the poor. But I have experienced the sense of entrapment and futility that office work can bring for periods long enough to enable me to glimpse their meaning. For this glimpse I feel peculiarly indebted, knowing that had my life gone according to my class, I would have known no work but office work; and had my life gone according to my plans, my knowledge of this kind of working life would have been almost nonexistent. In fact, this knowledge and my friendship with other office workers have been the only benefits of the experience.

* * *

I keep asking myself why I need to write this, what it is that I need to say. As often happens with my writing, the title comes first: "The Distances Between Us." The "us"—my sisters in the women's movement (however one defines it) and the women in the offices I work in, who talk disparagingly about that movement, about "libbers," about how they like to have doors opened for them, about the poor "spinster" living down the road.

I did not say my "sisters in the offices I work in" because I'm not used to writing or reading that phrase. My failure. Our failure. But sisters they are with a connection I feel strongly despite our different lives, our different levels of consciousness, despite the fact that most of the time I cannot be open about myself as a dyke, a Jew, a writer. But then, am I fully myself in the women's movement when the life I lead—the experience of office work and economic pressure—is not part of the feminist consciousness? So there is distance there too.

This essay represents my attempt to balance a perspective in a movement I am deeply committed to—the feminist movement. I want to view the world, or at least the immediate society in which I function, not only from the vantage point of a deliberate, conscious lesbian/feminist, but also from the vantage point of those women who seem to reject feminism theoretically, but obviously need a feminist movement because they are affected by women's issues—including class, work and economics— about which they are the experts and can teach us. Too often these women are excluded because they do not have the correct political language or consciousness. Ironically, much of our political theory addresses their condition and living circumstances. And yet how often do we dismiss them or put down their perspectives as uninformed and unenlightened because they do not talk like we talk, do not operate from the same framework?

* * *

March 11, 1983: The deadline for this essay is almost past and nothing that looks like an essay has yet emerged.[5] I have a pile of separate sheets of paper with first-draft notes: memories, observations, half-formulated ideas and theories, questions, suggestions for answers, reminders to look up certain passages. Most of these have been jotted down at high speed on my office IBM Selectric, usually when I should have been doing something else and was tense that I might be caught.

These separate sheets physically embody part of what it is I want to write about: what it is like to be an alert, thinking human being absorbed, assaulted by mindless, unintelligent work; the fragmentation; the sense of being scattered; what it is like not to have time to think, to consider an idea and follow it through to its logical conclusion. This condition—devoid of logic because it is irrational, devoid of structure because it is aimless, devoid of theme or thesis because it is pointless—is not unique to me just because I happen to want to write. Rather it is the common experience of many working people, an experience that I have observed and shared primarily with those who do office work.[6] Most of the office workers I have met are not writers and do not want to be, nor are they lesbians or conscious feminists. Yet how often between transcription tapes, during extended coffee or smoke breaks, on those Friday afternoons that seem endless—how often have I heard them speak of the sense of deprivation, of being robbed, the sense of loss that I happen to experience in relation to my writing. 8 hours a day, 5 days a week, we all lose possibilities, lose self.

I am stuck with this paradox. Those who do not share this life of aimless, meaningless work, those who do not sit and feel day after day go to waste, simply do not know, cannot, I believe, fathom the depth of its destructiveness. They do not know, and yet they think they know, frequently creating theories about it, stating how work and economic issues are important, yet how we must move past them toward "deeper" or "higher" ones. Poor and working-class women know that much of the time these are the only issues; no wonder they find such theoretical writing—not too difficult as some would have us believe—but too abstract, too divorced from their own daily struggles.

My own experience has taught me that work and economic issues are essential starting points for feminist discussions, ones which cannot be quickly skipped over. They affect us psychologically, affect our personalities, our creativity, our ways of thinking, affect our relations with each other. Unfortunately, those of us who understand this through direct experience—well, the experience itself frequently blocks us from communicating what we know. After all, how many of us have the time or space to pull together our knowledge and observations? How many of us have the energy, in fact, both to absorb the experience and to convey it to others in whatever form? And this is precisely the trap in which I now find myself. Knowing. Yet not being able to speak.

Fact 1: My life at this time does not allow me to write the traditional essay: beginning, middle, end—state your thesis clearly; develop the argument; illustrate appropriately; smooth out transitions; refine the logic, conclude. And I really do not want to produce such an essay, but rather something that is closer in form to my way of life and, equally important, close to the process of my writing.

The fragmentation of this piece, therefore, is not unlike the fragmentation of the lives of those of us who have no time to ourselves. The leaps, ellipses, zigzags are the result of a specially developed thought process, one that is not linear because it is always interrupted, frequently free-associative and haphazard, rarely schematized. We think. But we think differently. Sudden realizations, half-finished paragraphs, an outline, a sketch. But no smooth development, ordered philosophy.

Fact 2: If those of us stuck in these situations are going to say anything at all, then we must say it in nontraditional ways. We must speak in leaps, in zigzags, in incomplete parts. To wait until we can speak smoothly and completely is to doom ourselves to silence.

Inside and Outside

I frequently talk about being in the "real" world as opposed to the feminist or lesbian circle. What is the opposition I set up?

Everything outside the feminist movement is the "real" world. This consists of institutions, the office and office workers at my current job, my family and friends "from before." When I think this way, do I mean the feminist world is "unreal"?

Not so much unreal as sifted. To some degree. To a great degree. The "movement" world—the inside—is created through choices. We choose the people we want to work with, we choose the causes we want to work on, we choose the feminist institutions we want to create. None of this is absolute, but certainly it seems true to a greater degree than in the "real" world—the outside. Because we are so used to these choices, coalitions are frequently difficult to make. We think we have a choice about whom we work with. And there are people we choose *not* to work with.

Outside

I have no control over the circumstances in the office I work in. I look for a job and usually take what I can get, hoping for a decent salary or benefits or manageable travelling time—all the considerations surrounding work. But I do not choose the other people in the office, just as I do not choose other members of my family, just as I do not select who can be a Jew or a woman. These all come with birth. And working circumstances come with the job.

What always astonishes me is how quickly people whom I have never seen before begin to exert enormous power and influence over my life. My boss could be constantly proving his authority by demanding I let him know when I need to leave my desk and go to the bathroom. My supervisor might hate her job, be frustrated with the administration and take it out on me by constantly dropping in to see "exactly what you are doing." The supply person might take a dislike to me and not give me a good transcribing machine. When you consider that you must spend 8 hours a day, 5 days a week dealing with any or all of this, life can become a complete nightmare. It is not easy just to say: I guess I'll leave and find something else. Not in these times when jobs are scarce, when you're middle-aged and can no longer "pretty-up" some man's office, when you've been conditioned by poverty not to leave any job.

Given these circumstances, most women in offices know it's to our advantage to pull together. There are always exceptions, the ones sucking up to the supervisor or boss; but these individuals are easy to spot because of their isolation. There is no faking around this issue. Most of us know, even if we are very different from each other, who the enemy is. In the office, we rarely mistake what side of the line we are all on.

Inside

We act as if we always have a choice. We are insulted when asked to associate or join with someone we disagree with or dislike. We try as much as possible to pick and screen those around us.

This is probably an exaggeration.

This is probably not an exaggeration. Look at the in-fighting, the pulling apart, the trashing and back-stabbing. We confuse who the real enemy is, frequently fingering each other. We act as if we can afford to pick and choose. And we can't.

Two Episodes

Outside: I am being interviewed for a secretarial job. I have made a mistake in this application by admitting, not that I have a Ph.D. (which I know never to admit to in these situations) but that I have an M.A. The job as advertised seemed to require some research and editing experience. I misread. My prospective boss, a psychiatrist, worries that I'm overqualified. Would I be bored? he asks. I've been asked this question before whenever the issue of my education has come up. The implication is, of course, that the more educated you are, the more tedious the work will seem.

Does he think women with a high school degree find transcription and typing interesting and stimulating? What kind of hierarchical conception of human beings does this psychiatrist have? How is it that a well-educated man, supposedly trained in sensitivity, does not have any idea that every single secretary around him sees through his arrogance and condescension and is repeatedly outraged by them? And to what degree does he—and those like him—have to dehumanize office workers in order to maintain this limited view of them?

Let me put it another way: what deliberate ignorance and callousness to people—high school drop-out and Ph.D., secretary, housewife, athlete, construction worker, farm worker—would allow for the conclusion that anyone would find this work anything but boring?

Inside: Another writer has just finished reading my short story "The Journal of Rachel Robotnik." The story is about a woman office worker—and a writer—trying to find time to write, trying to cope with the tensions between other transcribers in her steno pool and their boss, trying to find some balance in her chaotic life. My friend, a political writer, proud of her political awareness and commitments, likes the story very much, but confesses: "I've always wanted to write about office work. But it's so boring. I've never been able to do it." At first I am stunned. Then I feel rage at the ignorance, insult of the remark. *Office work,* I know, *is very boring,* very boring indeed. But *the people* who do office work *are not.* Certainly not any more than any other people. My friend knows she must be aware of the "working class," must "reach out" to *them,* but in her own life, what she does is distance herself. For her the work and the people are one and the same; only boring people would spend a lifetime doing boring work. No wonder she—and others like her—can't build personal or political bonds with working-class women.

Inside and Outside: One night when I had a bad case of insomnia, I remembered these two episodes and suddenly realized that in both the word "boring" loomed large, though the judgment came from two people seemingly opposed politically and ethically. Neither my boss (he finally hired me) nor my politically correct friend with her guilt toward the working class sees the woman office worker for what she is: as complex a human being as the political writer wanting to make an impact on the world through her radical political analysis; as complex a human being as the head of a research department of a modern psychiatric hospital, claiming to have insight into the psyches of others. As complex and as simple. But only those who have allowed themselves to look beyond the occupation label and have made personal contact and shared experiences will know that.

* * *

I have encountered extraordinary arrogance and ignorance concerning working-class people, often from feminists who are well educated, of middle-class backgrounds, and who pride themselves on their political analysis, their raised consciousness and awareness, and their critical appraisal of privileges. Some examples:

—I review a novel about a waitress and ask for some feedback. On one note I receive the following question: Given that this novel is written in different voices and from different perspectives, should you not deal with the fact that a working-class woman will not understand it?

Why should she not understand it?

—I present a poem to a workshop that I am leading. It describes a working-class woman who, among other things, mentions that she believes in seeing things "aesthetical." Members of the workshop object. How could such a woman know such a concept, much less the word itself?

Why should she not know it?

—A woman tells me about a political group in which members decided to use the word "ain't" in their flyers so that the group would seem like "one of the people."

No comment.

—Another woman tells me of rewriting leaflets primarily in monosyllables so the "masses" could understand them better.

No comment.

—A downwardly mobile dyke tells me she's going to get unemployment. It's not very much, but she's decided to collect anyway even though it seems a lot of trouble and somehow, she implies, it is demeaning to fill out all those forms and stand on line once a week.

What must she think of the rest of us who line up obediently and to whom it never occurs that we should do otherwise because we have no choice?

Arrogance. Contempt. But above all, incredible ignorance. The "masses" out there are stupid, uneducated, unreachable unless you speak to them in kindergarten English. They are not people with a different way of living, surviving, with their own perspective. They are inferiors. To most middle-class feminists, as to most middle-class nonfeminists, working-class women remain mysterious creatures to be "reached out to" in some abstract way. No connection. No solidarity.

A Feminist Consciousness

A memory from the late '70s: I am teaching a course: Introduction to Women's Studies. It is summer and we meet four times a week in the evenings. The class is a typical New York City mixture of Third World and white women, middle-class and working-class, gay and straight, Jew and Christian, old and young.

Before I started teaching, I had been warned that women registering for it would probably have a low level of consciousness on feminist issues in general. This turns out to be too true. Though they live in New York City, not one has ever stepped inside a women's bookstore (at the time there were three) or attended a women's event (and there were dozens). Most are here out of a conscious curiosity as well as an unconscious pull toward feminism. And so we spend a great deal of time on what is basically consciousness-raising. After about three weeks they are much more sensitive, more aware of sexism, of feminist perspectives and analyses. Initially very skeptical, they are now frequently angry.

Midpoint in the course, I assign a story from the violence issue of *Heresies,* a story about a family outing at a lake.[7] As I remember it, no overt violence takes place; but throughout the outing the father bullies the wife and children incessantly. The class discusses domestic violence, the different degrees, levels, types. Without thinking very much about it, I ask casually: "Well, what about the mother? What do you think of her? After all, she's fairly passive. Do you think she can be reached?"

The answers come quickly. No. Absolutely not. She's beyond help. Maybe this is naive of me, but I am genuinely shocked. Most of the women in the class seemed in her condition only three weeks before. And now—they deem her a hopeless case: *She's the type that never changes.* Why, I wonder, do they give up on her so quickly? Why do they distance themselves from her?

Suddenly *I* am angry. Everything we've been doing for the past three weeks seems worthless. What's the point, if there is no identification, no empathy? So I return the next day and make a very clear statement: I refuse to let them give up on this character. I tell them I am willing to sit in silence for the remainder of the course until they come up with some kind of satisfactory answer in relation to the woman in the story.

And so we sit. And I wait. No one is particularly comfortable. The silence goes on for a long, long time. And then finally one woman blurts out: "What the hell is she supposed to do? Just pick up the kids and go? Where? And do what?"

And with that question, with what is clearly an identification with the woman's perspective and options, the class is off. They begin a serious discussion of choices. Of helplessness. Of indoctrination. Of breaking through the indoctrination—what makes it possible, what blocks it. Of available support systems. Of support systems that should exist but do not. Of the feelings that led them to register for the class. The fact that the class existed. The fact that they knew someone who encouraged them. And on and on.

What they bridged at this point was the distance their consciousness created between themselves and other women who had not reached the same point. They *remembered* and *integrated* their past experiences with their new perceptions. They realized that a young mother with two children, with no independent income or social support, will tolerate a great deal from a cruel husband. Her remaining with him might not be just stubborn resistance to feminist ideas of women's strength and independence, nor her "ineducability," but rather a realistic acceptance of the circumstances which allow her and her children to survive, if painfully.

A recent interpretation: When I described the episode to Melanie, she remarked that when people first discover new parts of their identity, their tendency is to strengthen their self-perception by separating themselves from those who do not share it. This solidifies one's new position. We see this frequently with just-out lesbians who can't bear heterosexual women, or newly-born radicals who scorn all who are not politicized like them.

Still, if this type of separating is a necessary stage of the process, it should be only temporary. For when consciousness does nothing except separate us from each other, it is useless. Maybe worse than useless. It is divisive.

I have watched feminists with such "raised consciousness" be contemptuous of the office worker who wears make-up and worries about her weight (never mind if these might be legitimate concerns in relation to her job). Such a judgment reveals: one, that the working-class woman is seen as completely passive, having to be changed by others and having nothing to offer; and, two, that her experience as well as her being are deemed too lowly. This analysis frequently passes for "consciousness" or "being political," again separating those who are from those who aren't. In this context, being political means being morally superior.

I am reminded of Anzia Yezierska who, in her story "Brothers," wrote: "Education without a heart is a curse." And raised consciousness without a heart is not only a curse, but a fraud.

* * *

February 22, 1983: Why do we always assume that having a "raised consciousness" or "political awareness" is desirable? I remember my initial exhilaration after finishing Tillie Olsen's *Silences*. Though much of the content was not new—my background had already clued me in to many of the limitations that this book describes—I had never really thought about silencing in such a systematic way, nor had I thought about how it applied to myself as a writer.

For example, I had always characterized myself as "not very prolific." This was not said defensively, just descriptively. I did not produce much. It hadn't occurred to me that the circumstances of my life did not lend themselves to my being prolific because most of my energy was expended on trying to support myself. Writing was, of course, important, but not *most* important. It was not anything I cried about. Who cries about such things? Certainly no one I knew while growing up. I was taught that everyone works. And no one expects any pleasure from it. You just do it. And writers are not exceptions.

I read *Silences* at a time when I was taking my writing more and more seriously. As I said, the initial realization of the various barriers—sexual, social, economic, racial—that silence us, that prevent us from externalizing our vision and experiences of the world was exhilarating: certain discrete perceptions suddenly fell into place and created a pattern in the midst of complete chaos.

But as the recognition took hold, as it sank deeper into my consciousness, as the true implications of that pattern became clearer, as I realized the full force of the "givens" of my life in relation to my writing, I began to experience a tremendous upheaval—a period of intense rage and pain. I became acutely aware, in a way I had not been before, of all my limitations.

I read *Silences* in 1979 during a short three-month "break" from work. Afterwards, I began working full time in a law office. I had begun to write the story "The Journal of Rachel Robotnik." Every day during that period, while typing, while transcribing, while xeroxing, while filing, I would think: I could be writing. I could be writing my story. I could be working on many stories, on many poems. I went through a period of intense self-observation, of focusing on the exact meaning of what I was living through. Day after day completely wasted in meaningless work. Getting up every morning. Crowding into the dilapidated subway. Other people crowding around me. Empty, bleak days. All I could think was: I am wasting everything in me. For almost a full year I counted and measured every minute, every second of my life that was being wasted. The constant calculating was excruciating.

The rage was soon accompanied by an envy that worked like a high-powered microscope, making visible and enlarging differences, magnifying what others had and what I did not have. A writer I knew who didn't need to work was looking for a room so she could write in seclusion and peace; her home, she said, was chaotic. I envied her, could barely look at her when she explained "her problem." Another woman was taking time off because she was feeling scattered and just couldn't focus (she had income from sources outside of her job). Someone else went away on vacation to unwind. Someone else was just staying home. I envied them and sometimes hated them. I could not forgive them for not being in my position.

These were the kinds of emotions that erupted in me as I awakened to the limitations of my growth as a writer. Envy is a horrible thing, especially when directed at what is not within our control. It is like raging at a thunderstorm. It is stupid. It eats you up.

But I felt it. And it came with the perception that consciousness brought. At the time, there was nothing I could do about my condition. And so I yearned for the time when I was oblivious to it.

* * *

I remember another feeling I experienced during this period. Every morning I would take the train from Brooklyn and get off at 42nd Street and Grand Central Station in Manhattan. I would hurry through the station surrounded by hundreds and hundreds of other people, all also rushing to get to work on time. Thousands of us would bunch up near the escalators that took us up into the Pan Am Building, a short cut to the Helmsley-Spear Building where I worked. As I waited, completely surrounded by masses of people, completely lost among them, and then as I began to move upward on the escalator and saw those above me getting off and those below me still crowded and waiting patiently, I would be overcome with a feeling I can only imagine as close to mystical. I, raised an atheist and completely nonspiritual in my approach to life, would be overcome with such a sense of oneness with the people around me, such a sense of being with them—a feeling I had never before nor have ever since felt. I knew we were all lost together, that we were all being eaten up, swallowed up as if we were on a large conveyor belt feeding us to oblivion.

At those moments, I neither envied nor raged. I felt enormous peace with everyone. I knew I was sharing a basic experience with thousands of people. I did not feel alone.

Wasting a Life

A memory: I am meeting a friend who is working for the "Fair Hearings Court" of the State of New York. She transcribes the court proceedings of welfare recipients who challenge decisions on a local level.

The transcribing pool is in the midst of a vast floor space—on the edges are crates filled with files, desks piled on top of each other. Smack in the center of this upheaval—there's no way to tell if they're moving in or moving out—there are ten transcribers sitting in two rows facing each other. At the head of the two columns sits the supervisor, a woman who used to be one of the girls. She has risen through the ranks and along the fringes. Behind each row of transcribers are a few other desks with extra space around them—state bureaucrats—and then the cartons, crates and stacked office furniture. Large windows look out on the state capitol. Outside, I can see the enormous towers built by Rockefeller in honor of himself. His labyrinthine highways run under this plaza, unnecessary highways which required the demolition of century-old bridges.

The transcriber who is my friend is also a sculptor of massive structures that seem to push themselves out of the studio, that always seem to demand more space than she can provide. Karen is sitting, one of the girls, dressed in typical "bohemian" fashion—bright green Indian pants, a burning pink blouse, her long black hair defiantly loose and the grey streaks quite unashamedly visible.

She sits the third one down. She is facing a young woman who has her hair cut punk, defiantly green. Karen sits and transcribes. She is wearing boots, her foot is on the pedal, the headset over her ears. I stand for a moment and watch her silently. She cannot see me.

Later she will tell me how not a single case that she has transcribed during the past three months, not a single welfare recipient who has come for a hearing in order to increase payments or be reimbursed for a refrigerator, for an electric bill, for nursing care, for food—*not a single one* has won a case in the state's "Fair Hearings Court." And how can they? she asks. The state picks the judge, the prosecutor and the defending lawyer. So why should anyone win?

I look at Karen and watch her foot press the pedal.

Stupid is not the word for it. Criminal.

And I know that I could walk along these two rows of women and stand and watch each one and say the same thing:

Stupid is not the word for it. Criminal.

* * *

I am attending a feminist brunch. An intense discussion develops around the issue of women's lives and the lack of opportunity, the repression, oppression, the exploitation. One woman becomes extremely upset, indignant because she cannot bear to think that her mother's life has been a waste. Some women try to comfort her. I do not say anything. I know, of course, that no person who has exhibited kindness, caring and support can be said to have wasted her life entirely. But I also know the bitter fact that most lives are incredibly wasted, that the opportunities for developing identity, for receiving pleasure, for achieving a sense of self-worth are limited and, not only underdeveloped, but in most cases not developed at all—because no one thinks that a housewife, or a mother, or a typist has anything to develop. It simply has never occurred to most people. And that judgment is passed on through the silence surrounding them.

I do not say anything. But I know that this woman's mother has probably wasted a lot of her life, just as I have wasted periods of my life. And there is no getting away from that knowledge.

Art and Other Callings

I have been asking myself why I always focus on the artist. I focus on her because art—in my case, writing—is the most obvious yardstick I have to measure the waste in my own life. I do not know what yardsticks to use for others, for most people have not been allowed to see their own possibilities. Art, after all, is not the only means to self-expression and though some of my co-workers might, given the chance, want to be artists, others might want to be organizers, engineers, philosophers, full-time housewives and mothers, physicists, athletes, activists, greenhouse keepers, animal doctors, furniture strippers.

How easily do I and many of the feminists I know accept the fact that some of us are born with "talent" that should be nurtured and supported, without considering the implications of labelling and naming only those talents associated with art or professions. In doing that, aren't we implying that those born without a specific, *visible* talent are automatically meant to be transcribers or xerox machine operators or factory workers?

Sometimes I wonder if, in fact, most formally educated people do believe just that. Just as an artist or doctor must have the proper, conducive working atmosphere to flourish, so the secretary or office worker must have the proper, conducive working atmosphere for her calling. So how can we help her? How can we nurture and support her? Musak perhaps? Good lighting? A self-erasing typewriter? A word processor?

When people think in these structures, when they separate the artist, intellectual, or professional and think of her as a person apart, as special, as disconnected from the "masses," from the assembly line, from the stenographic pool, they reveal their basic distance from working people. When feminists think in these structures, our commitment to helping the "nonartist," the "ordinary" woman becomes nothing more than a desire to make her *more comfortable in the current social order*, a failure to see the separate value of her life. Such distancing denies our connection to her. For while we place ourselves outside that order by virtue of our "unique talent," we doom her to remain forever inside the xerox room or steno pool. That is not radical thinking. That is plain elitism.

* * *

November 30, 1982: Talked to Nina this morning. She is the cook for the staff—psychiatrists, administrators, office workers. She makes our lunch. She works fast. Uses all her free time to read. I wonder about her. She's tough. Used to work in a gas station. Raised dogs. Yes, I wonder about her.

Said to me she didn't like working. Said she's wishing her whole life away. (She's only 22.) Isn't it terrible, she asked, to live just for 2 days out of 7, and to wish the other 5 away?

Bonding

Given external facts, friendship between Elizabeth and me would seem impossible. Born a Catholic in a small Massachusetts town where she lived all her life, she was the oldest of four children. Went to work immediately after high school at the same psychiatric hospital where I met her more than 20 years later. Learned about sex by typing charts. Married at 20. Did not say much about Kenneth except that he never complained and was a good father. Had three children. The oldest boy had visual problems, hated school, was denied graduation until he passed a certain reading test. Elizabeth had worked with him almost every day since he entered second grade. The second boy had just begun college, the first to do so in his family. The "baby," a girl, is still in high school. All worked. Elizabeth was exactly my age when we met:

41. She returned to work in this hospital about a year before I arrived.

I am a Jew, a survivor of the Holocaust, a lesbian, an author of two books of poetry, a Ph.D., a teacher and an activist. I have never married and I have no children. I knew a great deal about Elizabeth within a couple of months. Until I left, almost a year later, Elizabeth only knew that I was a Jew, a survivor, that I aspired to write, and that I had a roommate.

Yet Elizabeth and I did become close friends. I admired her and listened as she analyzed and reflected on her life at home and at the office. She taught me about the hospital and kept rejecting my suggestions for greater efficiency and accountability with: "Haven't you learned they're not interested in your opinion? That they don't care what we do or how often? That they simply don't care?"

She hated her job with a passion, but saw no way out. She was in constant crisis. Five adults, all needed transportation to jobs and schools, and cars and motorcycles were forever breaking down, kids getting into accidents, bills constantly popping up and out of control. She said she felt cheated because she could never enjoy the house whose mortgage she and Kenneth were killing themselves to pay off—she was either in the hospital typing or at home cooking and cleaning. Once, I came into her room when she was collating a long monograph and was moving from desk to table. She said, "Irena, I feel like a corkscrew, just driving myself deeper and deeper into the grave." And then she began to turn in place and say: "Work. Grocery. Home. Work. Grocery. Home."

She understood basic feminist principles, though she openly rejected any feminist labels. She analyzed the structure of male thinking in relation to organizations and stated that men simply could not diversify and do more than one thing at a time while women had learned to play multiple roles in the home. She was sure if the women took over the hospital, it would make more sense.

Yet she was devoted to her family and the job. I would try to convince her, for example, to take a day off because she was totally depleted and exhausted—that "sick" did not mean exclusively "physically ill." It was hard for her to accept this; she thought it a form of lying. She felt responsible to the doctors. They relied on her. She refused to fudge or shortchange anyone, even though they constantly shortchanged her.

I understood her attitude. She wanted to salvage some sense of integrity. It was through her job and her family that she saw any possibility for achieving self-esteem. And so typing a report, quickly and flawlessly, was important. Meeting all deadlines was important. Never lying was important. Though I had things outside of the office that gave me a sense of worth—my writing, my political work—I too would often set goals for myself so I could have some sense of achievement during the day.

Still, I lied all the time, determined to use every sick day I could. I had no shame about it and Elizabeth and the others knew what I was doing. Yet no one blamed me or guilt-tripped me. They simply accepted me and my behavior. Elizabeth was particularly giving, enjoying our differences. She liked hearing about my outings to New York City, about my mother, about the woman I lived with—though that relationship was never clarified. She sympathized when I was really bored or disgusted. She sympathized when I was broke. And I was always eager to hear about her life, about how she had grown up in this town, her pre-marriage innocence, the progress of her kids in school, and to give any kind of advice based on my own experience outside the office. She in turn advised me to have patience, showed me short-cuts and pitfalls of the institution, and became a model of how to live without envy and constant rage. I tried to help her make more room for herself, pointing out the kids were old enough to take over more responsibility. I also felt helpless and stymied, as with other friends, because I could not get her to break a lifelong pattern of self-sacrifice. At times I would feel angry and frustrated, especially when I found her asleep, her head resting on her typewriter. She countered: "It's not so much that we're not as good as we were. We're just not as good for as long."

Elizabeth made me feel privileged because I had reasonable hope that eventually, in a year or so, I could leave. I would get a break, if only temporary. I knew what one free week would have meant to her. Talking to her month after month, I realized over and over again, no matter how deeply unhappy I was, how depressed, that it was not the same as her unhappiness, as her depression. She made me feel the great difference between us, between our lives.

And yet this difference did not separate us. It was possible for us to share equally—to share the particular strengths we had developed from our different lives. We formed a close bond based on a common experience of trying to cope with nonsensical regulations and the callous behavior of our bosses. Elizabeth made me more conscious than ever that her life was like so many others—devoured by meaningless work. She made me conscious of the kinds of lives so many women lead and the waste of it. As she put it, "You know, Irena, when I got out of high school in '58, no one thought I should do anything but type."

1982: A Photograph

Source: A local upstate New York paper.
Content: Two people shaking hands.

He is older. The president of a college. It is obviously graduation. He is dressed in an elaborate cap and gown—inverted collar, tassels, colored stripes, a multitude of folds evoking complexity, emeritus, honorary, distinguished, doctor.

She is young, very young. She is wearing the plainer costume: black cap and gown. No frills.

It is graduation.

They are shaking hands.

She has just received an award from the Secretarial Arts Department for "outstanding achievement in typewriting."

A Soap Opera

She was not glamorous. That is important. Because receptionists are always supposed to be glamorous. But Sandy was 35, wore casual make-up, clothes that were clearly frayed at the edges.

It took me a while to piece together the full portrait. Initially, Sandy struck me as happy-go-lucky. She was always laughing and joking whenever I came into the main office to pick up mail or do my xeroxing. She talked a lot about her kids, about her baby, her 12-year-old daughter who was now wearing her "training" bra; about her 14-year-old son who had decided he was a "breast man" and not a "leg man." She was divorced and talked a lot about crushes she had and dreamed out loud about meeting someone, about trying to show interest without overstepping the limits of ladyhood, about the middle-aged man at the post office who was interested in her but whom she couldn't abide because, after all, he was balding.

She talked endlessly about all this. It all seemed fairly usual, simple.

But Sandy's life and history were complicated, so complicated that some people—mainly the administrators of this special school for boys—laughed behind her back and called her life a soap opera.

Her health, it turned out, was poor. She had kidney problems and she was taking special medication for arthritis. One day I noticed a black and blue mark on her arm and, without thinking, asked about it. She blushed, and then confessed that her brother had beaten her. Many family members were alcoholic, she herself was once, though she was sober now. The night before, one of her brothers had arrived drunk. She shrugged and blushed again.

She also had custody problems. The arrangement was not permanent. Custody was reassigned on a monthly basis. And it was partly contingent on her ability to support the kids, pay her mortgage, her fuel bills, etc. She kept reassuring me that her husband was really a nice guy and loved the kids.

Since she had been hired to replace someone who had gone on maternity leave, Sandy had no job security or benefits. She was earning $3.25 an hour working a 40-hour week (not including lunch).

Her "responsibilities" included switchboard, typing, xeroxing, collating, and filing. She worked in the main office of the school. I was a secretary, but in a different building. Compared to other secretaries—there were six of us in all—Sandy was not very good. Her work at the switchboard and xeroxing were fine. But her typing was filled with errors and misspellings, her filing sloppy and confused. Most of us would help her out whenever we were in the main office, but we could never give her all the help she really needed.

One day toward the end of the summer, she got sick—sunstroke complicated by the arthritis medication she was taking. She collapsed and was rushed to a hospital. She remained critical for a few days and then finally stabilized. After two weeks she was back home.

The day after she got home, the supervisor called and gave her two weeks' notice. Another secretary came to stay with her. She could not get out of bed yet. She had absolutely no money. She was worried about custody.

Another woman had been interviewed for the position. But when it came time to negotiate the salary, she refused the $3.75 (50¢ more than Sandy was getting). Not anticipating any problems, the supervisor had fired Sandy before the other woman had actually accepted. Now the school was stuck.

Shameless, as always, the supervisor called Sandy. Forget what we said.

And, of course, she did. What else was she supposed to do?

The other secretaries tried to make her deal with the situation, emphasizing that the administrators had no scruples, that this could happen again, that Sandy needed to get a firm commitment. It was obvious the woman she had replaced was not returning and that the administration was not going to offer the job to Sandy. She had to clarify the situation. If they refused to make a commitment, she had to start looking for something else—*now*.

Sandy listened, but was afraid to move. And then things changed. The supervisor gave notice and was replaced by a Mrs. Conroy. Everything got very quiet. We all sat tight and watched. It could get better. It could get worse.

We told Sandy that there might be some hope since Conroy was new. We urged her to talk to her and finally she did. Though it was now the end of October and Sandy had been working for the school since April (8 months!), Conroy told her she would be put on 3-months probation. If she did well, the job was hers.

We were appalled. We knew it was a set-up. Clearly they intended to let her go. We told Sandy she had to start looking for another job, had to start now. But she just smiled. She felt hopeful. She was going to work hard, get her typing speed up, and then she'd become a permanent employee.

A couple of weeks later, her car broke down. She had no money to fix it. She lived about 25 miles from the school. During the next week, she hitched, once walked 12 miles, a couple of times got rides from people who deposited her at the office at 7 A.M. and picked her up at 8 P.M. She was keeping up, but barely. She was beginning to apply for jobs.

And then one day, they fired her. It was November, the week before Thanksgiving.

Oppression

Inside: There's a romance about it, a romance by middle-class women who feel guilty about their privileged backgrounds. Downwardly mobile, guilt-ridden, they embrace the status of the oppressed and wear it like a badge. They point with pride to how little they have, able to measure it by what they've given up. They are, they claim, clerical workers, office workers, struggling with the injustices of the capitalist system.

Outside: I do not believe anyone really chooses to be a clerical worker, though I know many women might say they do. I believe that most people have never had the opportunity to examine what their true potential is and so the selection of clerical work is not done in a framework of complete freedom. Most women are told they are without potential—intellectual, athletic, artistic—are raised to fear responsibilities outside of the home and to question their ability to deal with nondomestic issues.

My experience in offices is that clerical workers, who are the lowest in status and pay in the hierarchy of office workers, despite all conditioning, dream privately and sometimes quite openly about doing something else. Most never do and instead spend endless years doing the worst office shitwork, 8 hours a day, 5 days a week. They spend this time in dead-end rooms, usually the useless corners of walk-in closets of large suites, rooms blocked off for files that don't need air or light. These women work for years stooped over folders, or climbing ladders to reach drawers close to the ceiling. Dusty, dirty, boring, unhealthy work, endless index cards, endless folders, staples, paper clips, punched holes, reorganizing, pulling, shuffling, filing.

They do this when they are nine months pregnant, when they can barely bend, when they are too exhausted to move, do it till the day before the baby is born. And then, two weeks later, after the delivery, they are back, while a sister or a grandmother takes care of the newborn. Whenever you walk into their workspace, that dark area that nobody else wants, they greet you eagerly, chat, show photographs of the baby, try to delay your departure.

There are some who hold 2 or 3 part-time jobs in different offices. Some sneak in books, take correspondence courses so they can develop new skills and perhaps one day become a secretary.

These are the clerical workers I have known. They do not think about their status with pride or with shame. It is simply where they are in this society. The work they do is not a ticket to anything. And the only thing they get for it is a very, very small paycheck.

* * *

In the hospital where I worked, *each* doctor received an $11,000-a-year *raise* between October, 1982 and January, 1983. In January, 1983, each secretary received a $10/week raise. Out of 13 women, not one had been earning more than $10,400 a year ($200/week before deductions) and, because health insurance went up that year, a number of secretaries took home less in 1983 than they had in 1982.

Victim

A woman was once describing a friend of hers to me, someone who was always hurrying from one part-time job to another, trying to piece together a living, always in a kind of frenzy and chaos that I know well. Perpetual deadlines. Different focuses. Irregular schedules. The woman concluded her long detailed description by commenting: "I don't think she'll ever get it together."

I swallowed hard. I had completely identified with the woman in the story. Get it together? I thought. With what assumptions does this woman operate? Who gets it together? How many people in this society ever get it together?

Most of us fail miserably at it. And we're meant to. Yet we cannot accept the concept of ourselves as totally victimized, totally done in. We must feel some measure of possibility in our lives, for how else could we ever hope to gain any degree of control?

So, victim? Yes and no, I suppose. I know a lot of people—skilled and hard working—who cannot get it together the way society wants them to. They do not meet current needs—whether that be typing skills or computer knowledge. They have many other skills—skills to care for the old, skills associated with compassion and patience, skills to build and construct, skills to teach and awaken. Are we to say they are playing victim, that they're not taking responsibility for their lives because they cannot, however hard they try, get their typing speed up or learn to use a word processor?

How glib. Would we ever say to anyone outraged at sexism, "you've got to accept the givens of this society"? But how quickly we say, "accept your lot because you've chosen it; otherwise you would have gotten out long ago and 'gotten it together.'"

Money

Feminists have barely learned to say the word to each other. How afraid we are to talk about it. Whenever the subject is broached, we run as if on hot coals and don't stop until we reach a cool spot. Talk about anything but that.

A woman I know has so much more than me. She has a good job—good pay, benefits. She is secure, takes vacations. Another woman doesn't have to work at all. Both leave, take long, what seem to me luxurious periods of time off. I say good-bye to them. Wish them well. And I mean it. But I also think, Why them, not me?

Another woman I know has so much less than me. In her eyes I am rich. She works as a chambermaid, is dependent on tips, is never quite sure how much she'll take home. She can never save, thinks it's a real luxury that I can take a day off with pay because I have sick leave. She thinks it's good that I have a day to write. And she means it. But she also thinks, Why her, not me?

Women sit around a table. Perhaps they're planning a benefit. Perhaps they're writing a statement. Perhaps they're organizing to participate in a conference in another city. One glances impatiently at her watch and calculates the cost of the babysitter. Another is thinking of the cost of a round-trip ticket out of town and whether she can afford to go. Still another feels depressed because she has to work that day and can't afford to take off. But they do not mention it. Some don't even think about the differences between them. Some do and feel guilty. Others want them to feel guilty. Others don't give a shit. But no one talks about it.

* * *

Shame and Humiliation:
When Need Becomes Shame and Asking Is Begging

November 10, 1984: I have postponed and postponed finishing this piece. I must finish it, I tell myself. But I am blocked, have been blocked for over a year now on an issue that sticks in my throat. It is the issue of shame and humiliation.

How can I write about this without exposing my own sense of shame? How can I write about this without confessing that just publishing this article about economics and money is intertwined with shame and humiliation? A shame that stems from early poverty. A shame that stems from my having internalized the worst of Jewish stereotypes. That because I'm a Jew, I must be rich. And if I say, no, I am not rich, then I am hiding my wealth, trying to get out of something.

I remember the first time I heard that some people would rather die in a burning building than run out and be seen naked. At the time, I could not quite grasp the depth of shame that could force someone to accept death rather than be exposed.

For the past year or so I have been thinking about this phenomenon, the power of shame over our lives, over my life—its power in stopping me from completing this essay, for example. I have been trying to sort out the times when I have felt ashamed as if I had done something wrong when, in fact, I had done nothing; to sort out the circumstances in which I have felt humiliated.

Need. I feel shame in feeling need, a shame that I associate with my early childhood of not having, of always wanting, of feeling that not to have a dress, a game, a toy made me somehow deficient, beneath, below, less than—*apart.*

That is, if those I am with have more. For if others share my circumstances, there is no shame. What occurs is complete understanding, camaraderie: a comparing of notes, of swapping suggestions, of exchanging strategies—how to write a check and not have it bounce if the account is empty; which gas station gives credit; how to get an advance, etc.

But when the need is visible and public in the presence of those who are above it, or who have power to choose to help or not, who could bestow their resources, use their privileges—call it what you will—then *need becomes shame and asking feels like begging.*

Why?

I think back to group situations where assumptions are made, assumptions I do not share. It might be a question of which restaurant to go to. Or whether we should go to an event I want to attend but can't afford. Or even a discussion of whether the price of a certain book is reasonable. And what is reasonable? *How can something be reasonable if I can't afford it?*

I think about these situations and my own sense of exclusion—of wanting to be a part of a group and feeling I can't, of having to draw attention to it, knowing I will embarrass everyone, knowing I will be the wet blanket and burst the happy bubble of togetherness.

And what is it I really want of them? To carry me? Do I have any right to ask anything, I who have not gotten it together?

Sometimes, I think, all I want is the issue acknowledged. That in itself. But above all, I want someone else to raise this issue, someone for whom money is not a problem, but who recognizes that her framework, her "reasonable cost" is not necessarily everyone's.

As feminists, we pride ourselves on our "awareness" of class. Our events invariably have the "more if you can/less if you can't" tag attached to the entrance fee, hardship rates for journals, sliding scales. And yet, I know that many women who cannot afford the standard price will not admit it because to admit it is to admit to failure, to inadequacy—to admit to something shameful—the fact of not having "gotten it together." Often it is the feminist with the middle-class background, downwardly mobile, who pridefully puts down her dollar at a five-dollar event. Many women I've known who stem from poor backgrounds, from a life of welfare and unemployment, a life of piecing it together, barely, week by week, day by day, would rather die than admit to their present poverty. Everything in their upbringing, everything in this society says that "failure" (and that is equated with economic dependence) is their own fault, a deficiency in them. They have not worked hard enough to "succeed" in the climb—it is all their fault, they should have tried harder.

> TRAIL OF TWO LIVES THAT DISINTEGRATED LED TO
> LONELY DEATHS ON AN ICY DAY by Nathaniel Sheppard, Jr. (*The New York Times*, February 3, 1983)

This article has been hanging over my desk now for a year and a half. The first few paragraphs read as follows:

> Chicago, February 2—The lifeless bodies of Norman and Anna Peters were found, wrapped in tattered blankets against the January cold, on the icy seats of the dilapidated 1971 station wagon that had become their home. With no resources and no place to go, they had died of carbon monoxide poisoning, presumably while running the car's engine in an effort to keep warm.
>   It was the sad final chapter to the tale of the disintegrating lives of two ordinary people, a struggling blue-collar couple who exemplified the lives of a sizable part of America. Theirs had always been a difficult existence, a constant struggle to make ends meet for a family of seven with an income from Mr. Peters' periodic employment as an equipment mover....
>   The Peterses had been a proud and private couple who had maintained a code of silence about their personal problems. It was a silence that often extended to their children.

The Peterses had lost their home—unable to keep up mortgage payments. Financially depleted by hospital costs to correct the birth defects of a child who had died 15 years before, plagued by alcoholism and unemployment, Norman and Anna saw no way out. Their life had been an endless series of crises. A member of the Riggers Local 136, the machinery movers union to which Norman belonged, commented:

> "There was no reason for them to sleep in a car. We would have figured out some way to help. If Norm had just come in. You can always get the guys to give five, ten dollars, fifteen dollars each. If only we had known."

But they didn't know. Norman did not say anything. Anna did not say anything.

* * *

When I decided to lead my first writing workshop in Brooklyn around the winter of 1976-77, I began to experience enormous anxiety when it came time to advertise. I needed to put up posters locally as well as in gay bars and women's bookstores in Manhattan. I felt enormous resistance to doing this and I kept procrastinating. Finally, a friend walked with me up 7th Avenue in Brooklyn and the signs went up.

POETRY WORKSHOP
led by
IRENA KLEPFISZ
author of *periods of stress*
an editor of *Conditions* magazine

My paralysis went beyond any insecurity over my ability to lead such a workshop. Like everyone else, I have self-doubt, but never to the degree of near incapacity. It was only after trying to sort it out and understand it that I realized that for me the placing of such an advertisement was a public admission that I needed money, that I was doing this *only* because I needed money.

And I really *did* need the money. It didn't seem to matter that I was providing a service. My name was appearing in huge, shameless letters and announcing, just as shamelessly, that I was broke. Of course no one necessarily knew; after all, there are many writers who lead workshops for the pleasure of teaching or for the prestige. And no one looking at my advertisement could distinguish me from them. Still, *I knew* of my need. I knew I was dependent on people signing up. And it was that sense of need, of dependence, that paralyzed me.

* * *

When my mother and I came to the United States in 1949, we lived on charity from Jewish organizations. We occupied one room—the living room of a one bedroom apartment—and shared the kitchen with an older Jewish woman who did piecework in the garment district. We lived in this room for four years and much of this time my mother earned some money as a seamstress—doing alterations (taking up hems, taking in waists, puckering shoulders, and tightening darts) and sometimes creating originals of her own design. It was a difficult existence—uneven in income, very crowded and depressed, completely suffused by what we had just managed to survive in Europe.

The charity we were living on was never clearly defined for me. My mother wanted to protect me and tried to hide it. But it could not be completely blocked from my consciousness, and instead what was strongly communicated was that we were not to refer to it. When pressed, we were, in fact, to lie about it. It was a source of shame.

Once someone she knew offered to print advertising cards for her. Since she wanted to build her list of customers, my mother accepted and soon there were hundreds of cards to be distributed.

ROSE KLEPFISZ
Seamstress
Originals and Alterations
Building 1, Apt. H-22

We took the cards and went out to the newer buildings of the cooperative complex we were living in. I was about 10 at this time and I found it all very exciting. We rode in the elevator to the 14th floor and then began slipping the cards under each door. For reasons I could not understand, if someone stepped out of an apartment, my mother would immediately slip into the stairwell. She did not want to be seen.

Everything about this endeavor seemed magical. The modern building, the elevators, the cards with my mother's name, the feel of the cold metal bannister as I ran down the stairs, skipping, jumping, leaping off the last four steps on to the next landing, rushing out into the hall ready to push more cards under the doors. But if someone stepped out of an apartment, my mother would immediately slip into the stairwell. She did not want to be seen.

She did not want to be seen.

✳ ✳ ✳

You must ask, a friend once advised.

Yes, I thought, she is right. But my tongue could not form the words and at different moments I have been like the person in a burning building *willing to die rather than stand bare with my need*. I know that I could pass up the opportunity of a lifetime because of this deep-rooted shame. Some, I know, would categorize such behavior as "playing the victim." I don't agree. The person overwhelmed by shame, unable to move while the flames inch closer and closer and the heat becomes more and more intense—that person is not playing victim. Rather she is paralyzed by a socially learned lesson so deeply absorbed it has become almost an instinct life itself cannot counter.

The opportunity of a lifetime. Let it pass rather than ask or inquire. It is too humiliating to acknowledge the power of others over you, your dependence on them. It is too humiliating to think that you might risk asking and they will turn you down. It is too shameful to wonder why you must go through this, why you do not have such power. Why it is that you have failed and have so little control over your own life.

You must ask, a friend once said.

Inside and Outside

What is real? What is feminist? What is inside? What is outside?

All are false distinctions, something I've known all along. There is no inside or outside. I do not live in two worlds. I live in one. The economics of the "real world" are not separate from the "feminist" world, even though the attitudes are often different. And this fact is one we ought to begin paying more attention to. For example:

—Women working in a battered women's shelter decide to unionize because they feel "their labor was exploited." The workers in Women Against Abuse (Philadelphia) stated that they did not view their problems as "isolated" and that "they have talked with staffs in other programs who have similar problems and concerns."[8]

—A feminist editor rejects a reconsideration of distribution of profits in an author's contract on the basis that such notions are "childlike" and inappropriate for the "real" world. The same editor sympathizes with protests of clerical workers over conditions and salaries, prints pamphlets about these injustices. Yet she tells an author to "grow up" and face "real" facts when it comes time to sign a contract.

—A political organization becomes financially stable enough to hire women to do the paper work. Immediately a hierarchy is established. Political activists—feminists—have become employers and now must relate to employees, in this case also feminists, whose work is inevitably more mechanical and less prestigious.

—A number of writers protest treatment by *The New York Native* and publish their statement in other gay papers. They maintain that gay institutions must have economic responsibility to their workers and are not exempt from the standards that would be applied to mainstream institutions.

—A Women's Studies Department has its "own" secretary, or "shares" one with another department. She is, of course, an employee of the school. But how do members of the department deal with her and *use* her?

—A writer complains she received only a token honorarium for her contribution to a feminist anthology, and that out of 25 contributors, only the editor made any money. Why, she asks, is this woman not sharing some of the profit? Isn't she living off the work of others? Isn't that what we fight against in all other places? Why should this be the exception?

—A collective gets a grant and is able to pay one of its members for some of the shitwork all have shared so far. On what basis is the person chosen? The neediest? Or the one with skills because she already has the experience? And when she messes up, another member, without thinking, says angrily, "But you're being paid!" And suddenly behavior that was tolerable as a volunteer is totally unacceptable. What happens when our commitment turns into a job?

—A three-day feminist conference is scheduled for Thursday, Friday and Saturday. All working women are automatically excluded from participating in two-thirds of the activities. The feminist organizers have forgotten that we live in one world and that some of us do not have the luxury of stepping out of it even for a minute.

But if society has taught us to be ashamed over not having money and privilege, some feminists' romance with oppression has also made them ashamed over having money and privilege. The result has been a kind of dishonesty, a fudging around economic issues, of falsifying backgrounds and current possibilities, of blurring distinctions, of ignoring or denying power and achievements. With all our emphasis on truth, on breaking taboos, why is it that so much lying occurs around economic issues?

I remember that among the first feminists I met some were downwardly mobile and considered oppression a status symbol. Some had higher degrees. Some were college drop-outs. A predominant criticism was directed at anyone who had any education beyond high school. Because I was new to feminism and still naive, because I wanted to be accepted, I did not challenge attitudes which even then, in my heart of hearts, I knew to be wrong. Instead, I went along to such a degree that in my first book of poetry I was too embarrassed to list the Ph.D. in my biographical note. I—an immigrant, a Holocaust survivor, despite economic obstacles, having worked 20 hours a week through most of graduate school and full time during the summers, having managed to overcome psychological odds and traumas—I, Irena Klepfisz, received a Ph.D. Truly something to be ashamed of.

How utterly crazy, when I think about it now. How utterly crazy.

* * *

The aspirations of most people—security, pleasure, leisure, meaningful work, creative and intellectual pursuits—are to be supported. These desires and dreams are not shameful. In supporting them, we are showing solidarity with working people, for whom these are luxuries and not givens.

* * *

Feminism cannot be separated from the economic realities of our society, and, as feminists, we need to face the economic unity of our lives; we must also learn to identify those of our actions that fall short of our best hopes. There is no such thing as purity. We must be willing to recognize and name powers and privileges that we do have and assess their significance and usefulness. And we must all recognize that these are not constant, but sometimes change in different contexts.

Sitting at various conferences, workshops, collective meetings, I have often marvelled at our ability to articulate perfect political theory while remaining insensitive and stubbornly ignorant to the life of the feminist sitting right next to us. At those moments, I have understood why so many women, deeply oppressed by sexism and economic necessity—find feminism and feminist theory abstract and irrelevant. At these feminist events, I too have sometimes felt alienated from discussions of sexism, homophobia, racism or anti-Semitism, though all these touch me personally. But the fact that there is no allusion to the working day from which I've just emerged or to the economic pressures which I carry with me has frequently made these discussions seem highly theoretical and left me estranged and angry.

* * *

It has occurred to me that it would be a good idea every once in a while to begin meetings with a ten-minute round robin so that each woman could say how she had spent the day and thereby ground the group. The differences between us, not only in terms of work, would then be clarified as each woman's assumptions, framework, and mental state on that particular evening became evident. The political discussion, no matter what its focus, would, I believe, be ultimately enriched and informed by the immediacy and concreteness of this information. We would then be not simply feminists speaking about feminist issues, but feminists rooted and bound in different ways in the same society, stating our frustrations as well as our pleasures and achievements. At the end of the meeting, members might want to do another round robin, this time focused on what each woman was going to be doing the next day. Thus, the political discussion would in some way be framed by and connected to our daily lives.

I offer this suggestion even though I know it is fraught with obvious dangers: self-hate, breast-beating, envy, anger, guilt-tripping, and lying. But I think, also, this kind of process contains the possibility of a much deeper view of our differences at any given moment and their relationship to our politics.

Above all, such a process might actually help all of us articulate the words we most fear and face the discomfort of our economic and class differences. For we need to put an end to the shame and guilt surrounding both power and powerlessness. We can begin with direct questions of ourselves and each other:

—What should I do with what I have? Share it? Keep it? Give it all away? Will you talk to me about your life? Will you help me understand? Can I learn from your strength? Will you tell me how I can be most useful to you? *Can you trust me?*

Difficult questions. As difficult as:

—Can I ask without shame? Can I show my strength? Can I stop equating all power with money? Will you listen to me? Will you give up some control? Will you see my need and not blame me—or fear me? *Can you trust me?*

And always the underlying question: *How do we work together?* For if we want liberation for women, then we're committed to building a society in which these distances—of class and economics—dissolve, and all our authentic differences—cultures, personalities, sexualities, talents, and aspirations—emerge and are equally nourished.[9]

Notes

1. City College of New York was free at the time, yet there was hardly any student I knew who did not work at least one part-time job.

2. My first collection of poetry, *periods of stress,* was self-published through Out & Out Books and later distributed by me directly. I borrowed money for this venture and never broke even. My contributions to *Lesbian Poetry, Lesbian Fiction,* and *Nice Jewish Girls: A Lesbian Anthology* have netted a total of $145 and a complimentary copy of each anthology. When Persephone Press went bankrupt, it had already distributed almost 2,500 copies of my second collection, *Keeper of Accounts,* but I had received no royalty payments. Ultimately, I borrowed $1,500 to buy the remaining 2,400 copies from Alyson Press, to whom the books had been sold. *Sinister Wisdom* is currently distributing *Keeper* and I am expecting royalty payments. The biggest royalties I have ever collected were for an essay anthologized in *Why Children?* (The Women's Press Ltd., London: 1980). Editors Stephanie Dowrick and Sibyl Grundberg shared profits equally with contributors; so far I have received approximately $550.

Since this essay was written, although I have received some royalties from *Keeper of Accounts,* my income from writing has not changed substantially.

3. This was not from a salary but from a $5,000 editorial grant, which the collective received from the Coordinating Council of Literary Magazines and split four ways.

4. This was awarded by the New York State Council on the Arts, 1984.

5. As this indicates, I have been trying to finish this essay for the past year and a half.

6. Gloria Anzaldúa pointed out that this is true of those who also do physical and factory work or for that matter any kind of work not involving the self.

7. Anita Page, "The Pleasure Outing," *Heresies* #6 (1978).

8. *Womanews,* July/August 1984.

9. I'm indebted to Melanie Kaye/Kantrowitz for her discussion of the feminist movement's failure to address class issues in her unpublished essay "Is There Post-Feminism Before Women's Liberation?"

II

Anti-Semitism in the Lesbian/Feminist Movement

(1981)

In the summer of 1981 I wrote to Womanews, *a New York City-based paper, about its silence and apparent indifference to the growing anti-Semitism in this country, a silence and indifference which I consider anti-Semitic itself. Though my letter was sparked by specific articles in one of its issues, it could in fact have been addressed to almost any of the major feminist or lesbian/feminist papers, most of which have been equally silent on this topic.*

In response to my letter, Womanews *focused its December 1981 issue on Jewish women and anti-Semitism. The article that follows (minus specific criticisms of* Womanews' *response to my letter) appeared originally in that issue together with other pieces by Jewish women.*

In *Prisoner Without a Name, Cell Without a Number*, the Argentinean Jew Jacobo Timerman answers the question "whether a Holocaust is conceivable" in his country, in this way:

> Well, that depends on what is meant by Holocaust, though no one would have been able to answer such a question affirmatively in 1937 in Germany. What you can say is that recent events in Argentina have demonstrated that if an anti-Semitic scenario unfolds, the discussion on what constitutes anti-Semitism and persecution and what does not will occupy more time than the battle itself against anti-Semitism.

Timerman's statement can easily be applied to the situation here in the United States where, I believe, an "anti-Semitic scenario" is on the verge of developing. And like so many other issues of the "mainstream," this one is being mirrored in the lesbian/feminist movement. Repeatedly, I find that I am preoccupied not with countering anti-

Semitism, but with trying to prove that anti-Semitism exists, that it is serious, and that, as lesbian/feminists, we should be paying attention to it both inside and outside of the movement.

My experience with this is much like shadowboxing, for the anti-Semitism with which I am immediately concerned, and which I find most threatening, does not take the form of the overt, undeniably inexcusable painted swastika on a Jewish gravestone or on a synagogue wall. Instead, it is elusive and difficult to pinpoint, for it is either the anti-Semitism of omission or one which trivializes the Jewish experience and Jewish oppression.

Even when confronted with these attitudes, the lesbian/feminist response is most likely to be an evasion, a refusal to acknowledge their implications. This was the case when I wrote to *Womanews* over its repeated silence on anti-Semitism. Though conceding previous omissions, the collective typically resisted a deeper analysis: "Your anger is understandable, but the tone of your letter is puzzling. *An oversight, considerable as it is, is not necessarily a sign of insensitivity, much less intentional silence*" (italics mine). In a movement that has focused on the meanings of oversights, silences, and absences and that has rigorously examined how they are functions of oppression *no matter what the intent*, this type of defense and excuse is very difficult for me to absorb, much less accept.

I am aware that there are many Jewish women actively participating in the lesbian/feminist movement and that makes the situation even more painful and dangerous. For it is clear that what I am confronting here is not just the anti-Semitism of non-Jews, but of Jews as well.

I recently heard a Jewish woman complain about what she perceived to be a lack of pride among Jewish lesbian/feminists. Though in agreement with her observation, I felt angry with her complaint. For what philosophy, emerging out of this movement, I asked, has encouraged the development and sustaining of such pride? What strategies evolved against the growing oppression in this country have included the strategy for countering anti-Semitism, a strategy that would enable Jewish women to feel some self-worth? What theory of oppression, formulated by either Jews or non-Jews, has incorporated an analysis of the history of anti-Semitism outside of the movement and within it, a theory that would reflect a caring for the fate of Jews? And how often have Jewish lesbian/feminists heard anyone declare: "I am committed to this struggle not only because I am a lesbian, but also because I am a Jew"?

The truth is that the issue of anti-Semitism has been ignored, has been treated as either non-existent or unimportant. And, therefore, I am not surprised that pride is low among Jewish lesbian/feminists. For that kind of evasion, that kind of stubborn refusal to focus can only breed low self-esteem, can only increase defensiveness about drawing attention to oneself, can only encourage apologies for distracting others from "more important" issues, can only instill gnawing doubt about whether anti-Semitism exists at all.

Yet clearly the opportunities to connect anti-Semitism with other oppressions have been with us for as long as we have been concerned with the rise of fascist activity in this country. On each occasion in which outrage has been expressed over the ideologies and goals of the Ku Klux Klan, of the American Nazi Party, of the accelerating fundamentalist Christian movement—on each of these occasions there was an opportunity to bring up the issue of anti-Semitism, for each of these has been and continues to be unequivocally anti-Semitic. Yet such interconnections have not been made. And Jewish women have not been insisting that they be made.

There have been a few who have sensed that something is wrong about this, but even they have been hesitant to bring it up, as if by doing so they would be just causing trouble. How is such hesitancy possible among women who have passionately devoted themselves to fighting *every* form of oppression? How can anyone, given our goals and ideals, even doubt the correctness of challenging anti-Semitism?

I believe that Jewish lesbian/feminists have internalized much of the subtle anti-Semitism of this society. They have been told that Jews are too pushy, too aggressive; and so they have been silent about their Jewishness, have not protested against what threatens them. They have been told that they control everything; and so when they are in the spotlight, they have been afraid to draw attention to their Jewishness. For these women, the number of Jews active in the movement is not a source of pride, but rather a source of embarrassment, something to be played down, something to be minimized.

For these women, it is enough that their names are Jewish. Their Jewishness never extends any further. Their theories and viewpoints are never informed by Jewish traditions and culture, or by Jewish political history and analysis, or even by Jewish oppression. In short, there is nothing about them that is visibly Jewish except their names—and that is simply a form of identification, of labelling. No, Jewish women have not been visible in this movement as Jews. They have been good, very good. They have not drawn attention to themselves. And I, a lesbian/feminist proud of her Jewishness, am as sick of it as I am sick about it.

I think it is time that Jewish and non-Jewish women focused on this issue and got it into perspective. I think it is time for all of us in this movement, Jews and non-Jews alike, to examine our silence on this subject, to examine its source. And Jews especially need to consider their feelings about their Jewishness, for any self-consciousness, any desire to draw attention *away* from one's Jewishness is an internalization of anti-Semitism. And if we want others to deal with this issue, then we ourselves must start to develop a sense of pride and a sense that our survival *as Jews* is important.

If someone were to ask me did I think a Jewish Holocaust was possible in this country, I would answer immediately: "Of course." Has not America had other holocausts? Has not America exterminated others, those it deemed undesirable or those in its way? Are there not holocausts going on right now in this country? Why should I believe it will forever remain benevolent towards the non-Christian who is the source of all its troubles, the thief of all its wealth, the commie betrayer of its secrets, the hidden juggler of its power, the killer of its god? Why should I believe that, given the right circumstances, America will prove kind to the Jew? That given enough power to the fascists, the Jew will remain untouched?

There are many, and Jews are among them, who do not accept my view. But I am firm in my belief. Not out of panic. Not out of paranoia. I believe it because of what I know of American history and Jewish history in Christian cultures.

I am a lesbian/feminist threatened in this country. I am also a European-born Jew, born during the Second World War, a survivor of the Jewish Holocaust. That historical event, so publicized and commercialized in the mass media, so depleted of meaning, has been a source of infinite lessons to me, lessons which I value.

Fact: It took *four* years before the Jews of the Warsaw Ghetto could learn to trust each other and overcome their hostilities toward their divergent political philosophies; it took *four* years before they could pool their energies and resist the Nazis in what has become known as the Warsaw Ghetto Uprising. And before that, while the Zionists would not speak to the Socialists, and while the Socialists would not speak to the Communists, the Nazis were creating more and more efficient death camps and more and more Jews were being exterminated.

Fact: When the Jews finally staged the uprising in April 1943, the Polish underground refused them almost every form of assistance. Even though they were facing the same enemy, even though their country was occupied, the Poles could not overcome their anti-Semitism and join the Jews in the struggle for the freedom of *both* groups, and instead chose to stage a *separate* Polish uprising more than a year later.

These two facts concerning this event in Jewish history are permanently etched on my consciousness. (1) The oppressed group divided against itself, incapacitated, paralyzed, unable to pull together while the enemy grows stronger and more efficient. (2) Two oppressed groups facing a common enemy unable to overcome ancient hatreds, struggling separately.

And I think about these two facts whenever I hear about a completely Jewish demonstration against the American Nazi Party in the Midwest and then hear about a completely Black demonstration against the same American Nazi Party, this time on the East Coast.

And I think about these two facts also in terms of this movement, the lesbian/feminist movement, consisting of diverse groups with diverse needs and diverse experiences of oppression.

I want the issue of anti-Semitism to be incorporated into our overall struggle because there are lesbian/feminists among us who are threatened in this country not only as lesbians, but also as Jews. If that incorporation simply takes the form of adding us on to the already existing list of problems, then it will be mere tokenism and lip service. But if it includes self-examination, analysis of the Jew in America, and dialogue between Jews and non-Jews, then I think this movement will have made a real attempt to deal with the issue.

* * *

The following are some questions that I think both Jewish and non-Jewish women might consider asking in trying to identify in themselves sources of shame, conflict, doubt, and anti-Semitism. They should keep in mind that the questions are designed to reveal the degree to which they have internalized the anti-Semitism around them. I hope that by examining their own anti-Semitism, Jewish women will conclude that anti-Semitism, *like any other ideology of oppression,* must *never* be tolerated, must *never* be hushed up, must *never* be ignored, and that, instead, it must *always* be exposed and resisted.

1. Do I have to check with other Jewish women in order to verify whether something is anti-Semitic? Do I distrust my own judgment on this issue?

2. When I am uncertain, am I afraid to speak out?

3. Am I afraid that by focusing on anti-Semitism I am being divisive?

4. Do I feel that by asking other women to deal with anti-Semitism I am draining the movement of precious energy that would be better used elsewhere?

5. Do I feel that anti-Semitism has been discussed too much already and feel embarrassed to bring it up?

6. Do I feel that the commercial presses and the media are covering the issue of anti-Semitism adequately and that it is unnecessary to bring it up also in the movement? Am I embarrassed by the way anti-Semitism/the Holocaust is presented in the media? Why?

7. Do I have strong disagreements with and/or am ashamed of Israeli policies and, as a result, feel that I cannot defend Jews whole-heartedly against anti-Semitism? Is it possible for me to disagree with Israeli policies and still oppose anti-Semitism?

8. Do I feel guilty and/or ashamed of Jewish racism in this country and, as a result, feel I can't defend Jews whole-heartedly against anti-Semitism? Is it possible for me to acknowledge Jewish racism, struggle against it, and still feel Jewish pride? And still oppose anti-Semitism?

9. Do I feel that Jews have done well in this country and therefore should not complain?

10. Do I feel that historically, sociologically and/or psychologically, anti-Semitism is "justified" or "understandable," and that I am, therefore, willing to tolerate it?

11. Do I feel that anti-Semitism exists but it is "not so bad" or "not so important"? Why?

12. Do I believe that by focusing on the problem of anti-Semitism I will make it worse? Why?

13. Do I feel that Jews draw too much attention to themselves? How?

14. Do I associate the struggle against anti-Semitism with conservatism? Why?

15. What Jewish stereotypes am I afraid of being identified with? What do I repress in myself in order to prevent such identification?

Resisting and Surviving America
(1982)

As a child, my first conscious feeling about being Jewish was that it was dangerous, something to be hidden. For years I agonized over my visibility as a Jew, over the fact that I lived in a Jewish neighborhood, that my name was on lists of Jewish organizations and schools, that at a moment's notice I could be found, identified, rounded up. My sole comfort during that time was that I did not "look" Jewish—something which I clung to as my only means of escape.

My sense of danger was rooted in a total physical and emotional knowledge of the war. Yet this knowledge was acquired only after I came to America in 1949 at the age of eight. It was in New York—at the annual memorials for the Uprising of the Warsaw Ghetto, during conversations among my mother's friends, in the books I was encouraged to read—that I absorbed the full horror and insanity of the camps and ghettos, absorbed them in such a way that they became first-hand knowledge. I reacted and lived as if I had been an adult in 1945, instead of a four-year-old child. It was especially in these early years in America—when the pain of survivors around me was unguarded and raw—that I learned in minute detail the ingenuity and capriciousness of the torturer, the powerlessness of the victim's reason and logic, and the necessity of a rigid life/death morality. As a child, I was old with terror and the brutality, the haphazardness of survival.

Ironically, those who taught me "not to forget" also provided me with a way of coping. And as melodramatic as it may seem, it was through literature. My first felt response to literature was in my Workmen's Circle Yiddish *Shule* No. 3 in the Bronx. There I absorbed an endless

---
The first section of this essay was originally written in 1979 as a statement for *Anthology of Contemporary American Jewish Poets* (unpublished).

variety of Yiddish poems and songs. I found that they touched me in a way that neither "The Rime of the Ancient Mariner" nor "Evangeline" (which I was reading then in public school) ever touched me. Predominantly the poetry of labor, of poverty and ordinary struggle, their open rhymes and bare meters transformed what was painful into something not only bearable, but beautiful.

> I have a little boy
> A child so rare and fine
> That when my eyes behold him,
> I think the world is mine.
>
> But seldom, oh so seldom,
> I see him when he's at play;
> I see him only fast asleep
> When I return from a hard, hard day.*

As I grew older, I learned the full breadth of Yiddish literature; but this early introduction with its inherent political vision became as powerful an influence in my life as did the war.

Of course neither influence was always reflected in the American Jewish life around me. I was repeatedly dumbfounded by other children who insisted on calling themselves Jewish, but who did not know Yiddish, were not avowed atheists and socialists and knew nothing of the war or the Jewish Labor Bund. I tended to be quite cynical about them and dismissed them as fakes.

Things merge in strange ways and I do not want to falsify by making unnatural distinctions. Experience has obviously taught me that Jews are not the only ones in danger and that what is "undesirable" in me is not limited to my Jewishness. As an adult I have nurtured what I consider to be a mature, healthy paranoia, one which I cling to as an important means of survival. As a writer I still cherish poetry that tells a story, especially the dramatic monologue. I still value most a poetry that deals with people, especially those alienated and out of the mainstream—the overworked and dreamless, Third World, women, gay—a subdued, earnest poetry that expresses their feelings, their struggles, the conditions of their lives.

* * *

---

*From Morris Rosenfeld's *"Mayn yingel,"* (My little boy).

February, 1981

Dear Evelyn:

You've asked me to add something to the statement I wrote for the *Anthology of Contemporary American Jewish Poets*. To add something about being a lesbian, a Jewish lesbian.

As usual with this kind of thing, I feel I can't simply add a statement, that I have to start over again, to start from the very beginning. And as usual, my feelings are not exactly the same as when I first wrote over a year ago.

It is not that I have re-evaluated or have changed my ideas, only that at different moments I focus on different aspects of some of the issues. My feelings about being a Jew, especially being an American Jew, and more recently about being an American Jewish lesbian, are not all completely clear or logical to me. They seem for the most part to be tangled and interlocked and I guess I will present them that way—not to do so would seem to me to falsify. I am sure certain statements will seem contradictory. Perhaps to some even offensive. But I will try to be honest here, as honest as I can allow myself to be.

One of the things most evident to me about my feelings is that I have rarely expressed them. It is not that I have disguised them, but merely that I have for the most part remained quiet about them. There are many reasons for this. For one, I have sensed that people are simply fed up with what Jews feel. Sensing this, I have not been eager to make myself vulnerable. I have also been silent because, unlike what some people might assume, I feel critical of certain segments of the Jewish population and how they function in America. I do not often express these criticisms because of the persistent and more recently flourishing climate of anti-Semitism in America. Since I have not seen any strong concern over this anti-Semitism (except perhaps from the most conservative elements of the Jewish community, those often labelled extremists and hysterics), I have been afraid to express my own misgivings lest they be interpreted as anti-Semitic. To criticize in an atmosphere of dislike or even indifference is to play into anti-Semitic strategies. I refuse to do that.

One reason I am willing now to write about the mixture of feelings that I have is that I trust you and trust the anthology. It feels safe to say many of the things I want to say.

Let me begin with the silence that stems from my sense that people are tired of hearing about what Jews feel. This silence hides my extreme pain, frustration, and rage with non-Jews and Jews alike. The source of people's impatience, I believe, is the Holocaust. I find it almost impossible to write that word because here—in America—the word has lost almost all meaning. And the fault lies with both non-Jews and Jews. It lies with the "American way of life," with the process of Americanization, with American Big Business, with commercialism, with posing, with artificial feelings.

I am convinced that the reason that people are turned off of the Holocaust—I can barely believe that I just now wrote *"turned off of the Holocaust"*—and yet that seems the most appropriate language to describe the phenomenon because the Holocaust has been like a fad, a rock group losing its original sound, a fashionable form of dress that outlives its popularity—I am, I repeat, convinced that people are turned off of the Holocaust because it has been commercialized, metaphored out of reality, glamorized, been severed from the historical fact.

Yet despite this "turn off," I find—and am repeatedly stunned by it—that people (including non-Jews) insist on dredging it up. Writers, for example, who have no feelings or connection to the war, insist on it as literary metaphor, as an epigraph, as some kind of necessary addition. A casual allusion to Auschwitz. An oblique reference to the Warsaw Ghetto. Somehow this "sprinkling" of Jewish experiences is thought to reflect sensitivity, a largeness of heart. And of course it does not. It is simply the literary Holocaust, the Holocaust of words that has nothing to do with fact. It is nothing more than a pose. I must say that my teeth grind whenever I see these gratuitous gestures—usually devoid of any Jewish context, devoid of any sense of the Jewish experience or history.

I am also furious with the Holocaust of American Big Business. The Holocaust of glamour. Of movie stars. TV stations. Of sloppy books that sell millions of copies and make reputations and millions and millions of dollars. This Holocaust is awarded Emmys, Oscars, Tonys, Best-Jewish-Book-of-the-Year awards. This phenomenon of co-opting is, of course, not atypical. It is very, very American. It is the process of mainstreaming whatever seems real and genuine, whatever seems threatening. It is a process of dilution, of wringing any reality or feeling out of true suffering or need or ideal. It is cheapness, vulgarity. And repeatedly it rouses my rage and disgust.

Am I making any sense? It is hard to write about this. But I've been thinking a lot about it lately, about the corruption here in America, how everything becomes big business, how everything becomes diseased. Everything. Manufacturers roll up their sleeves and we're inundated with buttons, slogans, black arm bands, yellow ribbons, six candles.

Both Jews and non-Jews have depleted the meaning of the word Holocaust in this way. But Jews, by themselves, have also had their own special role. Their own Holocaust has been preserved as the Holocaust of spectacle, show biz, of song and false ritual. Of services at Temple Emanu-El on Fifth Avenue amidst silk scarves and fur coats. Of condolence telegrams from candidates on the campaign trail. Of Presidential declarations. Of operatic arias. It is the Holocaust of finally organizing, of having meetings and dues and committees. Of gaining status and respectability through incorporation and tax exemption.

I am sick of all of it. Sick and angry because I know it has absolutely nothing to do with what my family and I experienced during the war; it has nothing to do with what millions of Jews experienced during the war.

And so I rage internally when I hear or sense that people are tired of or fed up with the Holocaust.

And worse. I feel robbed, robbed of a true sense of loss, a true sense of mourning, a true sense of suffering and surviving. I am not sure I can explain this properly. But this hype of the media, of publishing houses, etc., has robbed me of the possibility of really mourning the losses of my life, of even defining them or articulating them properly. How can I say to people that for the survivors with whom I grew up the Holocaust never ended? That all my life I will feel the loss of never having known my father, never even having a photograph of him after the age of seventeen. That all my life I will feel the loss of aunts and cousins and grandparents I never knew. That my mother still stacks shelves and shelves of food—*just in case*. That twenty years after the war, when some plaster fell down from the living room ceiling, she froze with fear because she thought we were being bombed. That when a friend's child died—the mother, incredulous, said to me: "Irena, I thought I had already paid for all my children's sins. I paid for them during the war. I told God. This, what I went through, is for my children's sins." That another friend committed suicide just when it seemed she had settled into her American life. That even I, just recently, after surgery, expressed my sense of violation through dreams about the war.

None of this has anything to do with the Holocaust that people are "turned off" of. It is ordinary, undramatic and ever present. The Holocaust was not an event that ended in 1945—at least not for the survivors. Not for me. It continued on and on because my mother and I were alone. Because my father's family no longer existed and I was its sole survivor. It continued on in the struggle of extreme poverty that we experienced in the early years in this country. It continued on and on, coloring every thought I had, every decision I made. It continued on in the Bronx, on ordinary streets, at the kitchen table. It continued on invisible.

So you can understand that when I see that experience exploited, co-opted, when I sense people are fed up, how I want to rage at everyone: "You're fucking around with my pain, with my real pain, my real life. Forget the metaphor. Think about reality."

The real mourning, the real sense of loss has hardly ever been evoked or expressed, at least not recently. And as I said—Jews have participated in this falsification. I am not an expert on what happens to immigrant groups in America, but I have often felt that one way of assimilating, of entering the American mainstream, is to learn to package, to adopt Big Business techniques, to market. It is, of course, also the way to lose your spiritual identity. It's obvious how this has happened to labor and various minority struggles in this country. And it's happened to Jews as well. And I am pained by it, frustrated by it. It is such a horrendous mistake. But Jews have done it. Have pushed into the mainstream and thought themselves safe, deluded themselves—for no matter what, they are not part of the mainstream, no matter the money or the position. When it comes to the bottom line, the Moral Majority is Christian. So is the Ku Klux Klan. So is the Nazi Party. And I am completely stymied that large segments of the Jewish population have not absorbed these simple basic facts.

I am also angry that Jews have somehow, during this process, gotten stuck—I'm not sure if that's the right word, but I don't know how else to express it. They have been unable to absorb the experience of the Holocaust, have not learned how to transcend the catastrophe. They've mistakenly thought that to transcend means to forget the past, that to think about the present is to abandon the past. That too is a painful mistake, a grave mistake for Jews in America, because it's kept many of them from universalizing their experience, from joining with others who have experienced oppression—not perhaps an exact duplication of Jewish oppression, but nevertheless oppression. Jews have made the mistake of thinking that we all must experience exactly the same thing; in doing so, we've severed ourselves from many other people's suffering. And so I become angry because of course I want Jews to "know better"—feel they should "know better"—and am repeatedly disappointed when the evidence shows they are just like most people—they don't learn from experience or from history.

This is perhaps the most painful aspect for me of being Jewish, for I identify strongly as a Jew, am proud to be a Jew. And yet I sometimes feel so torn—so torn from the Jewish community, from the Jews I grew up with, who nurtured me, helped me. And yet I don't understand what America has done to them and how it has seduced them. The conservatism is there and really hard to accept. But it is there, definitely there with the mainstreaming.

So when you ask me to say something about being a Jewish lesbian, what can I say? You know of course that there are no Jewish lesbians because, to begin, with Jews are not supposed to be sexual. Especially Jewish women. So what the Jewish lesbian encounters are the typical conservative stances. Closed doors. Silence. Disgust. For this reason I have not publicized my lesbianism in Jewish circles. That is probably wrong. Probably homophobic. I have thought it pointless, self-defeating in certain instances. Often I have not said anything out of simple fear. I didn't want to experience the closed door, the disgust. At the same time I've been perfectly aware that you can't write and publish and keep these things a secret, especially if some people are already in on the secret. And so the secret spreads. Irena Klepfisz. Oh yes, she wrote those poems about the Holocaust. But you know she wrote those other poems too. Well, we can always pretend we didn't read them. No need to mention them. Let's just talk about those poems about the Holocaust. Powerful stuff. But did you continue reading past the first section? Did you read those other poems too?

At that moment I am an outsider, a lesbian, a *shikse*. The Jewish community is not my community.

But as a Jew—as a Jew in a Christian, anti-Semitic society—the Jewish community is, and will always remain, my community.

Enemy and ally.

This is the confusion. Being Jewish. Being a lesbian. Being an American. It all converges. It is like feelings about one's parents. Love and embarrassment. The painful realization that they are not perfect.

As I perceive the danger from the Right increasing, my identification grows even stronger. I want to buy a Jewish star to wear around my neck. I can hear my mother's wry comment: "What? Have you become a pagan?" Not unexpected from a Jewish-socialist position. But it is true; for the first time in my life, I want to wear a Jewish star. The time seems right for it.

But if the time is right for it, it is not only because reactionary elements in this country have made it so. There is a danger, I believe, from the Left as well, and this includes the Jewish Left—especially those in the Jewish

Left who are embarrassed about being Jewish. Who will only say that Jews are guilty of this or that. Who never express any pride or love or affection or attachment to their Jewishness. Who only declare their Jewishness after making an anti-Semitic statement, as if ending such a statement with "Well, I'm Jewish" makes it all right, acceptable. That too enrages me and frightens me. Those of the Left, Jew and non-Jew alike, seem to believe what the Right has always maintained—that Jews run the world and are, therefore, most responsible for its ills. The casualness, the indifference with which the Left accepts this anti-Semitic stance enrages me. It is usually subtle, often taking the form of anti-Semitism by *omission*. Its form is to show or speak about Jews *only* as oppressors, never as anything else. That is anti-Semitic. And I think it's prevalent and it scares me, the repeated fault-finding in an atmosphere of indifference.

I cannot end without affirming as strongly as I can my deep feelings of identification and pride in being a Jew. It was Jews who first instilled in me the meaning of oppression and its consequences. It was Jews who first taught me about socialism, class, racism and what in the fifties was called "injustice." It is from Jews that I adopted ideals that I still hold and principles that I still believe are true and must be fought for and put into practice. It was from Jews that I learned about the necessity for resistance. It was from Jews that I also learned that literature is not simply fancy words or clever metaphor, but instead is deeply, intimately connected to life, to a life that I am a part of. It is really almost impossible to compress this inheritance into a single paragraph. But I know its depth and vitality, and I know that I have absorbed it thoroughly into my consciousness.

I know also that often some Jews have not lived up to what they themselves have expressed and taught others. I do not like that and will not apologize for it. And I generally argue and fight with them whenever I am with them and find they are lacking. But I will not deny them. I am clearly their product, the product of a Jewish upbringing, of Jewish teaching, of the Jewish experience both here in America and Europe. That is not *shmalts,* or nostalgia, or sentimentality. It is simply acknowledging and crediting Jews with what I consider to be my best self.

I said from the start it was not going to be very logical. Strong identification. Pride. Disappointment. And fear—fear of what is happening to the Jewish community from within, as well as what is happening to it from without. And these feelings are always with me. I write as much out of a Jewish consciousness as I do out of a lesbian/feminist consciousness. They are both always there, no matter what topic I might be working on.

They are embedded in my writing, embedded and enmeshed to the point that they are not necessarily distinguishable as discrete elements. They merge and blend and blur, for in many ways they are the same. My poem "Death Camp." My poem "From the Monkey House and Other Cages." Alienated. Threatened. Un-American. Individual. Defiant. To me they are ever present.

Irena

Jewish Lesbians, the Jewish Community, Jewish Survival

(1988)

I am pleased to have been invited to speak today as a lesbian, a feminist and a Jew. Pleased because fifteen years ago, when I first came out as a lesbian, I could never have imagined such an invitation coming from a Jewish organization or conference committed to close ties with the mainstream Jewish communities, observant and secular. Five years after that, when I retreated from the Jewish world, I found it impossible to be both a Jew and a lesbian and to be accepted in the Jewish world. And this was a real source of anger, pain, and sorrow to me. The secular Yiddish world which had nurtured me suddenly felt alien and strange. I found myself for the first time afraid—afraid of its disapproval, of its rejection, if I publicly claimed my lesbianism. In these early years as a lesbian I learned the terrible power of homophobia. Certainly I was the same Jew I had always been, committed to my people and to their survival. How, I wondered in anger, could such fear arise?

I had been raised in a secular Yiddish environment, one peopled mainly by Holocaust survivors and members of the once strong and influential Jewish Labor Bund in Poland and Russia. As a child I learned my political lessons by listening to the conversations of the adults around me, *'khob zikh kaseyder tsugehert tsu di dervaksene*, and by attending Yiddish schools, *arbeter ring shul dray*, where Yiddish culture or *yidishkayt* was *undzer yerushe*, the rich legacy left to my generation. As a child I internalized the values of this world, its politics of the oppressed to such a degree that as an adult I took them entirely for granted and have never doubted their validity. They were part of the

---

This speech was delivered at "Jewish Feminism—A Call to the Future," a symposium sponsored by the American Jewish Congress and Spertus College of Judaica, in Chicago on November 13, 1988.

universal and eternal *emes,* a truth which I assumed everyone would eventually accept. I learned that *dos lebn fun poshete mentshn,* lives of ordinary people, *iz tayer,* were precious, that they needed both protection against the powerful and greedy, and sustenance through *muzik, gezang un lider,* music, song and poetry. I learned of the deep ties every Jew should have with her Jewish community, of the importance of Yiddish as the medium through which our cultural and political life is expressed. This was my inheritance.

And yet when I came out as a lesbian, I suddenly faced the fact that this legacy did not include gay people among the oppressed. I knew that the moment I declared myself a lesbian, I would become a stranger. As a lesbian I would be left standing outside the tribe and the Jewish world where I had always sought and found safety. Suddenly I was filled with fear that my true identity would be revealed, and once revealed, I would be immediately disinherited and sent into permanent exile.

Ten years ago, the conflict between my love for other women, my dedication to feminism, and my love of both *yidishkayt* and my Jewish community had no resolution. My Jewish community simply was not ready to deal with me as a lesbian. At this time I had been working at the YIVO Institute for Jewish Research and I was teaching Yiddish—in short, I was deeply immersed in Jewish life. But I had also co-founded and was co-editing *Conditions,* a feminist publication emphasizing writing by lesbians. I was in two worlds which never overlapped or even touched, which seemed eternally split from each other. And so rather than be damaged by that split, rather than erase my life, I chose to withdraw from the Jewish world.

I know some of you are thinking: But why does she have to let everyone know? Isn't sexuality a "private matter"? Why does she insist on being public about her lesbianism?

But lesbianism cannot be isolated, for it touches all aspects of private and public life. If you are heterosexual, imagine how it would feel if you had to keep your heterosexuality a secret. Imagine having to omit all references to a date, a boyfriend, a husband, a live-in partner. Imagine never being allowed to even whisper that there is a connection between you because such a connection would be deemed disgusting or even criminal, that it could cost you your job, the custody of your children. Imagine also having to be silent about your joys and sorrows, your pride in the other person when he achieved something, your concern when he was ill or in trouble. Think about the pressure you'd be under not to let anything slip, the constant fear you would live with. Imagine—better yet, try to keep your secret for just one week. Perhaps then you will begin to understand what you're asking of gays and lesbians when you tell us to keep our lives "private."

When I am closeted I have to present myself in a void: alone, without a partner, without a community, without a life rooted in that community. I have to omit any references to books, to conferences, to meetings, to political activities. I have to "edit" a funny incident at the laundromat where my lover's wash got mixed up with someone else's. I have to "edit" the volleyball game I play every weekend with other lesbians. If I were currently at a job where I was forced to be closeted, I could not even reveal that this weekend I had flown to Chicago. Try to imagine me on Monday morning having to come into the office and suppress the pleasure I feel at having attended a Jewish feminist conference, having been asked to speak, having met interesting women, having heard stimulating talks, having felt energized. And though it is not true of my situation at the moment, I have worked at many jobs, including ones in the Jewish world, where I would not be able to reveal my role here without dire consequences. It is a terrible way to live. Perhaps it is hard for you to imagine. But certainly as Jews, we all know the terror and pain of passing, the toll it takes.

But why should I accept this toll when I carry Jewish concerns wherever I go? I am still devoted to the values of *yidishkayt*, to a strong Jewish identity, to making Yiddish literature, particularly its women writers, accessible to American Jews. And my commitment is not unusual. Lesbians have been fighting Jewish battles wherever they need to be fought. We have been in the forefront of fighting anti-Semitism in the women's movement, a phenomenon which I am sure you are familiar with. For whether you accept us as Jews or not, we certainly continue to see ourselves as Jews and are seen as Jews by others. And because we continue living as Jews, because we do participate in Jewish struggles, such as the fight against anti-Semitism and assimilation, because we continue fighting for *all* women's rights in the Jewish community, many of us have come to feel a bitterness against the heterosexual Jewish communities for their exclusion of us. For by excluding us they limit our experience only to the pain of being Jewish in a world that often does not accept Jewishness as a positive value; by excluding us they deprive us of the joy that accompanies full participation in our rich Jewish culture and Jewish life. And this is neither just nor necessary.

My knowledge of Jewish lesbians, from having led dozens of identity workshops, is that they do not want to be alienated from the Jewish communities of their origin. Quite the contrary—they care deeply about them. This is manifest in the many Jewish groups—secular and observant—that have sprung up in the last fifteen years. These gays are proud of their Jewishness, want to feel involved in the community, need the community to keep their Jewishness vital. Though they may establish their own *rosh khodesh* groups, their own synagogues, their own *havurah* circles, they, like all other Jews, want to feel a tie to the larger community, need the larger Jewish community as a lifeline, as a partner in an ongoing dialogue that nurtures the individual parts and keeps the whole alive and vibrant. Many of us have formed our own base institutions because we share certain viewpoints, interests and concerns and do not want to be erased by heterosexual assumptions—much as a Sephardic community might decide to establish its own cultural club so as not to be erased by Ashkenazi perspectives. Nevertheless we do not want to feel alienated for doing so. We need to know that when the leaders of Jewish institutions meet, the leaders of our gay and lesbian institutions will also be invited to deal with whatever issues the larger community is addressing.

What I have been trying to express is that lesbians want to rely on the Jewish community, on the nourishment it can offer, on its institutions—educational, cultural, political, religious—as sources for strengthening our Jewish identity.

So perhaps you are somewhat reassured that an alternative lifestyle does not preclude a commitment to Judaism or to a Jewish life. But that is not all I want to express here today. Because if, in a relationship between two parties, only one ever experiences a need for the other, then the relationship is unequal and easily slips into patronization and condescension. Lesbians certainly don't want that. What we do want is respect and a sense of being valued, of having something to offer. And so in addition to accepting us, I am also asking that you think more deeply on this issue of relations between lesbians and the Jewish community. I would like you to think of your own needs and I would like to suggest today that *you* need us.

Perhaps that is not clear to you and surprises you. Perhaps it offends you. Yet I firmly believe it is so. You need our energy, our special vision, our fresh perspective. You need us in every sphere of Jewish life, which for a long time now has been in grave crisis. Certainly Jews are living through an important period in Jewish history. A portion of

Jewish history is being played out in the Middle East, another here on American soil. American Jews are in the process of redefining Jewish identity, culturally and religiously, and are struggling to adapt to the special characteristics of this age and this country. We are redefining the role of Jewish women in our synagogues and secular institutions; and we need to unravel the complex relationship that has evolved between Jews and people of color. And for American Jews it is also urgent to formulate a productive role for ourselves in resolving the violent and destructive conflict between Israelis and Palestinians. These are serious issues which require imagination and creativity. Lesbians and gays have these to offer and perhaps even more.

We can make a valuable contribution because there are many similarities between Jews and gays. Like Jews, gays live in every culture and class, reside in every country on this planet. Like Jews, gays have at various times been identified as the pariahs of society. Like Jews, gays have been held responsible for society's ills. Like Jews, gays have been stigmatized and stereotyped by both the Left and the Right: the Left identifying us as the decadent products of capitalistic and imperialistic society; the Right as immoral deviants living contrary to Christian principles. And though it is not popular to point this out, gays, like Jews and Gypsies, were victims of Hitler's extermination camps. Like Jews, gays understand the perils of passing, its destructive nature, its capacity to undermine the core of an identity, to rob us of spirit. I am sure many of you may be uncomfortable with the analogy; yet it is not strained. Much of gay experience parallels Jewish experience. And because of our particular position in society, gays have developed a sharp political consciousness, one which gives us a special vantage point from which to challenge mainstream assumptions. Thus, Jews and gays have a great deal in common, have a great deal politically in common, and Jews need and can use the political savvy that the gay community has to offer.

Consider also the energy lost in remaining closeted. In my own case, I know I wasted a lot of time and energy that could have been devoted to Yiddish and Yiddish literature, had I not been preoccupied with hiding who I was. Had I stayed and not withdrawn from the Yiddish world ten years ago, an anthology of Yiddish women writers that I have been trying to work on would have been finished by now and been of benefit to Jewish feminists; Yiddish women writers might be better known; Yiddish literature might be viewed from a newer, more complex perspective. I don't think I'm being immodest in saying all this. I know precisely what my interests and talents are and I know when they are being stifled. And prejudice has a way of not only stifling one segment of a person's life, but undermining the whole. To be productive, to be effective, gays and lesbians, like all human beings, need breathing space; we do not want to be absorbed by fear, for fear always inhibits and in the end we give only a part of ourselves.

So I perceive a mutual need when I speak about the relationship between Jewish gays and the Jewish community or between Jewish lesbians and heterosexual Jewish feminists. The Jewish community needs to reach out to Jewish gays not only because it is the humane and moral thing to do, not only because we are legitimate members of the Jewish community, not only because we need the larger community, but also because the larger Jewish community needs us. And until the Jewish community recognizes its own need, until then there will never be equal relations between gay and heterosexual Jews.

I know that Jews have special concerns which color their attitudes toward gays and lesbians and I would like to address two of these today. The first is the issue of demographics. There is great concern that intermarriage, the loosening of community ties and the weakening of Jewish identity are decimating the Jewish population. The Holocaust or *der khurbn* ravaged us; our children and the future generation are a major preoccupation. Certainly those of us who are children of *di lebn geblibene,* survivors, who have lived among survivors, understand *di benkshaft,* the longing, yearning for continuity that was and remains the fabric of *undzere elterns khaloymes,* our parents' dreams. *Ikh bin di eyntsike lebn geblibene fun dem tatns mishpokhe.* I am the only survivor of my father's family. I know the keen sense of loss in *di khaloymes,* those dreams: the desire to pass on the names of dead relatives, the desire to regenerate the family.

I also know that the entire burden of fulfilling *di khaloymes* has fallen on *di yidishe froyen,* Jewish women, and has put great pressure on Jewish women to bear children. And though I understand the emotions and concerns which lie behind that pressure, I feel it is imperative for us to resist this special form of sexism which reduces a Jewish woman's value simply to a biological function. We have to resist the view that the most significant contribution a Jewish woman can make to *undzer folk,* our people, is to give birth to a Jewish child.

This is an important issue and one that can serve as common ground for Jewish lesbians and their heterosexual Jewish sisters. Jewish lesbians are often confronted with the argument that we do not care about

Jewish survival because we do not want to bear children, an argument which, of course, ignores the fact that many lesbians *do* have children. But aside from that, it is outrageous to suggest that those of us who have chosen to be childless are indifferent to Jewish survival. In fact we have a critical function to play in maintaining the survival of our community in every sphere of Jewish life, and bearing children is not always the best contribution we can make. I know of many women who possess hardly any Jewish identity, are entirely ignorant of Jewish history, religion, culture—they could have a dozen children but these children would be raised in a void.

Clearly the act of bearing a child does not guarantee Jewish survival, for *der khurbn*, the Holocaust, not only ravaged us physically through the murder of six million, it ravaged *undzer kultur, undzer gayst*, our culture and spirit. If Jewish identity is weakening in the United States, one cause is the destruction of Eastern European culture, a culture on which American Jews were extremely dependent, to which they turned for nourishment and strength. The result is that assimilation, alienation, a thin fading Jewish identity have become our greatest enemies.

Yet Jewish women and lesbians have a great deal to offer to counter these by the art they produce, by the institutions they establish and nurture (secular and observant, cultural and religious), by their acute political sense. I am thinking of my own commitment to Yiddish and to building a strong Jewish identity. I am thinking of my close friend and collaborator, the lesbian/feminist Melanie Kaye/Kantrowitz who lives and teaches in a graduate program in Vermont and with whom I worked for four years on *The Tribe of Dina: A Jewish Women's Anthology* so that all Jewish women could discern their role in Jewish life and culture. Throughout the year Melanie gives workshops in the women's community on Jewish identity and relentlessly challenges anti-Semitism whenever and wherever she sees it. I am thinking of my friend, another lesbian, Evelyn Torton Beck, the mother of two, a teacher, scholar, and chair of Women's Studies at the University of Maryland in Baltimore. It was Evi who identified the influence of Yiddish theater on Kafka's writing and who brought to the surface Bashevis Singer's misogyny. I am thinking of my friend Clare Kinberg, a lesbian recently settled in Seattle, who works tirelessly to further peace between Israelis and Palestinians. I am thinking of my friend Bernice Mennis, a lesbian who lives in upstate New York and teaches non-Jewish students at the local community college about Jewish immigrant life through the stories of Anzia Yezierska. I am thinking of my friend Marianna Kaufman, a lesbian who is a librarian in Atlanta, Georgia, who always makes sure that her library is up-to-date in its Judaica section. I am thinking of my friend Sharon Kleinbaum, a lesbian who lived in Amherst, Massachusetts and for a number of years served as the assistant director of the National Yiddish Book Center which is helping to keep Yiddish and Yiddish culture alive. Sharon is now completing her rabbinical studies in Israel. I am thinking of Rabbi Linda Holtzman, a lesbian who teaches in Philadelphia and prepares men and women for their roles as teachers and rabbis. I am thinking of Elana Dykewomon who, with other Jewish lesbians, founded a writer's group in Oakland which is trying to create a new American Jewish literature, one that acknowledges the lesbian presence in the Jewish community. I am thinking of the Jewish lesbians in Northampton, Massachusetts who, with their Jewish heterosexual sisters, are translating the biographies of Yiddish women writers so that they will finally become known to the American Jewish community and take their rightful place in Yiddish literature and history. I am thinking of the Jewish lesbians in Boston who are editing an anthology of their experiences as daughters of Holocaust survivors; they are determined the past will not be forgotten and are working toward a future that will help Jews heal. And I am also thinking of all the other Jewish lesbians who are afraid of being identified, but who work in mainstream Jewish organizations like the American Jewish Congress, the American Jewish Committee, Hadassah, the National Council of Jewish Women, the Workmen's Circle, YIVO Institute for Jewish Research—lesbians who live in fear of the community, but who nevertheless serve it through endless council and committee work in these organizations as well as in neighborhood synagogues and community centers.

What the Jewish community needs is more women, more lesbians like these, for it is they and their work that will help us be a proud, strong community, one able to resist the pull of the homogenizing, Christian mainstream. It is lesbians like the ones I've just named who are actively helping guarantee Jewish survival.

I would like to raise one more issue that often emerges in a discussion of lesbians and gay men in relationship to the Jewish community. Frequently I have heard that Jews need to be careful whom they form alliances with, that they need to keep a low profile and, because of the unpopularity of gays, they need to be careful not to be associated with such a group. Again I understand the fear behind the argument. I, too, worry about Jewish visibility, especially when that visibility is associated with unpopular causes. I think any people that has been traumatized as we have been by the Holocaust or has experienced genocide would naturally feel cautious and tentative in taking public stands. And yet we need to resist these fears and always strive toward the moral good, toward justice. In a way we have no choice. We are, after all, a small minority in this country and we cannot struggle successfully if we struggle alone. This is the hard political reality. We need to be able to form alliances and to do that we must understand not only our own needs, but the needs of others.

When gays are threatened, the Jewish community ought to be ready to defend them, for surely a threat to gays will ultimately extend to other minorities. At all times, including times of crisis, the Jewish community ought to be able to say: "Gays are our children, our parents, our friends and neighbors. We love them. They are our own." When the Jewish community can say that, when its leaders begin to speak out against homophobia, against sexism, against prejudice, they will become true allies. The Jewish community will not only be protecting all gays, but it will be enriching itself by guaranteeing that the gays among them are able to participate fully in Jewish life.

I have been asked to be specific about courses of action in the future. So let me end with some guidelines. Heterosexual Jews need first to admit to the presence of gays in their midst and make us feel welcome, make us feel that the community is our home. The community needs to welcome not only us, but our lovers, our children and friends. Heterosexual Jews need to include gays in their activities, need to make sure that activities are structured in a way that allows us to participate. They need to be able to do this themselves and not wait for lesbians to point out limited assumptions and inhibiting structures. I think it particularly important for Jewish lesbians and Jewish heterosexual feminists to sit down and speak openly, frankly. We need to identify conflicts and differences as well as points of agreement and common ground. I have no illusions. Such a dialogue will not be easy, but I believe it is a necessary one.

Above all, heterosexual Jews need to familiarize themselves with gay life and gay culture and sensitize themselves to gay issues. Let me give one brief example. Last year I was invited to participate in a Jewish conference in California. The people there were kind and quite open to my speaking as an advocate for Jewish gays. Yet during the two days of the conference, I was never asked a single question about my life. I had been frank about the fact that I had just separated from a very long relationship and had moved from the country to the city. Yet no one asked me about the difficulties of adjustment, about the gay community in the city as opposed to the country or how it felt to be single again. Though everyone was generous and extremely hospitable, they were afraid to ask the kinds of natural, personal questions that are part of all friendly, easy conversations, and which they would not have hesitated to ask a heterosexual woman. The inability to ask such questions reflects an alienation, a fear on the part of heterosexuals to deal with lesbians and gays. This fear needs to be addressed honestly and overcome.

I began this talk recalling the situation between gays and the Jewish community as I experienced it fifteen years ago. *'Khvil endikn mit der itstiker tsayt un mit der tsukunft.* I want to end with the present and the future. The fact that you invited me to speak gives me great pleasure and I am sure gives pleasure and hope to many Jewish lesbians and gay men who yearn for the breaking down of barriers between themselves and their Jewish communities. In the last couple of years I personally have come to feel less inhibited in the Jewish community and much more welcome. I am able to function as a Yiddish teacher and an activist and not hide my lesbian identity. Clearly things have changed in the past fifteen years and have become easier.

Yet despite this, you will still hear complaints and anger from lesbians and gay men because the Jewish community has not moved far enough. These days I am frequently asked to speak at Jewish functions, but I almost always find that I am the only lesbian invited—in other words, I am a token. Though creating space even for a token is in itself a sign of progress, it is but a faint one. I do not represent all lesbians. I happen to have been born in Europe and have been directly touched by *der khurbn*, the Holocaust, and many Jews are moved by this. *Ikh red yidish, ikh bin a tuer in der froyen bavegung.* I speak Yiddish and am an activist in the women's movement. Not all Jewish lesbians are like me. Some are observant. Some speak Hebrew. Some are Sephardic. There is as much variety among Jewish lesbians as there is among heterosexual Jewish feminists who in turn are as diverse as the international Jewish community. I urge you all to become more familiar with that lesbian diversity, to make use of the great resources that it offers you. I also urge you to open your community centers and synagogues to those Jewish lesbians who, through no fault of their own, were raised in assimilated environments, who feel the pain of their ignorance and alienation—but who want to return home. I urge you to welcome us all.

When planning a conference, don't invite one of us. Invite many lesbian speakers on every issue being addressed. Don't be satisfied by a limited pool of expertise, of perspectives. Allow the Jewish community to broaden, to flourish. *Bakent zikh mit undz ale.* Get to know all of us. *Lomir arbetn tsuzamen tsu helfn ale yidishe froyen un oykh undzer folk.* Let us work together to help all Jewish women and also our people. *A dank.* Thank you.

III

Oyf keyver oves: Poland, 1983
(1983)

April 19, 1983 marked the fortieth anniversary of the Uprising of the Warsaw Ghetto. Early that spring the Polish government announced plans for official ceremonies to commemorate the event and invited all Jews, Jewish leaders, and government representatives from around the world to participate. These plans were controversial among some Jews who have remained bitter over the lack of sympathy and support by Poles during the war. Other Jews objected for very different reasons. Marek Edelman, a member of the Jewish Labor Bund[1] and an organizer and participant in the Uprising was, in 1983, the only Jew from the Uprising to be still living in Poland. A nationally known cardiologist who lives in Lodz and an ardent supporter and activist in Solidarność *(Solidarity), Marek called for a boycott of the ceremonies because of the Polish government's repression of the* Solidarność *movement and the imprisonment of its leaders. He himself had once been arrested and held for three days.*

Marek's insistence on a Jewish boycott on this important anniversary became itself controversial and most Jews—including the Israeli government—did not adhere to it. Nevertheless, Marek himself conducted a separate ceremony attended by some Jews from other countries—friends, survivors and resistance fighters (many of them Bundists)—and Polish Solidarność *members.*

In honor of the anniversary, the American Joint Distribution Committee offered its archivist, Rose Perczykow Klepfisz, the opportunity to attend the fortieth anniversary ceremonies. My mother had not returned to Poland since she'd left with me in the spring of 1946 when we emigrated to Sweden. Because of various commitments, she did not want to go until July and asked me if I wanted to come. I did. We spent seven days in Poland—almost exclusively in

---

Oyf keyver oves: (Yiddish) The custom of paying tribute to the dead by visiting their gravesites.

Warsaw. One day we spent in Lodz and one day in Treblinka. Though I had wanted to go to Auschwitz, it proved too far—a day's drive to Cracow.

I took some notes during these days, but it was only after we left for Switzerland to recover that I sat down quietly and wrote a journal which reconstructed the activities of each day of our stay. As soon as I got home, I typed the journal exactly as I wrote it in Switzerland. Since then, I've been barely able to relate to it. I have "lost" all or parts of it innumerable times. And when I first began planning this book of essays, I had totally forgotten about its existence. I remembered it suddenly, a while after I'd sent Ruth Gundle a tentative table of contents. The journal retains an emotional charge for me that is elusive. I have decided to publish it because the trip to Poland in July 1983 was an extremely important event in my life and I feel more able to reflect on it now.

What follows is not the exact journal I wrote in Switzerland. I have had to make a few deletions and changes because in certain instances the original impinges on individuals' privacy. I have also added some material which, because of Solidarnosc illegal status in 1983, I was afraid to write down. This might seem overly paranoid—but that's how I felt. I have also added explanations and facts and embellished on episodes that I remember clearly, but which for some reason I did not describe fully. Though I have edited the text, I have tried to retain its awkwardness, and, in some instances, the distance which characterized the original writing.

I have also included some footnotes which support or expand upon the material. But in order to make reading easier, I would like to identify at the outset some of the people I refer to.

Marek Edelman, whom I mentioned earlier, was a friend of my father's. Like Marek, my father, **Michal Klepfisz,** was an activist in the Bund (as were his parents) and was a member of Di yidishe kamfs organizatsye (Jewish Fighters Organization—ZOB) and a participant in the Warsaw Ghetto Uprising. My father was fair and blue-eyed and, therefore, able to smuggle people out of the Ghetto in the years before the Uprising; in early 1943 he took out both my mother and me to the Aryan side. She got a job as a maid to a Polish family—she was able to pass—and I was placed in a Catholic orphanage. I was one and a half years old. My father smuggled weapons into the Ghetto and was responsible for obtaining materials and organizing small "factories" that produced the Molotov cocktails that were used in the Uprising. On the second morning of the Uprising, April 20th, he and a group of resisters were trapped in an attic in the brush factory district of the Ghetto. A German with a machine gun on the opposite roof covered their exit. My father killed the German, but was simultaneously killed himself. The killing of the German cleared the exit and the group escaped. Marek was with them. This occurred three days after my father's thirtieth birthday. The next day Marek returned to bury my father's body in the courtyard. The events are described in numerous histories of the Uprising.[1] When the Ghetto was totally destroyed my father's grave became part of the rubble. We have photographs taken right after the war of Marek placing flowers on the debris where he had buried my father. I once heard that the Chinese Embassy in Warsaw now stands on this spot. I have no idea if this is true and have never tried to verify it. In 1966 my mother had a symbolic gravestone erected for my father in the Jewish cemetery in Warsaw. Until 1983 we had only seen photographs of it.

My father's older sister, **Gina Klepfisz,** was also a Bundist and active in the resistance. She became known for smuggling people out of the umschlagplatz *(place of deportation)* just before the trains were to leave for Treblinka. Gina, who was a nurse, died while undergoing surgery in a hospital on Warsaw's Aryan side. She was buried in a Christian cemetery under a Christian name. After the war, my mother had her real name carved into the stone, but the grave was never moved (as I erroneously state in my poem "Solitary Acts").

Marysia Sawicka is Polish and before the war was active in the Polish Socialist Party (PPS). She was one of Gina's closest friends. Before the war there were strong ties between the PPS and the Bund and Marysia knew my father and his family well. Her sister Anna, like Marysia, helped Jews during the war. They both survived.

I also refer to **Elza Frydrych,** the orphaned child survivor—daughter of **Zygmunt** and **Cyla Frydrych**—and **Gaby Fryshdorf,** the son of **Chana** and **Gabrys Fryshdorf.** Chana and Gabrys Fryshdorf and Zygmunt Frydrych were active members of the Bund and members of the resistance. It was Zygmunt who was given the assignment to confirm reports that Treblinka was an extermination camp and he accomplished this mission. All three participated in the Uprising and survived it. Gabrys and Chana became partisans. He was later ambushed and killed; Chana was already pregnant with their son Gaby. Zygmunt was killed later that year. After the war, friends were able to identify Zygmunt and Gabrys's separate graves and their bodies were reburied together in one grave in Warsaw's Jewish cemetery.

Elza Frydrych was adopted by the Shatzkin family in Peekskill, New York. She committed suicide in 1962 right before her twenty-sixth birthday.[2] Chana and Gaby survived the war and later emigrated to the United States. Chana became the Executive Secretary of the YIVO Institute for Jewish Research, in New York City. She died in 1989. Gaby lives in Los Angeles. I consider both Elza and Gaby my siblings and family.

Much of my family died in Treblinka: my mother's mother, **Rikla Perczykow;** my father's parents, **Miriam** and **Jakub Klepfisz** (Gina could not smuggle them out) and my great-grandmother "Babcia" Salamon. Three of my mother's sisters also died during the war. Sala or "Krysia," the youngest and the one my mother "raised," probably died in Treblinka. The oldest, Genia Dubnikow, probably died in Dubno with her husband and nine-year-old son Majus (who was apparently already a gifted painter). Guta Rosenfeld and her husband Bernard also perished; she died in Lvov while giving birth to twin girls and he died in Janowski Camp, right outside of Lvov. The twins died two days apart shortly after their birth. One sister **Anka,** her husband Hershel Bachrach and their daughter **Dina** survived via Shanghai and Japan and emigrated to Australia after the war. My mother's brother **Beniek**, his wife Nacia and their son Szlamek survived in Siberia and after the war passed through Sweden and emigrated to Australia.

In presenting this journal, I am extremely conscious of how context influences our perceptions, our feelings. For the whole year before our trip I had been absorbed by Israel's invasion of Lebanon and struggling with new perspectives on Jewish power. Returning to Poland in 1983, I was plunged back into a period of history in which Jews were powerless. Complicating my feelings even more was my acute awareness that the country to which I was returning was a Poland almost empty of any Jews, a Poland absorbed totally by contemporary political tensions and problems. The Polish government had long declared Solidarnosc illegal and the movement had been forced underground. Its leaders and many members were in prison. About a week before our arrival, Pope John Paul had visited his homeland and there were rumors that he had negotiated some form of amnesty for political prisoners. In fact, amnesty was the main topic of conversation among the many Solidarnosc supporters that Marek introduced us to. People were tense and cautiously optimistic. All the store windows were filled with photographs of Papiez and it was not uncommon to see his photograph leaning against a building or propped up in a small square surrounded by wreaths and flowers in what were obviously makeshift altars.

Finalizing the manuscript in January 1990, I can only think of the changes that have taken place since that summer of 1983. Solidarnosc is not only legal, it has power. There has been a great deal of feeling expressed about Polish-Catholic-Jewish relations as reflected in the controversy over the convent at Auschwitz. The latter has added meaning for me because in 1988 I was able to go to Cracow and see the camp. My visit to the Jewish cemetery in Warsaw on this second trip to Poland reaffirmed the feelings of the first, but also deepened my understanding of the special significance this country has for *me and for the people among whom I was raised.* Poland remains **undzer heym**, *our home, no matter how bitter the memories, how filled with disappointment and betrayal.* Amerike iz goles, *America is exile, a foreign land in which I speak a foreign tongue. But I will never live in Poland. I do not want to, though I do not see an end to the mourning.*

At the time of the trip, I was living in upstate New York and working as a secretary in a psychiatric hospital in western Massachusetts. Before leaving, I explained to one of the secretaries, who was not Jewish, why I was returning. She, of course, knew about the Holocaust and was, I think, surprised to realize that I was directly connected with it. I told her my family was killed during the war and that it was basically going to be a trip to meet the dead. A few days before I left, Betty asked: "Are you going to be staying with relatives or at a hotel?"

Sunday, July 3, 1983

Arrived in Warsaw in the afternoon. Customs. The woman asked me if I had anything that was gold or silver. I showed her my ring with my name on it. Then pointed to the gold chain around my neck with the Jewish star. She wrote in Polish: *Złoty łańcuszek z wisiorkiem.* "One gold chain with pendant." I had no idea whether she knew what it was and didn't want to identify it, or perhaps had never seen one before.[3]

I had hoped that either Marek or Marysia would be there, since we had heard that in April, when we had originally planned to come, they had waited all day at the airport. But they were not there. We went to the Victoria Continental Hotel, which looked quite deserted.

Monday, July 4, 1983

We took a taxi to the Jewish Cemetery. I was overwhelmed by the size. Later found out it is more than 60 acres. One area on the right as you walk in is completely clear, grass clipped neatly like a lawn. Toward the back of that section is a statue of Janusz Korczak with the children.[4] There are benches all around. The clearing and statue were apparently set up for the 40th anniversary.

My mother and I went immediately to my father's stone and the area of the Bund fighters' monument. My father's stone is already cracked. The inscription appears both in Polish and Yiddish, but I am presenting only the Yiddish:

Inzh. Mikhal Klepfisz
1913—1943
tuer fun yugnt-bund "tsukunft"
fartreter fun der
yidisher kamfs-organizatsye
in der poylisher
vidershtand-bavegung
gefaln in bavofntn kamf
basn varshever
geto-oyfshtand
koved zayn ondenk!

Engineer Michal Klepfisz
1913—1943
Activist in youth Bund *"Tsukunft"* (Future)
Representative of the
Jewish Fighters' Organization
in the Polish resistance movement
Fell in armed battle
during the Uprising
of the Warsaw Ghetto
Honor to his memory!

Among the Bund group is the stone for Gaby's father and Elza's father. Their bodies are actually buried here in a group grave. We thought we would be able to buy flowers right by the cemetery. But the area is fairly deserted. My mother cried. I didn't, though I felt constantly on the verge.

I was utterly unprepared for the size, the seeming endlessness of the cemetery, and its abandoned condition. Most of it is completely overgrown, not just by grass, but trees, huge trees growing unchecked since 1939. You look down an alley and it is almost completely dark from the overgrowth, the gravestones are barely visible. Really jungle-like. Along the main alley— which is, of course, completely cleared—I found Esther Kaminska's gravestone and Peretz's and also Pola Elster's, which I photographed for Melanie.[5] Also found a grave of a 13-year-old girl who died in a bunker in 1944—probably in the Polish Uprising. Also a stone—which I'm not sure I photographed—and I couldn't find it the second time I went—placed by a woman and it said something to the effect: "This is for my parents, sisters, brothers, husband and children. And I remain alone, uncomforted."

We spent maybe an hour, an hour and a half, in the cemetery and were about to leave. My mother stopped at the entrance to talk to a man, a Jew. She asked about the crack in my father's tombstone. He called Bolek Szenicer who is in charge, who turned out to be about 30. His father was in charge before him. He has a brother who left Poland and now lives in Israel. He recognized the name Klepfisz and became quite attentive. He told us the crack was a natural one in the stone and that it would not crumble. He showed us the areas of the cemetery that had been worked on, like around the Korczak statue and another area straight back as you come in. As part of the restoration a wall was created of fragments of gravestones, a kind of mosaic. Bits and pieces of different colored stones, marble, sandstone. Detached dates, names, places. An attempt to salvage what was left. It's symbolic, of course. It's a miniscule reflection of the chaos and destruction.

Then Bolek showed us an area that was completely hollowed out on two sides. In other words, two enormous valley-like depressions overgrown with grass recently mowed and a number of 30- to 40-foot trees growing in these hollows. Between the hollows was a raised, grassy pathway. Bolek explained: At one point during the war, the Germans started to remove soil from this area of the cemetery (destroying, of course, the graves) for some use in factories. Eventually these two pits became bigger and bigger. When the Germans decided to liquidate the ghetto, they just started snatching Jews who probably were too troublesome to transport to Treblinka—mainly children, the old, disabled— and they brought them directly to the cemetery, shot them, and buried them in mass graves in the open ditches. Bolek said that more than 10,000 Jews lie buried in these two spots in mass graves. I kept looking at the trees growing in the midst of this.

Bolek said that now some money has been designated by the government for restoration. But most of the money comes from Jews outside of Poland. Probably 95 per cent of the cemetery, maybe even more, is simply wild growth; the gravestones are sinking deeper and deeper into the ground. The cemetery is just disappearing. Bolek did mention that one group of young Dutch Jews had come to help with the restoration. He also pointed out how uneven the ground of the cemetery was and explained that before the war it was customary, when space ran out, for Jews to pour new soil over gravesites and place new graves on top of them.

Bolek also showed me a book in Yiddish, English, and Polish, *Jewish Cemetery in Warsaw*.[6] I bought two English copies for $5 each. Everybody wants dollars. My mother asked him about how to get to various places in the old Ghetto and he offered to drive us around the area. My mother didn't recognize anything. We saw the Ghetto Fighters' Memorial—on a large plaza surrounded by a complex of apartment buildings. At least it stood out. Then we went to the Mila 18 bunker (the address of the headquarters of the ŻOB) which is on a small grassy hill in the midst of a group of apartment buildings and barely visible. It seemed in disrepair and unintegrated with its surroundings. But the small wall and plaque marking the *umschlagplatz* was the worst. Just stuck there, with a gas station right behind it. There was a candle and I lit it.[7]

We also went to where my mother lived with my father on 52 Ogrodowa. But her building was gone, though the one next to it, No. 50, was there and my mother said it was exactly like the building she lived in. I should have photographed it, but somehow felt very scattered all day and I think I lost a lot of material. It turned out to be the *only* place, and not even the exact one, which was left from my mother's whole life before the war.

My mother didn't recognize any of the areas Bolek took us to. She would mention a street and Bolek would say, "It's right here." But what she saw were not the same narrow streets she remembered, but broad, often grim boulevards which had completely different names. There is simply no trace of the Ghetto or old Jewish section of Warsaw.

This was the "Jewish" part of the day. My mother paid Bolek $10 for the tour.

We went back to the hotel for dinner and then walked around *Stare Miasto* (Old City) and it is quite pretty and charming. That too had been bombed, but has been completely restored. I saw a plaque which referred to Marie Curie. We walked around the fort, which my mother remembered, and she told me a bit about it. Polish history—like all European history—seems terribly complicated when compared to the brevity and relative simplicity of U.S. history. But my mother knows it letter perfect. We also passed a large church which had a cross of flowers with notes about *Solidarność*. In the evening, a friend of YIVO's librarian Dina Abramovicz came to visit. He is a Jew and he wanted to send Dina materials for the library. He declared himself a Polish patriot. He said that anti-Semitism stems from the government and radiates from the top down.

In reviewing the "Jewish" part of the day I concluded: the major Jewish activity in Warsaw occurs in the Jewish cemetery and consists of the unchecked sinking of gravestones into the ground. Deeper and deeper. It is clear that at this rate, there will be no trace left in 20 years and all evidence of Jewish life in Poland will be completely obliterated.

Tuesday, July 5, 1983

We went to the American Consulate to register. And there we met Marysia Sawicka. I had never realized how close she and Gina had been. She and her sister Anna helped Gina and my father during the war. Today she is 78 and remarkably energetic. She is a beautiful woman, gentle, with a wonderful soft smile. We had seen her last in 1946, and I didn't remember her at all. She said she thought she knew who I was because of my "American pants." After we met, we went immediately to the Christian cemetery on the other side of the Vistula to see Gina's grave. We brought flowers and first went to Anna's grave and Marysia cleaned it up and we placed flowers. Then she took us to Gina's grave, which says:

Kazimiera Jóźwiak
Gina Klepfisz
Żyła Lat 32
U 1 XII 1942
Cześć Jej Pamięci
Drogiej Ginie
Lodzia

Kazimiera Jóźwiak (Gina's Aryan name)
Gina Klepfisz
Lived 32 years
Died December 1, 1942
Honor to her memory
Dearest Gina
Lodzia (My mother's Aryan name)

Directions to Gina's grave: The cemetery is Na Pradze (Praga) Cemetery. Walk in the main entrance and turn right. Walk along the wall. The wall ends. Continue walking straight ahead till you reach an intersection where a cross has fallen on a grave. Then you turn right. Eventually you come to another intersection; on the left are two graves: Okrasa and Wolas. Turn left here. Gina's gravestone lies flat on the ground. On its left side is Regina Michalowskich Lipska and on the right Feliks Frankowski. I give these specifics so if others are ever in Warsaw they will be able to find Gina's gravesite and place flowers on her grave.

I weeded around the grave very thoroughly. I thought, here I am at my favorite activity, weeding. We washed the stone and placed flowers. Took photographs. And then suddenly Marysia asked us if Jewish law allowed for the placing of one grave on another. My mother said no. I said I didn't know. Anyway, it turned out that Marysia wants to be buried with Gina. She said something about being mad at her mother and not wanting to lie with her and something about her sister Anna and, again, the main point: she wants to be buried with Gina. We agreed immediately, though I was somewhat shocked at first and felt kind of trapped.

I also experienced real pain at the thought of any disturbance of Gina's grave. I kept seeing Gina's body wrapped in a shroud. I felt that any movement might cause her pain. It was an eerie feeling. It's the only time I've stood at a grave of anyone in my family.

I wonder now whether Marysia would want a cross on the stone or if only her name would be added. I have to speak to my mother about this. I couldn't tolerate a cross. Marysia said to my mother: "After the war you gave me a place to live (my mother passed on the Lodz apartment to her when she left) and now you've given me a place for death."

Marysia told us a story about her and Gina. They were in the mountains with a group on some sort of trip or vacation and there was a young girl who was horribly homesick and crying uncontrollably. So she and Gina comforted her and told her she could sleep in the same bed with them. The girl was delighted and she was all right after that.

My mother didn't know Marysia before the war. Marysia knew Gina and my father. She was a member of PPS and that was the connection to the Bund. She said Gina would come to her house during the Jewish holidays (she mentioned *pesakh*) because she was sick of matzoh and my grandparents, Miriam and Jakub, were being strict about food because of my great-grandmother (my grandmother's mother, "Babcia" Salamon).

Marysia helped Michał and Gina during the war. Gina stayed with her when she was sick and my father came to her apartment after he escaped from the train headed for Treblinka. In 1942 my father had been caught and forced on the train. The train went first to Malkinia and then to Treblinka. He jumped before Malkinia and injured his leg quite badly. He spent the night in a cemetery and managed to return to Warsaw on the Aryan side. He went straight to Marysia's apartment. Marysia recalled that at the time they had a little dog that barked at strangers. But that night it stood and whined by the door. They were all afraid. But when they opened the door, it was my father. And Marysia told how overjoyed they all were that Michał was safe. And she began to cry as she related this. I am moved by her gentleness, an unusual sweetness. I wonder about her, her aloneness. She has never married.

I did not know that Marysia had been declared a Righteous Gentile *(Hasidei Haumot)* by *Yad Vashem* and that she receives a small monthly allowance from the Israeli government and has been to Israel at least twice.[8] Her sister Anna was also named a Righteous Gentile. Marysia showed us a letter from *Yad Vashem* asking her to certify that another woman and her brother had helped Jews during the war. Marysia said she knew the woman had, but that the brother had done nothing. Why should he get anything? she asked. She was asking my mother what to do.

She and my mother talked about Gina again. My mother claims that Gina did not have to have the surgery and did not have to die. But she insisted on the operation. She had something like a bleeding ulcer, which caused a lot of pain but was not fatal. My mother quoted Gina as saying she had to take care of my mother and me and she needed to be strong. She didn't tell my mother she was going into the hospital for the surgery because she knew my mother would try to stop her. When my mother found out and went to the hospital, Gina was already dead. My mother couldn't believe it and went to speak to the doctor even though it was dangerous. And the doctor made some analogy to clean plates and plates in water. I didn't understand it.

Everyone says I look like Gina. Everyone also says she was very strong, independent. Someone once said: She should have been a doctor, not a nurse. She was my father's older sister and they were close. She never married and was apparently very attached to me and my mother.

I placed a pot with begonias on her grave and hoped it would rain. I knew that whatever I left there would eventually dry up.

This cemetery is also enormous. I have never seen so many crosses. I was unused to the photographs on the graves. Marysia told us that after the war people threw stuff on Gina's grave because it didn't have a cross or Christian symbol on it.

We had to leave. It was hard.

We went to the Jewish Historical Institute which had put on an exhibit on the Uprising in honor of the 40th anniversary. The building was large and deserted. My mother spoke to someone in charge. According to this man, it has a staff of four. I asked for a catalog of the exhibit, but there was none. The man said the show was a rush job and a catalog had never been written. The exhibit itself was good, the material familiar. They displayed pictures of Marek and Chana and Gabryś, Zygmunt, and Michał. There was a photograph of Artur Zygielbaum.⁹ I took photographs of some of the displays and tried to take close-ups of some of the women Melanie mentioned in her *Nice Jewish Girls* piece. But now I think she must have seen them in *They Fought Back* though I had not seen them before.¹⁰

The emptiness of this Jewish Institute, the fact that there was no one there to see the exhibit, was very depressing. There was a display case of books, but nothing for sale or in stock. The man who spoke to us said that they can't cope with the massive archives. They are hoping to get at least a Xerox machine to copy their materials. But they don't seem to have enough people even to do Xeroxing quickly enough. I'm in error. Xeroxing, he said, was not good because some materials are in such poor condition, they don't reproduce well. Instead, they'd like to microfilm everything. Apparently it's a project that could take a few months at the very least.

We then returned to the hotel. My mother and Marysia went to see someone I didn't know—"Dziatka"—grandma. I felt too exhausted and went to sleep. Later Irena L. came and stayed quite late talking and gossiping. I liked her a lot. Her Yiddish and English are good. But I mainly spoke Polish to her. She talked about Elza. She told me that the Shatzkins had thought it wouldn't be good for Elza to maintain contact with Poland and that when Irena came to the States they didn't want Elza to see her. But Bernard Goldstein arranged it—and she and Elza spent a few hours together.¹¹ She had seen Elza during the war and knew her parents Zygmunt and Cyla. She said Elza had an incredible memory and remembered a number of things and corrected her. This was the first time I heard about the Shatzkins' attitude. My mother had not heard this before either. There was the usual talk about politics, economics. Dina Abramovicz's friend popped in with stuff for his daughter in the States.

I don't remember all the conversation with Irena. She talked a little about what happened after the war. How Bundists in the States had originally *encouraged* Jews to stay in Poland. This included Patt and Stolar, who came to Poland after '45 to help the surviving Jewish community.¹² And many Jews, in fact, wanted to, planned to stay. But then the Kielce pogrom occurred.¹³ I'd never heard of it before. Dozens of Jews—survivors—were murdered by Poles. That pogrom finally pushed most Jews to leave (we had already left). Only about 60,000 Jews remained behind. There were over 3,000,000 Jews in Poland on September 1, 1939—the day Hitler invaded.

My mother said that our apartment in Lodz was searched once. They were after a Jewish man and Bolek was home and she said they were all very frightened.[14] Later, when we left Poland with Chana and Gaby, we went with a "protective escort," a Polish woman who sat on the train separately with me and Gaby just in case there was any trouble. Chana was dark and thick featured and beautiful—but she looked so Jewish. Halinka and Fishke also came along and sat in another compartment as guards.[15] We were travelling to Gdynia, a seaport. We were emigrating to Sweden.

Irena told us her son doesn't identify as a Jew, but doesn't deny it either. He is married to a Pole and they have a little girl.

When Irena left the hotel it was almost midnight.

Wednesday, July 6, 1983

This morning we met Marysia at the main train station and took the train to Lodz, over two hours, maybe two and a half. I stood at the window all the way. The Polish countryside is spectacular, the wheat fields golden. And there are endless dark, rich forests. What is amazing is that I didn't see a single piece of farm machinery anywhere during the entire ride. Not one! Everything is done by hand. You see the farmers cutting hay and wheat with scythes. Women working slowly in the fields. Horse-drawn wagons. People resting under trees, sleeping. It all looked like a nineteenth-century painting.

When we got to Lodz, Marek was waiting for us at the station. It was wonderful to see him and I felt quite excited. He looked exactly like I remembered him, a mixture of real images from childhood memories, photographs, and from his visit to the States in the '60s. He and my mother immediately had an argument about why she didn't telegraph that she wasn't coming in April, etc., etc. I think it was a way of deflecting their emotions—but he sure yelled and she stood her ground. It was kind of funny and I was completely floored. After all they hadn't seen each other in maybe 25 years. What a greeting! Anyway, first he drove Marysia home and we were able to see the apartment she lives in. One room with a kitchen. She gave me a book called *The Polish Jewry: History and Culture*, which had just been published. It was in Polish and so I couldn't really read it.[16]

Then we left her and Marek drove us to the apartment building where we had lived after the war—18 Żeromskiego, Apartment 26. *The actual building completely intact!* Standing in the courtyard, I could see our kitchen window on the third floor.

My mother told us that once I came home very upset and said: *"Mamusiu, chlopak mnie nazwal sydowka. Co jest sydowka?"* (I should have said *zydowka*—I guess I had a slight lisp.) Mommy, the boy called me a Jewess. What's a Jewess? I remember quite clearly how the boys fought in one of the cellar rooms, and how I sat obediently on a bench watching them. Also how the blood running from their noses made me ill. This was the apartment my mother and I shared with Bolek and Ania. I remember the white tile oven which heated the main room. Also the small room where I had my crib and my mother her bed. I remember Pani Helena visiting us here.[17] She is the wild woman with the red hair in my poem *"Bashert."* After she read the poem, my mother told me Pani Helena's hair was really completely white. She brought me my first orange, which I didn't like and spat the juice out in her face. They hung a swing for me in the doorway between the two rooms. My mother said that Pani Helena would come and swing in it. She claimed she was practicing for the ocean crossing to Sweden.

During that year in Lodz in '45 to '46, Bolek seemed to be always meeting other survivors—friends and acquaintances—and bringing them home. And Ania would look out of the kitchen window and see him coming with someone new and say: "Add more water to the soup." It was my job to put newspapers on the floor for them to sleep on. It was in this apartment that I had my fourth birthday party and I even have photographs. For this event, Halinka stuck a big bow in her hair in my honor, just like mine. We also have a photograph, on another occasion, of Gaby and me by the oven. The day the photograph was taken I got the measles and everyone thought Gaby would get sick. But he didn't.

I remember this Lodz apartment well and it felt quite incredible to be standing in the courtyard, to be actually there. I have very warm feelings about this place and am amazed it is real and was not destroyed. I guess I felt safe there and there must have been a sense of exhilaration of having survived at the same time as deep depression over everything that had been destroyed.

Throughout the early afternoon Marek kept worrying that his car was bugged. We stopped a couple of times. It's not in great shape, so there were a lot of wires attached to the fenders and lights. I got down on the ground at one point for a careful inspection, but could see nothing. Still, he wanted to feel free to talk to my mother, so he decided to take us to the Jewish cemetery where we would certainly be undisturbed.

The Jewish cemetery in Lodz seemed even more enormous than the one in Warsaw. We went through a back entrance because the front gates were locked. This cemetery is in worse shape than the one in Warsaw, because it's not used as a showcase.

It has unbelievably gigantic mausoleums and tombstones. All I kept thinking about was "Ozymandius." Lodz was an important industrial city and there were many Jewish industrialists, some incredibly wealthy, completely assimilated. Not a Hebrew letter or symbol of any Jewishness. Many gravestones were in Polish and adorned with Greek sculpture. Marek and my mother talked and talked. But I rushed around taking pictures—having this sense that I had to photograph it before it all disappeared. A woman, who I think might be a caretaker, was taking a couple to a grave. As she passed me, she told me it was forbidden to take pictures of any gravestones except those belonging to one's family. And I wanted to say: "All of them are my family." But I didn't. I just waited for her to leave. She was just harassing me. So I continued taking pictures. At one point I became terrified because a huge bird suddenly flew out from between two graves, as if a ghost had risen.

The cemetery was very overgrown and wild. Some stones were really beautiful, but difficult to photograph and I did a lot of pulling of weeds which, most of the time, were as tall as the gravestones themselves. The whole time I had an eerie feeling and wondered: where am I stepping? on what? It was so hard to distinguish and find the stones. Then I heard my mother calling me. Very faintly. I had been completely absorbed and she apparently had been calling for a long time and had become frightened I'd been murdered. We finally found each other.

The cemetery is robbed and vandalized on a regular basis. And it is rapidly deteriorating just from lack of repair. There is a monument to the six million but it is crumbling. One of the candles in the candelabra is broken off. It's pathetic. It's enraging.

Marek then took us to his house for dinner with friends. I saw the garden I played in and where I first saw Elza—brushing her beautiful hair. I was bald—I assume I must have had lice, though no one will admit this to me. My mother insists that I never had lice, that my head was shaved to make my hair grow thicker. I'll never get at the truth.

I had no recollection of the garden at all. It seems incredible that Marek's been living in the same house since '46. It was good to see it—

and not have to try to remember it. People had planted vegetables and it was pretty to look at.

Marek then insisted he and I take a walk and he told me how good my mother looked and then asked me about her health and work. I wanted to ask him about my father, but couldn't bring myself to. Don't quite know why.[18] He also reminisced about Elza and talked about how the Shatzkins had asked her not to write him after she got to the U.S.

When Marek and I came back, we had dinner with his friends, who were very pleasant. There were a number of sweet children running around. This group, I assume, is all *Solidarność*. After dinner, he took us to the train station and we went back to Warsaw. We got in around 9 o'clock and decided to walk to the hotel.

Thursday, July 7, 1983

A friend of Bolek Szenicer's drives a cab and Bolek arranged for him to take us to Treblinka. He is a Pole, probably in his late twenties, married, father of a young son. Says he sometimes helps Bolek in the cemetery. He seemed to know quite a bit about Jewish matters and told us he'd show us typical Jewish homes and also another Jewish cemetery in Warsaw.

The drive to Treblinka took a little over two hours. I had somehow always imagined that the train ride was much longer. I had read many accounts of the horrors of the train rides, but these were mostly about journeys from distant places outside of Poland. I naturally assumed all the trips to camps were very long, days long. The short drive seemed bizarre. One moment you're in a city and a couple of hours later you're in a camp being gassed.

We got to Treblinka and didn't quite know where to go. Signs are very unclear. We looked at the main "display"—which had a map and huge photographs. The one that struck me most was the one of massive marble crosses. Next to that was a picture of Janusz Korczak. This was interesting to me because the cab driver had told us that he had learned about Korczak in school but *had never been told he was a Jew*. I didn't read what it said about him under his picture. In general, I think I lost a lot of details this day because I felt so off balance. I think I felt somewhat frightened.

My mother was feeling extremely nervous and barely spoke. I know she was thinking about her mother, my grandmother Rikla, who died here. I think I was feeling impatient and angry because the site was so vaguely marked and there was no one to ask. We did not know where to go, so we decided to drive down the main path, but then met another car coming from the opposite direction. The family stopped and said they'd driven for two kilometers and there was nothing to see. But we continued driving for a while and finally saw some huge stones and stopped and began to walk. We decided the rows of cement blocks were symbolic railroad tracks. This was strictly an interpretation, which we found out later was correct.

At the entrance of the memorial site are enormous stones on which are carved the names of the countries victims (Jews are not specified) had come from. There is a huge memorial in the middle which I think has a candelabra and some writing on it. All around it is a huge, huge area full of roughly carved stones of different sizes—little ones for children, I suppose. Some are marked with names of cities. I stood in front of the one that said *Warszawa* (Warsaw) and listed my grandmothers, my grandfather, and my great-grandmother. I also thought about my father, who jumped from the train and managed to escape before the train reached Treblinka.

My mother and I walked around separately. She seemed to want to be alone. I was disturbed by this, felt helpless. Could not totally understand it. But I let her alone. I remember in the corner of my vision I saw a man working by hand in the fields.

I wanted there to be more Yiddish or Hebrew lettering on the stones. I'm not sure what was on the main monument. The names of the cities were all in Polish and I just didn't think there was very much of a sense of Jewish loss.

Near the candelabra-type monument, in the ground, was a kind of rectangular symbolic sculpture. It was supposed to represent burnt bodies. I could barely look at it. It made me sick and I couldn't bring myself to take a picture of it.

We drove on to the site of the slave labor and also the site of the Polish barracks. The area where the slave labor took place is enormous and endless—like an open rock quarry. The prisoners dug for stones, pebbles. I gathered some to bring back. I'm not good at judging distances, but it was extremely far, as far as you could see. Deep down. At the sides in a couple of places were bunkers for guards who stood as lookouts.

There was also a wooden cross on one spot with a sign that indicated

Polish laborers had been shot there. This was near the Polish barracks and that is probably why the cross was there. I don't remember seeing any Jewish stars anywhere.

There are no buildings in Treblinka. The Germans burned the whole camp when they retreated. The Polish barracks area is identifiable only because the cement floors weren't destroyed by fire. So the cement bunkers at the side of the rock pit were the only original structures in the entire camp.

There were two different groups visiting. One was of Polish children who were climbing the sides of the pit. One girl was sitting on a ledge and playing a guitar. Many wore American T-shirts. Another group—lying under trees in the shade—was of Polish women, and they had a large cross.

The experience was such a mixed one. The monument and the surrounding rocks are very beautiful and appropriate for what they're intended to represent. But somehow I've had my fill of symbols. Jews are not rocks and rocks are not Jews. And burnt sculpture metal/plastic—no matter how closely it duplicates reality—is not skin and bones. And I was deeply disturbed that there was so little specifically Jewish at this memorial. Maybe I'm wrong about this and am simply going through that self-doubt about my perception of other people's indifference. Maybe my photographs will prove me wrong. Probably not.[19] But I am really sick to death of symbols. Rocks may have their own lives. Jews certainly have theirs. To substitute one for the other and to say it is a close approximation, that somehow the "art" transcends the difference, is wrong, and a real evasion of history. And I kept thinking of that Polish family we met who said they'd driven two kilometers and that there was nothing to see.

One other thing I want to add here. And that is how beautiful the country around Treblinka is. Woods and farm fields. Lush and rich. I'll always keep that image of the farmer working in the field next to the memorial site.

We finally left. On the way back, the driver mentioned the Wyszków woods, which my mother told me were known for partisan activity. During our entire stay in Poland, whenever I saw woods I thought immediately of the partisans—Chana and Gabryś—and what it meant to live in the forests and to try to survive.

The cab driver stopped at a small town called Ostrów Mazowiecki and showed us what he said were typical Jewish houses—beautiful wooden structures. Very large. Before the war a number of families shared them at the same time and they were considered poor. To me now they look quite wonderful, almost magical. I took a number of photographs. I assume the driver was telling us the truth about this town.

The final part of this trip took place in Warsaw. The driver offered to show us the oldest Jewish cemetery in Poland—Bródno at Praga. (It turned out be right next to the cemetery where Gina lies buried.) It had been completely destroyed in the 1960's(!!!) during the anti-Semitic purges. It was illegal to go there, and the driver made us promise not to say he had taken us there. We climbed up a hill—a back way of getting to it. Along the way we noticed a few bits and pieces of gravestones. But at the actual site we found that all the gravestones had been pulled out of the ground and lined up in various places on their sides, fairly neatly. They were going to be shipped somewhere else, but the plan was apparently abandoned and they were just left there. There is no marking to indicate that any cemetery existed there. Everything, of course, is overgrown. Later I looked at *The Jewish Cemetery in Warsaw*, written in 1983, and it does mention the Bródno cemetery at Praga, but doesn't say it was destroyed. I was so upset by it all and so confused having just come from Treblinka that I kept thinking I wasn't understanding the driver's Polish. I kept asking: Who did this? And he kept saying: "*My, Polacy!*" (We, Poles). He also said that there is some talk about putting a *symbolic* monument there.

My mother finally said she wanted to leave. She appeared exhausted, a bit off balance. She had difficulty walking through the high grass. Treblinka had been very hard on her and, I think, coming to this other cemetery was ultimately too much. So we left and drove back to the hotel.

That evening I walked through one of the corridors in the lobby that I hadn't been in before and noticed a case displaying Polish books. Three shelves had books about the Pope, another about Polish jewelry, and the fourth exhibited *The Polish Jewry* in Polish, German, and English (the book Bolek had sold me).

Pani W. came to visit but I hardly spoke with her because I didn't know her. I took a bath and later left for a walk. When I got back, Jerzy, a close friend of my father's, was visiting; he and my father had been in the *Politechnicum* together. He was extremely nice, said I looked like Michał. Some of the talk was the usual—economics, etc. When we told him where we'd been, he said he arrived at Treblinka right after the liberation and saw two things that he'll never forget. One was a barrack completely filled with children's shoes. The other was a barrack filled with eye glasses. They should have preserved those barracks and not bothered with the monuments. Those were real and not symbolic. They would not have needed translation or interpretation.

Jerzy has relatives everywhere: Canada, America, Israel. His mother escaped to France in 1939 and managed to get by till six months before the end of the war. Then she was taken and shipped to a camp, but jumped from the train and committed suicide. Someone, obviously, must have told him that. Jerzy's first wife was seized by the Ukrainians. My mother told me that she was a sculptor and very beautiful and was taken to a brothel, then disappeared. The assumption is that she was killed. Jerzy is still close to her sister, who is a painter.

After the war, Jerzy remarried and now has two sons, both living in Denmark. The older one made the decision to leave Poland in '68 because of two specific anti-Semitic incidents: one, when a girlfriend of his was forbidden by her father to see him anymore because he was a Jew; the other, when a stranger cursed him on the street. The younger son was 16 at the time and he decided to leave with his brother for Denmark. The Danes took good care of them. The older one is a businessman, married to a Pole and has two children. Does not really identify as a Jew, but doesn't deny it. The children speak Danish and Polish. The younger son just finished studying dentistry, is married to an Eskimo, and they speak only Danish with the children, so communication between Jerzy and these grandchildren is difficult.

I liked Jerzy a lot, wanted to take photographs, but didn't. I think I felt shy. He left quite late.

Friday, July 8, 1983

As planned, we went back to the Jewish Cemetery this morning; it was only open till noon. We went down to breakfast and immediately met Sam and Raymond Webb (from Melbourne, Australia), cousins by marriage. (Dina, daughter of my mother's sister Anka, is married to Bill Webb, and Sam is his brother.) We had breakfast with them and planned to see them later. It was really bizarre meeting these Australians in Warsaw.

We went to buy flowers and then took a cab to the cemetery. Bolek wasn't there yet. We placed flowers at my father's grave and also at the collective grave of Zygmunt and Gabrys. I wrote notes with my mother's and my names and placed them with my father's flowers; one with the name of Chana and Gaby at Gabrys'; another for Zygmunt from my mother and me. Then I went to Pola Elster's grave and put flowers there with a note from Judy, Melanie, and Michaele and me and then put flowers on the grave of the 13-year-old-girl who died in a bunker in 1944 . And I placed a note from the *DVC* and then rewrote it and included Gloria's name.[20] Somehow felt I couldn't leave her out.

One thing I noticed in the book about the cemetery: the Zionists seemed completely absent. But maybe they themselves didn't want to be there.

I don't want to forget one incident. There are a few workers at the cemetery, maybe six or seven Poles. One woman was near the Bund monument and she was washing down tombstones. She had two huge pails and a watering can. I had a small jar and wanted to fill it up for Gabryś and Zygmunt's grave and so I walked over to her and asked if I could have some water. She said okay, but added "The pump's down there. *Pani tutaj tylko spaceruje.*" ("You're just here for a little walk. I'm working here all morning.")

I want also to mention that I understood for the first time why my father's stone says he was an engineer. There are many stones which say professor of anatomy, physics, mathematician. And, of course, books are very visible, often for *gelernte* (scholars), or rabbis, or writers. There are also symbols of scissors and needles for tailors, etc. I took a lot of photographs of all of this. Bolek explained some of the symbols. I'm sure there are a lot of these photographs at the YIVO. When I get back I want to write to Marek Web and find out.[21]

My mother had arranged to meet Irena and Inka here. And they came and sat by the Bund monument and talked. I rushed around taking photographs as usual. Bolek came and showed me some gravestones that were particularly interesting, including ones for Hassidic rabbis. I hope all my pictures come out because I discovered that for one roll I had set the wrong ASA on the camera which really depressed me. I took photographs of everything. My most intense feeling was how to keep a record, how to preserve all this in the midst of the present crisis, both in Poland and in Israel, how to find a place for this preservation among all the other priorities.[22] Bolek allowed us to stay after the official closing. But finally we left. I feel I will come back here some day.

Inka said she'd see us later in the evening at the hotel and we asked her to bring her daughter Alina too. She is a member of the the National Jewish Theater.

In the meantime the three of us took a tram to where Irena lives and started to walk. It turned out we were on Nowogrodzka Street, the street of the orphanage where I was placed (*Sierociniec Księdza Boduena*). It is not an orphanage now, but a Children's Home (don't quite know the distinction). Irena and my mother sat on a bench while I walked around taking pictures. Ironically, my mother had never been inside this courtyard. When it was decided that I was to be placed in this home, it is true that my father took me, as I had always heard, but what I learned now was that Gina went with him. And he did watch from a distance, but Gina was the one who made the contact and gave me away. Michał couldn't bring himself to do it. The Polish woman my mother worked for, Rouba, was the sister of Dr. Zachert (a woman) who worked in the orphanage and she arranged it all. My mother would sometimes come and watch me when the children were returning from a walk. Once she came over to me and took my hand, but one of the nuns reprimanded her and said: "Don't touch the children. You might infect them." So she let go of my hand and started to leave. But I called out "Mamma" and she became frightened and never came near me again.

Halinka Ellenbogen worked there and brought news about me all the time and, because of Dr. Zachert, I got special candy and food. Once my father came to bring me chocolate—or rather hand it over—and was told very severely by Dr. Zachert that he was never to come again or she would release me.

I have no memories of this orphanage, but in my twenties I wrote obsessively about someone being killed there, someone whose face was bandaged, whom the nuns had hidden. The person (and I've always assumed it was a man) was finally shot—I think—as he went over the wall. I also wrote that the Germans gave us red candy. I don't have any memory of this now, but I tend to think that it happened because for years as a child in Sweden and the United States, I could not see any violence in movies without actually vomiting. It was an automatic reaction. So I think I must have really witnessed something violent.

After seeing the orphanage, we walked toward Irena's house and shopped for presents at Cepelia. I wanted very badly to get Judy a book on architecture—urban or rural—but could find nothing. I finally found a used bookstore but it was closing for the afternoon break. So we went on to Irena's apartment. It was very pleasant there. Irena, by the way, had read *Keeper of Accounts* in England when she visited Vlodka and Nelly.[23] In fact, it was she who told me I'd still be able to see Marek's garden—referring to my poem, "Solitary Acts." But she made no comment about the book. She herself had a lot of books in her apartment and offered me some in Polish, which I really can't read. But she also offered postcards of Treblinka which are no longer available. I accepted those. We had tea and cherries. It is a two-room apartment, meaning one room serves as the bedroom and living room and the other is an eat-in kitchen. Her son is married to a Pole and they have a little girl. They've spent time in England. I don't think there is a Jewish question here.

I went back to the used bookstore and found a book about the work of a Polish sculptor Witosz. It seemed ironic because it was so utterly Christian—the last thing I wanted to buy—but it seemed so right for Judy because I thought she'd like the photography and the sculpture. Maybe I'm wrong. I sometimes tend to misjudge these things. Anyway, it's quite big and heavy and beautiful and I only paid 200 zl. for it. I think it was a real *mitsiye* (bargain) because Irena seemed quite stunned. I think she thought it cost thousands.

Later we took Irena back with us to the hotel and had dinner. She and my mother went upstairs and I went for a walk and when I came back Inka was there. The three of them gossiped for a long time about everyone. Afterwards Inka's daughter, Alina, came. She is in her twenties, a single mother of an infant son. She is an actress in the National Jewish Theater. They're rehearsing Manger's *Megile lider*.[24] Right now the theater is performing *Der dybuk*.[25] But we couldn't see it because it wasn't playing again until July 13th. Alina seems very pleasant. Her circumstances, financially, are extremely difficult and she relies on her mother to help her. She's hoping the troupe will be invited to the States. Something is in the works, but even if it happens it is not clear she'll be among those chosen to go with the company. They all talked about the fact that *Fiddler on the Roof* was about to open in Polish in Lodz. There have been difficulties because the authorities (censor?) did not allow the inclusion of the pogrom scene and it's been cut.

We talked about the usual—economics, etc. They left quite late.

About the Jewish theater. Apparently most of the actors are Poles, some of mixed Polish/Jewish parentage. Alina is one of the few with any Jewish heritage—her mother Inka is a Jew. Most of those with mixed backgrounds have "identity problems." The plays are performed in Yiddish, but the actors only know Polish, so they speak Yiddish kind of parrotlike. And then the Polish audience listens to their Yiddish and can't understand it and must use earphones for simultaneous translation into Polish.

Saturday, July 9, 1983

We had breakfast with Sam and Raymond. And we waited for Marek. He came around 10:30 with a Polish friend who wore a large cross around her neck. He wanted to get out of the hotel room. I guess he was suspicious. We went for a ride and he and my mother talked and later we walked around. We went to an apartment project where a very, very young woman presented me with a copy of *Jewish Cemetery in Warsaw*. I'm sure she was from *Solidarność*. I wasn't even told her name. There was genuine gentleness in the gesture. I think Marek had told these people about my father and who we were.

Marek drove us to the Polytechnic where my father studied and then we drove to the new synagogue which is right next to the Jewish theater. We walked into the lobby and there was Alina (a completely unexpected meeting) and she took us to the synagogue, which turned out to be closed. But two men who work there were willing to open it up when they heard we were American Jews. The synagogue is quite beautiful and is sparkling new. Of course, all this was prepared for the 40th anniversary. Marek put on a *yarmulke* and I took photographs. I joked with him that I would blackmail him.[26] Later Marek took us to visit a Polish poet, who, I gathered, was "one of us"—*Solidarność*.

Marek then took us out to dinner. We went to *Stare Miasto* and, on the way, stopped at a church which collects provisions for families whose lives have been disrupted, i.e., whose family members have been imprisoned or gone underground. They all knew Marek and he was very friendly with the nuns and, in the Polish manner, kissed the women's hands in greeting. And then we had a duck dinner in a *kawiarnia* (cafe). We walked around some, took photographs.

At one point, Marek took me aside and gave me a copy of *Getto Walczy* (Ghetto Fights), an account he had written right after the war describing the Uprising. In honor of the 40th anniversary, *Solidarność*

Walczy (Ghetto Fights), an account he had written right after the war describing the Uprising. In honor of the 40th anniversary, *Solidarnosc* had reissued it illegally using as a new preface his statement calling for a boycott. The small booklet carried the *Solidarnosc* imprint. Marek asked me to take it and show it in the States. I decided not to tell my mother until we were on the plane and on our way.

And then Marek and his friend left. I wondered when I'd see him again.

At this point I felt very depressed and physically sick. The worst migraine in a long while. My mother went to meet Sam and Raymond. I joined them much later for a snack while they ate dinner. Sam was born in Poland very poor and left for Australia when he was 7. Raymond was born in Paris and was 12 when the war broke out. She told incredible stories about going over the border to Switzerland, being separated from her family, staying in a Lutheran home for a couple of years. Her immediate family managed to survive. She said the Italians were the ones who warned them in France to get out. She said they were the only ones who were not anti-Semitic; the Swiss Jews did little to help. She didn't get to Australia till she was 15.

It was interesting. These are Jews with whom I feel I have very little in common. Extremely wealthy, politically different. I was taken aback by Raymond's history. What does her history mean in terms of today? in relationship to me?

We came back to the room, packed until 1 A.M. and set the alarm for 6.

Sunday July 10, 1983

We got up at 6. Ate breakfast and came back for our bags. Took a cab to the airport. Driver tried to rip us off— 1,000 zl. My mother refused and gave him 400. He grumbled and left.

Marysia and Halina, her niece, (we had met her in Lodz), came to say good-bye to us at the airport. Customs was a nightmare. Some people were being searched very thoroughly. One woman had to open every jar of face cream in her suitcases. I was becoming nervous about Marek's *Getto Walczy*, not even clear what the implication was of taking it out of the country—for me or for him. I slipped it into an envelope with photographs and passed the envelope over the gate to Marysia telling her I wanted her to look at the photographs. I'm not sure she understood what I was doing or even saw the booklet. After we got through customs—we weren't checked—I went back to the gate and Marysia gave me the envelope. My mother came over too. We all cried.

When my mother and I boarded the bus for the airplane, Marysia was standing on an overpass and waving. She was the last one that we saw.

Notes

1. Accounts of my father's actions include: Lucjan Blitt, "Hero of the Ghetto Awarded 'Virtuti Militari,'" *The Polish Review*, 4, 27 (July 19, 1944), p. 14; George Creel, "The Heroes: Michal Klepfisz," *Collier's* (November 11, 1944), pp. 46-47; Vladka Meed, *On Both Sides of the Wall* (New York: Holocaust Library, 1979); Bernard Goldstein, *The Stars Bear Witness* (New York: Viking, 1949); Hanna Krall, *Shielding the Flame: An Intimate Conversation with Dr. Marek Edelman*, trans. Joanna Stasinska and Lawrence Weschler (New York: Henry Holt, 1986).

2. For information about Elza's life and her short story, "Przemysl," describing her experience being hidden in a convent, see *The Tribe of Dina: A Jewish Women's Anthology*, eds. Kaye/Kantrowitz and Klepfisz (Boston: Beacon Press, 1989) pp. 165-67.

3. My Bundist upbringing disparaged the wearing of religious symbols. But after Israel's invasion of Lebanon in 1982 I decided, for a variety of contradictory reasons, to buy a Jewish star. I did not wear it all the time. When we decided to go to Poland, I was determined to wear it during the entire trip.

4. Janusz Korczak (1878-1942) was an internationally known child psychologist and children's story writer. Highly assimilated (his name was Henryk Goldszmit), he eventually moved his orphanage into the Warsaw Ghetto. In 1942, the Germans decided to liquidate the orphanage and deport the children to Treblinka. Because of his international reputation, Korczak was told he could stay behind. He refused and went with the children to Treblinka, where he was killed.

5. Ester Kaminska was the founder of Warsaw's Yiddish theater and famous for her portrayal of Gordin's Mirele Efros. Her daughter, Ida Kaminska, continued working in the Yiddish theater; later in life, she came to the U.S. and starred in the movie *The Shop on Main Street*. I. L. Peretz (1852-1915) was the "father" of Yiddish literature. In her essay, "Some Notes on Jewish Lesbian Identity," in *Nice Jewish Girls: A Lesbian Anthology* (Boston: Beacon Press, 1989), Melanie Kaye/Kantrowitz gives Pola Elster as an example of Jewish women's resistance during the war.

6. Warszawa: Panstwowe Wydawnictwo Naukowe, 1983.

7. When I returned to Warsaw in 1988, the gas station was gone. A huge memorial of white and black marble walls now marks the place from which half a million Jews left for Treblinka.

8. *Yad Vashem*, the Holocaust museum and research center established in Jerusalem in 1954, also honors Gentiles who helped Jews during World War II.

9. Zygielbaum, a member of the Bund, was sent by the Jewish resistance to mobilize help for the Uprising. He reached England and the Polish Government in Exile, but was unable to arouse any support. When news of the ghetto's destruction reached him, he committed suicide to draw attention to the plight of Polish Jews. See, Aviva Ravel, *Faithful Until Death: The Story of Arthur Zygielbaum* (Montreal: Workmen's Circle, 1980).

10. See Yuri Suhl, *They Fought Back: The Story of Jewish Resistance in Nazi Europe* (New York: Crown Publishers, 1967).

11. Bernard Goldstein, Bund activist and organizer, resistance fighter during the war, wrote *Tsvontsik yor in varshever bund 1919-1939* (Twenty Years in the Bund in Warsaw) and

Finf yor in varshever geto, translated as *The Stars Bear Witness* (New York: Viking, 1949) and reissued as a paperback under the title *Five Years in the Warsaw Ghetto*.

12. Jacob Patt and Abram Stolar, Bund leaders who emigrated to the U.S. right before the war and then returned to Poland to help survivors.

13. The largest post-war pogrom by Poles. Forty Jewish survivors were murdered in Kielce. There is a lot of controversy about this pogrom and who was actually responsible. But for most Jews in Poland, there was only one interpretation, and the majority decided to leave.

14. Bolek Ellenbogen, Bund activist and organizer, resistance fighter during the war. It was Bolek who brought food to my mother after he learned where she was hiding with me. After the war, we shared an apartment with him and his wife Ania and we all went together to Sweden. He and Ania now live in New York City.

15. Halinka Ellenbogen Kahan (Bolek's sister) and Fishke Najman. Fishke was murdered in 1946 in Warsaw. Halinka now lives in Chicago.

16. Warsaw: Interpress, 1982. I later bought a copy in English.

17. Helena Shefner, a Bundist and my father's French teacher. She was with us in Sweden, and then emigrated to the U.S.

18. In 1989, Marek came to the U.S. to receive an honorary degree at Yale University for his freedom work for Jews and Poles. I mustered my courage and asked about my father. Marek was very warm and expressive, said Michal was a good comrade and companion, a fine man to have a drink with. I felt Marek was sincere and not repeating myths. I was pleased I had asked.

19. My photographs did not prove me wrong.

20. *Di vilde chayes*, a lesbian/feminist group of which I was a member (1982-83). DVC addressed issues of Jewish identity and anti-Semitism in the women's movement.

21. Marek Web, head of the archives of YIVO Institute for Jewish Research (New York City).

22. Israeli troops were still in Lebanon.

23. Vlodka and Nelly Blitt were twin daughters of the Bund leader and writer, Lucjan Blitt. My father smuggled them out of the ghetto. They survived and after the war, emigrated to be with their father in England. Vlodka remained in London and Nelly now lives in New York City.

24. Itzik Manger's *Megile lider* are a series of satirical poems based on the Book of Esther in which *shtetl* Jews represent the major figures of the story.

25. *Der dybuk* by Sh. An-ski is about a young girl possessed by the ghost of a rejected lover and the exorcism which frees (and kills) her.

26. The Bund was antireligious.

Yom Hashoah, Yom Yerushalayim:
A Meditation

(1989)

Wednesday, January 18, 1989: A breathless week. Monday met Rita Falbel and Donna Nevel to review text of new flyer for the Jewish Women's Committee to End the Occupation. We sat in a Jewish deli and after a while I noticed that the waiters were eavesdropping. Turned out they were Palestinians. One of them had been imprisoned. Can imagine the history and finally his exile. Listening to him made our work seem less abstract.

Talked with Rita and Donna about trying to reach the mainstream community. We're thinking of organizing women rabbis, reaching Hadassah women, planning monthly events. We're reassessing the vigils, trying to figure out how to make them more effective. It's hard to believe we've been doing this for over nine months.

On Tuesday went to a reception for Dr. Mariam Mar'i and Edna Zaretsky, the Palestinian and Jewish Israeli women of New Jewish Agenda's "Women-in-Dialogue Tour." I became upset because someone made analogies to the Holocaust and Nazis, said that Israeli leaders had to be put on trial and sit in glass cages, an allusion to Eichmann's glass cage. I am always aggravated by such remarks. I tolerate certain Israelis being called fascist and I feel clear that there are fascist elements in Israel, but I can't bring myself to call them Nazis. It's wrong. Since this was a reception, I decided not to question it.

I discussed it later, with little clarity, with some women when we were heading downtown to the Village Gate to hear Mariam and Edna speak publicly. Mariam and Edna talked about indoctrination, the failure of the educational system, the stereotyping prevalent in Israel. They were excellent, but I felt exhausted and left early. Had a lot of work waiting at home, including a speech for today's rally to protest the arrest and harassment of members of *Yesh Gvul* (There's a Limit), Israeli reservists refusing to serve in the Occupied Territories.

Got up at six-thirty this morning. Wasn't that happy with the speech, but it was okay. Hard to keep writing statements. Kept reminding myself about the waiters in the deli.

Rally was at noon in front of the Israeli Consulate. There were news people from Channel 4 and they spent most of the time with a woman who said we were disgusting. I really lost it when she called us anti-Semites. I can take self-hating Jew, but I can't take anti-Semite. So I screamed back and everybody started trying to cool me out. I was in a rage. Turned out she was a survivor. I expect the news people felt she had a special view on the subject or was more informed or had more of a right to have an opinion. I don't know quite what. But clearly whenever any issue about Israel is raised, survivors and the Holocaust come to the foreground almost immediately. Why not? They're permanently linked. But the rally was good. Excellent press coverage, solid attendance. It was a beautiful day. Everyone energetic, up, despite the fact that we're all on overload.

This afternoon planned to finish some poems and to work on my Yiddish translations. But Deborah (editor at Beacon) called about *The Tribe of Dina*. She added that the deadline for the Israeli piece for *Nice Jewish Girls* is February 1st. I panicked. Israel has taken over my life. One more speech, one more essay, one more press release. Another meeting, another rally to prepare for. My Yiddish work and poetry get postponed again.

I have not resolved this tension within myself. Beginning with Israel's invasion of Lebanon I have become increasingly involved in peace work. Since the *intifada* (Palestinian uprising) began, I haven't been able to pull myself away from it. I can't bear what Israel is doing. I can't bear that teenagers are being killed, homes demolished, all education brought to a halt. I feel an urgent need to deal with this. At the same time, I'm never quite comfortable doing direct political work. I am most at ease in my role as poet and writer. I want so badly to return to my poetry and translations. I believe American Jews are engaged in a spiritual life-and-death struggle. The dissolution of secular Jewish identity, the rupture created by the Holocaust, still not healed, the disappearance of Yiddish, the death of the generation of survivors linked to Yiddish culture—all have contributed to this crisis. But I have not found a way to balance my concern for the Israeli/Palestinian struggle and the one here. Most of my energy, my passion is now directed toward peace work. And there seems no end to it. I felt relieved that the rally went well and was worthwhile. But then felt despondent after seeing the *Times* article about Israel becoming tougher in the Territories. Plastic bullets are killing more Palestinians than regular bullets ever did. December and January have had the heaviest tolls since the *intifada* began. 31 in December. Over 20 already this month—and it's only the 18th. There's no way to turn away from this.

* * *

As I reread this journal entry, I am conscious of how different my life is now compared to what it was when *Nice Jewish Girls: A Lesbian Anthology* first appeared in 1982. I think back to a certain day. Wednesday— late afternoon. Spring. About eight contributors to *Nice Jewish Girls* were gathered in a coffee shop on New York City's West Side to prepare for that evening's reading at Womanbooks. We had just heard that Israel had invaded Lebanon. We felt bewildered. Should we go on with the program? If yes, should we acknowledge what was happening? How? But beneath these lay the quintessential Jewish questions: Why did the actions of one group of Jews in one part of the world affect another? Were we, American Jews, responsible or accountable for the invasion by Israeli Jews? We knew, of course, that many would claim we were. We ourselves were unclear, and fluctuated between complete dissociation and intense guilt.

The evening was fraught with irony. *Nice Jewish Girls* represented a major step toward claiming pride in Jewish and lesbian identity. It was spurred by the women's and lesbian/feminist movements' tolerance of anti-Semitism and indifference (sometimes hostility) to Jewish attempts to strengthen Jewish identity. Sometimes anti-Semitism was expressed through rigid anti-Zionist statements that demanded dissolution of the Jewish State. Much of this was beneath the surface, but many Jewish feminists and lesbians were conscious of it, sick of it; increasingly Jewish lesbian/feminist groups were being organized both as a defense against anti-Semitism and as a source of nourishment for discovering Jewish attachments and the past. A number of these groups were also assessing the spiritual wounds left by the Holocaust. Jewish lesbians were frustrated by the fact that many viewed the Holocaust as an event limited to European Jews, with no connection to American Jewish life. All in all when *Nice Jewish Girls* was first published, Jewish lesbians were angry both at the women's movement, and at the Jewish community for its homophobia. Though anti-Israeli sentiments were a concern to us, they were not our sole preoccupation.

Israel's invasion of Lebanon changed everything. Those of us present for that Womanbooks reading faced a new and ponderous question: How were Jewish lesbians to express pride in their Jewishness when Israel was invading another country, killing another people? That night at Womanbooks I made a statement for the group, acknowledged what was happening in the Middle East, expressed our concern, and then— because there was nothing else we could do—we went on with the program. None of us was ready to have a full discussion of the Middle East and the facts about Israel's invasion were few and very scattered. I still remember how terrified I was when I made the statement. I was afraid someone would scream at me, throw something. Nothing like that happened, but from then on throughout the invasion and occupation I experienced constant fear whenever I called attention to my Jewishness in public.

All of us became better informed that summer and fall, though no one was prepared for the news of the Sabra and Shatilla refugee camp massacres. During that period, *Di vilde chayes*, a Jewish lesbian group that I belonged to (six out of seven of us were contributors to *Nice Jewish Girls*) put out three statements, each one as mistimed as the next.[1] The first, written before but not published until after the invasion, made us seem indifferent to the brutal events. The second, written before but not published until after the massacres, again made us seem indifferent to the plight of the Palestinians. Both statements were criticized by Jews and non-Jews for not taking a position on a Palestinian state and the question of the Occupied Territories. It was not until we wrote our third and final statement around November that we were able to pull together our concerns about anti-Zionism, anti-Semitism, and a Palestinian state alongside Israel.

Like *Nice Jewish Girls*, our statements were directed at the lesbian and women's community. They were published all over the country in feminist papers and they provoked heated debate among Jewish and non-Jewish lesbians and feminists. *Di vilde chayes* felt beleaguered, constantly under fire. Often we were misunderstood because we insisted we were still proud of our Jewishness even though we abhorred what was happening in Lebanon. We refused to back down on our belief that Jews, despite everything, deserved a Jewish state; yet we were becoming more explicit in our expression of solidarity with Palestinians and those who were fighting for the Palestinian right to a homeland.

I remember this period as being particularly painful. Jewish women, Jewish lesbians seemed bitterly divided. No one had a formula for uniting us. I had no formula for uniting what seemed to be contradictory parts of myself. I felt confused, often ashamed, and could not bear to read the news. I also felt disoriented. I did not know how to switch my focus away from anti-Semitism, from the wounds of the Holocaust, from my work on strengthening Jewish identity. The events in Israel had pushed me in directions that I would have never predicted. Wanting to show solidarity with Zionist sisters whose Zionism did not, I felt, make them automatically racist, I called myself a Zionist—even though I had been raised as a Bundist and taught that Jews did not need a separate Jewish state. Wanting to feel solidarity with other Jews, despite what was happening in the Middle East, I attended my first synagogue service—even though I was raised and have always remained anti-religious, intransigently secular. This occurred in the fall of '82 right after the camp massacres, and there was great anxiety that Jewish institutions would be attacked. In New York City police had to guard many synagogues during the High Holy Days. I was living in upstate New York and felt an intense need to be with Jews, so I went with three other lesbians to a small synagogue in Glens Falls for *Yom kipur*. It was in this context that I heard my first Jewish service and was surprised to find that I recognized music I had not realized I knew. Being Jewish seemed different at that moment from anything it had ever been before. It felt unfamiliar, even alien. When a few days later I heard that the Glens Falls synagogue's walls had been painted over with swastikas, my Jewishness felt familiar again.

* * *

In the winter of 1984-85 I traveled with Melanie Kaye/Kantrowitz to Israel and a lot of my confusion abated. Our trip had a specific purpose: to find material from progressive Israeli women for a book we were co-editing, *The Tribe of Dina: A Jewish Women's Anthology*. Melanie and I made contact with Israeli activists, met Israeli lesbians, visited the West Bank. The situation at that time was very bleak, worse than we had imagined. We had expected to find a strong, energetic Left movement. But the recent Israeli elections had placed Meier Kahane in the Knesset, and Labor and Likud had been forced into a paralyzing coalition. We found most people were depressed, frustrated, unclear what direction to take. We paid tribute to the Holocaust by visiting *Yad Vashem* and later learned of the bitter anger of the Sephardim about the way the Holocaust of European Jews was memorialized and the oppression of Arab Jews ignored. I was particularly impressed with this as I listened to Sephardic women describe their experiences and their treatment by Ashkenazis. On the West Bank we found, not surprisingly, Palestinians living in Palestinian cities. Hebron, Ramallah, Bir Zeit—how could anyone claim these were Jewish territories? The Jewish settlements, surrounded by barbed wire, seemed bizarre, out of place. Though I had understood the politics of this long before, the trip made the politics more concrete.

Despite this, I came back more knowledgeable, more solidly grounded in my belief that it was possible to be strongly Jewish identified, to believe in the necessity of the State of Israel, and to fight for Palestinian rights. The activists that I met gave me confidence that a peace movement existed, that many Israelis wanted the establishment of a Palestinian state and that they needed American Jewish support. I also felt a new, strong connection to Israeli activists, particularly the feminists and lesbians. The trip was a turning point in my commitment to the issue of peace in Israel and in Palestine. I had moved very far from that night at Womanbooks.

* * *

The 1984 trip was not my first. I had been to Israel in 1963. I stayed with my friend Pearl, whom I had met when she was studying in the States. Like me, Pearl was born in Poland and was a child survivor of the Holocaust. Pearl had once told me that when her family first settled in

Israel, they were given a house, and that for weeks, perhaps months, after they moved in, a Palestinian woman would come and sit on the steps and weep. It had been her home.

Pearl's story brings the Holocaust again to the forefront in dealing with Israeli politics. Jewish survivors and Palestinians who are stateless press against each other although I would wish them to become disentangled; the powerful lessons each evokes and teaches me remain intertwined.

I was particularly conscious of this in 1987 when I attended the International Women Writers Conference in Jerusalem. Toward the end of my stay, a group of American and Israeli Jewish writers and I met with two Palestinian women in East Jerusalem. One of them had been in Nairobi in 1985. She, like the Palestinian woman in Pearl's story, was born in a neighborhood in which one of the Israelis was living, a neighborhood now completely Jewish. During our meeting, the Palestinian women asked us to promote the cause of their people. I was deeply moved by this encounter and by the knowledge that women who had attended the Nairobi conference had been affected by it and were now trying to make contact with Jewish women. The next day I took a tour of the Jewish settlements around Jerusalem. I was shocked at their size; they were cities, fortresses. I realized for the first time that the term "settlement" was a euphemism.

This last trip took place in April, the month when Jews commemorate the Holocaust. While there, I became aware that the Israelis were already preparing to "celebrate" the twentieth anniversary of the reunification of Jerusalem. I saw the two holidays as symbolic and wanted to put them in perspective. I remembered what the Palestinian woman had said: "Write about what you see. Write what is happening to us." And I did.

Yom Hashoah, Yom Yerushalayim (1987)

In late April, Israeli Jews and Jews all over the world observed Yom Hashoah, *the day commemorating the Holocaust, the murder of their six million.*

As a Jewish child-survivor born in Warsaw during the war, mourning the Holocaust is an important part of my yearly cycle. Coming in the beginning of spring, it reaffirms my belief that Jews need a safe homeland in a world that for centuries has proved hostile; it makes me consider once more the enormity of our loss, the irretrievability, and the moral lessons to be drawn for the present and future.

One of these is that the cry "Never Again!" applies not only to ourselves but to others. Never again are we Jews to be deprived of the life, culture and religion we choose to be ours; never again are any other people to be deprived of their life, culture and religion.

Yet as we move toward summer, as Peres and Shamir struggle for power, as peace and security for all in the Middle East remain elusive, the Israeli government prepares for another holiday on June 5, Yom Yerushalayim—the reunification of Jerusalem. That this day is designated for celebration ought to cause deep sorrow, for Yom Yerushalayim veils a reality that should be mourned—the twentieth anniversary of the Israeli military occupation of the West Bank.

I know that there are American Jews and allies who deny out of fear and shame the validity of the term "military occupation." Yet as hard as it is for those of us who are rooted in our Jewish communities, who share a commitment to Jewish survival and a Jewish state, we need to use this term openly.

The Israeli military occupation is just that: the Palestinians on the West Bank are under military law, without a civil judicial system, frequently denied rights to lands on which they and their ancestors were born. Like any military occupation, the Israeli one is brutal and arbitrary. It arrests and detains without charges hundreds of "suspicious" civilians. In twenty years, it has generated over a thousand regulations, which only recently were coded, published and made available by Raja Shehadeh, the Palestinian attorney. Like any military occupation, the aim is to divest the occupied of will, collective identity, and cultural autonomy. This is done through the disruption of daily life, the control of educational institutions, and the systematic degradation of the Palestinian people. Predictably, the response and counter-response have been escalating violence and oppression.

One insidious example: The act of tree planting, so cherished by American Jews as a way of supporting Israeli and Jewish aspirations for nurture and stability, has been perverted. Today on the West Bank, the presence of olive trees is often considered illegal. Palestinian orchards, as well as newly-planted trees, are being uprooted and transplanted on Israeli soil. Why? If the land remains uncultivated for three years, the Israeli government can claim it. If the land sports no house, it too can be claimed; and if there is a house, the house may be bulldozed. Land on the West Bank is slowly being dragged from Palestinian control. Slowly, slowly push "them" back and back until the land is empty—as some have pretended it was from the start.

Need I say that this contradicts what I have always been taught were Jewish values: the sense of justice, of legal order, of respect for other human beings, the *necessity for culture, roots, and self-determination? And we need to keep hold of this contradiction as we move from* Yom Hashoah *toward* Yom Yerushalayim *to remind ourselves that the six million who died were ordinary men, women, and children who simply wanted to go on with their lives and were not permitted to do so.*

Yet it is in their name that both the U.S. and Israeli governments (for different reasons) justify current Israeli policies on the West Bank and thereby deny the decent and ordinary life that each Palestinian, like any other human being, yearns for. American Jews and non-Jews must recognize that the invocation of the Holocaust by our government does not necessarily express a concern for Jewish survival. Certainly the Iran/contra affair has proven the cynicism with which U.S. policy makers regard Israel—a puppet that carries out actions declared illegal by Congress.

During a recent trip to Israel with a friend who was visiting for the first time, I saw a dramatic enactment of the way the Holocaust is pitted against the occupation. On her last afternoon, my friend was given two choices: to tour Yad Vashem, *Israel's museum and research center for the Holocaust, or to tour the "settlements"—a euphemism for the stone fortresses that ring Jerusalem outside the Green Line. There was not time for both. In this instance, the forced choice between honoring and mourning our dead and acknowledging and addressing present wrongs was simply a matter of bad planning.*

Both the American and Israeli governments present us with a similar false choice. They play upon real fear of genocide and desire for security and they press us to choose "us or them." They pretend that the military occupation on the West Bank is somehow an answer to Yad Vashem. *It is not, for the last twenty years have brought neither safety nor security. Sabras, Holocaust survivors, and later refugees fleeing anti-Semitism have lost sons and daughters in the struggle to contain the Palestinians. Hardly a single Israeli Jewish family has been spared. And the violence continues.*

Some will consider my words disloyal to Jews and to Israelis. But many Israeli Jews acknowledge these things openly. In April, more than twenty thousand Israelis and Palestinians came to a peace festival in Neve Shalom, the Israeli Arab/Jewish town, to express their support of the possibility of Jews and Palestinians living in peace. In May, Arab and Jewish university students together protested discriminatory tuition charges. Most American Jews and allies ignore such realities. They ignore the very present, if splintered, peace movement in Israel made up of more than fifty Arab/Israeli and Palestinian/Jewish peace organizations that are groping toward a nonviolent, political solution (a fact rarely discussed in the American media). They forget that thousands of Israelis do not want to see another generation killed or maimed, but want peace now and an end to the present occupation; they forget that many of these Israelis support self-determination for Palestinians side by side with Jews. Our loyalty should be to these Israelis and Jews, for they are the repositories of the values we call Jewish.

Some maintain that you can't talk to the Palestinians; they're all terrorists. Yet talks between Israelis and the PLO have been going on for years; it is only governmental hypocrisy that obscures this reality, most recently with the government choosing to press charges against Israelis who met openly with PLO representatives in Rumania.

I have also heard many urge the Palestinians simply to emigrate to other Arab countries. This shows ignorance of (or disrespect for) the political and cultural diversity of the Middle East. Would anyone suggest to Swedes that they resettle in Norway because it too is a Scandinavian country?

Other debates about Israel focus on innocence. But there has been so much violence on both sides that such debates have no meaning. The issue is no longer who is to blame, is most innocent, or has fanned the hostilities. The issue is to recognize the undeniable fact that the Israeli military has wielded power over the West Bank for the past twenty years and that it must stop.

The Jewish Women's Committee to End the Occupation

In April 1988, exactly a year after my trip to Israel, I helped found a new political group, the Jewish Women's Committee to End the Occupation of the West Bank and Gaza. It happened like this: since the *intifada* began in December 1987, there were intensified efforts to pressure Israel to withdraw from the Territories and to recognize a Palestinian state. In February, New Jewish Agenda had staged a protest opposite the Israeli Consulate in mid-Manhattan. A short time later we heard news of Beita, where Israeli teenagers had been protected by Palestinian villagers from extremists. This did not stop the Israeli Defense Forces from blowing up houses in the village in retaliation for the death of an Israeli teenager who had been shot by her Israeli guard after he had been hit by a stone thrown by a Palestinian. Grace Paley called me and wanted to stage a vigil in protest. I was unenthusiastic. We'd hold the vigil and the next day we would read of more outrageous actions.

In analyzing my response, I realized that an ongoing vigil might be more effective because the situation was continuous. Clare Kinberg from New Jewish Agenda and Grace agreed. We were, however, unclear about the makeup of our vigil. Should it be just women, or men and women together? That week, Lil Moed, peace activist in Israel, gave a talk at Agenda's office and brought news of the work of two Israeli women's groups: Women in Black, who were holding weekly vigils in front of Shamir's house protesting Israel's actions in response to the *intifada*, and SHANI, Israeli Women's Alliance Against the Occupation. It made sense to organize an American Jewish women's vigil in solidarity with Israeli women working for peace.

That is the genesis of the Committee. We needed endorsements for the first flyer, so I began calling Jewish women in New York City. Everyone on the list was already sympathetic, so I did not hesitate to state our position: end the violence now, support an international peace conference and a two-state solution. But whenever I had to say what we were actually going to do, I would take a deep breath, for our weekly Monday night vigils were to be held at 515 Park Avenue, the offices of the Conference of Presidents of Major American Jewish Organizations, an organization that claims to speak for American Jewry and always endorses Israeli government action in regard to the Occupied Territories. I knew the deep feelings most Jews—including myself—have about public criticism of other Jews even when they disagree with them.

By selecting the Conference offices as the site of the protest, we had decided that instead of pressuring Israel directly, we would pressure the established American Jewish community that promotes, justifies and supports the policies of the Israeli government. American Jews need to start dealing with their involvement with Israeli policies. Given the support American Jews extend to Israel, we cannot claim neutrality on this question.

So, within a space of six days, the Jewish Women's Committee was formed and on Monday, April 25 at 5 o'clock, the day after the first major Jewish rally protesting Israeli policies in the Occupied Territories, eleven Jewish women—a number of them lesbians—gathered in front of the offices of the Conference of Presidents. At first it all seemed just like other demonstrations. You confer with the police, establish the rules about where you stand and where you leaflet. You approach people. Some take the lavender flyer, some don't. Some Jews don't like it and crumple it in disgust. All of this was expected.

What I did not expect was the intensity with which my doubts kept surfacing. I did not doubt for one moment that the occupation in Gaza and the West Bank and the second-class status of Palestinians within the Green Line were evils to be struggled against. No extenuating circumstances could justify morally what we had witnessed during the past five months of the *intifada*—Palestinians (many of them children) killed, maimed, illegally imprisoned and tortured, their homes demolished, their schools and shops closed. Yet despite my conviction that these evils had to be stopped, I found that standing in front of a Jewish organization, *publicly* questioning its integrity was not easy. A number of Jews came by and asked, "Aren't you ashamed?" and I wondered if what we were doing was right. In the past, I had always felt secure in my devotion to my Jewishness, to the Jewish people; I had never felt shame. Yet standing on line those first few weeks, I felt shame over what Israel was doing and also some shame about myself. This was a sense of my Jewishness that was completely new to me.

The confusion I felt during the initial vigils was intense. But equally intense was my reaction to those Jews who insisted on referring to the Holocaust, insisted that the Holocaust precluded our taking this kind of political action. Their fears and anger were unqualified. That first day a Jewish man came up to me and said: "I wish you were buried in Poland like my parents." Other Jews also wished another Holocaust upon us. Still others said our action would only lead all Jews, including us, "back to the ovens." Over and over again, in one form or another, we were told that the vigil was not only disloyal, but a form of collaboration with contemporary and historical Nazis. We were told that to give the Palestinians a state was to give Hitler his final victory, that our behavior was desecrating the Holocaust of the1940s and ensuring the Holocaust of the 1990s, perhaps even the 1980s. I was stunned and offended by these extreme remarks, but I did not find them ridiculous. Shame was a new feeling for me as a Jew, but, like the Jews who cursed us, fear has been my Jewish companion for as long as I can remember, and I understand its power. I soon came to recognize that the strange mixture of both shame and fear was the basis of a new aspect of my Jewishness, a mixture that brought into stark relief my feelings about Israel and about my background as a survivor.

* * *

I want to come to grips with this mixture, the shame, the fear and also the anger, for I have a lot of anger toward the Jewish community. It's a community I fight for and deeply love, but which, I remind myself, loves me only conditionally. I need to remind myself how I feared this community's rejection when I first came out as a lesbian. My being a child survivor, my family's activism in the Jewish underground during the war, my own strong attachment to Yiddish and activism in promoting *yidishkayt* and strong Jewish identity—none of these were sufficient armor against homophobia. Today I feel I have gained acceptance, but it was a tough process; I have scars and remember with bitterness many moments of pain.

The vigil brought new fears and anger to the surface. At the big April 24th Passover Peace rally I had feared the counterdemonstrators and their propensity toward violence. They screamed with such venom, such hatred for others—Arabs, Palestinians, Jews who disagree with them. They were ready to send us all to gas chambers and relished the idea. These Jews deliberately evoked fear: "Think, be like us—or die!" My fear of these Jews, the militant Right, is rational. They are dangerous.

But I fear not only these Jews; I fear also those kinder Jews who taught me my moral and political lessons, and this fear is more difficult to describe and explain. Do not speak ill of a Jew in public, they taught; and I have always obeyed. The command had nothing to do with social graces or pride. It was a command meant to help me get through life more safely. Publicly criticizing Jews gives fuel to the anti-Semites and endangers the Jewish community. It's a centuries-old rule for survival. Backed by the knowledge that anti-Semitism can turn into the Holocaust, the rule has even greater force for us in the post-Holocaust era than it did for our parents and grandparents. Anyone who breaks the rule places the Jewish people in danger and shows lack of respect and love for them. The response must be murderous rage. By participating in a vigil in front of the Conference of Presidents, I break the rule. I am afraid of the rage this may unleash as well as the unintended danger it might bring to Israel. After all, I might be wrong.

But the tangle of emotions does not end here, for I also fear history. I fear that I will misinterpret the present and not recognize my rightful role. This is a fear I have had all my life. Knowing that the world was passive and indifferent while six million Jews died, I have always considered passivity and indifference the worst of evils. Those who do nothing, I believe, are good Germans, collaborators. I do not want to be a collaborator.

So in trying to determine the right actions for myself in regard to

Israel, I too leap to the Holocaust for analogies and models, and I am trapped. On the one hand, I face the wrath of my own people; on the other, the wrath of history. I don't know how to find a balance. I want to be able to act with conscience, I want to remain part of the community. I don't know how to decide, how to feel certain and centered in my decision. These are the knots of feelings that emerged in the early days of our vigils as I listened to the remarks and arguments of passers-by and staff workers from the building.

In reviewing my feelings, am I being finicky? Palestinians are dying. Israel seems ready to break apart. Jews and Israelis worry about possible civil war. Should I be spending time examining my Jewish fears? I think I should because they remind me I have not left the tribe, that I am not as far from some of those Jews who confront us on line as I would like to think. I have to understand their emotions, if I ever hope to reach them. They form the bond that connects us across the great political chasm that separates us. To deal with the Israeli/Palestinian situation effectively, I need to calm their fears as much as I need to calm my own. I need to convince them of what I have to convince myself again and again. That Jews must choose and risk for peace. That we must choose justice despite our fears. That our fears are real, rooted in history, but that they cannot control us or stop us from making just choices.

Choices

During the Holocaust, choice was the nightmare. Whether through direct order by a Nazi or through the tangled strategies for survival, making decisions—who to take on a journey, who to leave behind, to set out early or late—was always the nightmare.

When I was little, I asked my mother over and over: "If the Nazis made you choose between me and my father, who would you choose to be killed?" At age ten I had absorbed the full horror of the choices Jews faced—of the life/death choices. I knew the idea of the third way was myth, romance. Someone stood and pointed and said: *"Choose! Choose now or they both die!"* I was, of course, testing my mother, trying to find out how much she loved me. In my fantasy, I mistakenly thought she had power. "And if you had to choose between me and Elza," I would persist, "who would you pick?" Elza, orphaned daughter of family friends, my almost-sibling and, therefore, a rival for my mother's love. *"Pick me! Pick me!"* my ten-year-old heart would beat and yearn, never fully understanding what it was I was asking, but clearly tapping the core of the Holocaust nightmare.

For most of my life, making decisions has been fraught with tensions way beyond what others regard as appropriate. I frequently experience as crisis what seems much simpler for other people. It is a psychology rooted in the past, not the present. It is something I need to watch.

Have Jews in the Diaspora and Israel permanently adopted this life/death psychology? Are we unable to see the present for what it is? Are we always looking at it through the immediate past, through the Holocaust? Is this why we do not perceive that the third way is not myth, that there *is* a third way in Israel, that there must be?[2]

Israel and the Holocaust: Analogies

I was always taught: never use Holocaust terminology to describe other situations; *never* in relation to Israel's own actions. Never, that is, unless you want to support Israel, justify its policies; then always bring up the Holocaust, point to what we have endured, claim that we will never again endure it. For this reason fundraising for Israel is frequently done in the name of the Holocaust. That is considered legitimate.

But what is not legitimate is expressing concern for Palestinians, for criticizing Israeli policy in the context of the Holocaust experience. Over and over we are told not to make comparisons, and most Jews balk when they hear them. Yet isn't it impossible *not* to make comparisons? Two events—the Holocaust and the creation of Israel—occur during the life span of one generation and are historically linked. Israel, after all, became the asylum for survivors of the Holocaust, many of whom were not Zionists, but had decided they were better off taking their chances in a Jewish state.

So whether we like it or not, the Holocaust and Israel are intimately connected in our minds and history. I think of the Holocaust and wonder what would have happened if Israel had existed in 1939. I think of Israel and wonder if it would have existed without the Holocaust or what kind of a country it would be now without the European survivors and their children. In what way would its national character, its psychology, its consciousness of tragedy and its self-image, rooted in fending off a second Holocaust, be different? Israel and the Holocaust form a natural association. What is problematic is the hardening of that association into an analogy between Israelis and Nazis, an analogy that enrages because it nullifies the Holocaust. If Israelis or Jews are really Nazis, then the murder of six million of their parents and grandparents is not so tragic after all.

When anti-Semites use the analogy, their intent is to negate German and world guilt. But when concerned, passionate Jews use the analogy, they are not only saying what they believe, they are also trying to express their outrage over Israeli action and to shake other Jews out of their apathy over the fate of the Palestinians. As a strategy the analogy is misguided; it detracts from the issue. Instead of focusing on the Palestinian struggle, Jews spend all their energy disproving the analogy and finding satisfaction and comfort in the fact that Israelis are not Nazis. This is disturbing and makes me wonder how close Israelis need to get to being true Nazis before other Jews begin to voice their objections. When we reject the analogy (as we should), and say that Israel is a democratic state and then turn away from the Palestinian struggle, are we not saying we are willing to object to Israeli policies *only when* Israel does finally resemble a completely fascist state? Do we want to wait that long? Exactly how many Palestinians must die before we speak up? One million? Shall we wait till the whole Palestinian population on the West Bank and Gaza and all those in camps are murdered? Is there not evil that we must object to *before* it reaches the level of Nazism?

"What does it remind you of?" I ask my mother, and read her the *Newsday* article about the Palestinian men in Rufus: rounded up by the Israeli police, they're told to lie face down in a nearby field. "I know what it reminds me of," she answers and says nothing more. Given the images etched on our collective consciousness, how can this *not* remind us of the Holocaust? What is it that we have been asking everyone to remember? Is it not the fields of Ponary and those nameless fields on the outskirts of dozens of *shtetlekh* that we've all pledged to remember? Am I to feel better that the Palestinians from Rufus were not shot by the Israelis but merely beaten? As long as hundreds of Palestinians are not being lined up and shot, but are killed by Israelis only one a day, are we Jews free from worrying about morality, justice? Has Nazism become the sole norm by which Jews judge evil, so that anything that is not its exact duplicate is considered by us morally acceptable? Is that what the Holocaust has done to Jewish moral sensibility?

* * *

I was especially conscious of Jewish sensitivities around using the Holocaust in analyzing Israeli policies toward the Palestinians when, in April 1988, I was asked to speak at a ceremony marking the forty-fifth anniversary of the Warsaw Ghetto Uprising. I accepted because I considered it an honor. But I was also conscious that the *intifada* was already in its fifth month, and I couldn't imagine speaking without making reference to it. I had to find a way to bring up the *intifada* without offending the survivors and without disrupting the memorial itself. I had to find a way to express my morality which is rooted in the Holocaust without evoking the hated analogy.

Though I had fears that I would not be skillful enough and might offend despite myself, more than anything, I felt angry at myself for being fearful and also angry at this community of survivors with its rules and taboos that restricted open discussion, that always threatened excommunication, that was willing—if I did not please—to label me the enemy. Even more, I was angry that there should be any question at all as to the rightness of condemning Israeli actions in regard to the Palestinians.

The evening of the memorial, the Norman Thomas High School auditorium is crowded with five to six hundred people, mostly survivors and children of survivors. I am sitting on stage. I am nervous, but as often happens, anger fuels my courage.

But from the start, I'm caught off guard. The evening begins with the ceremony of lighting candles for the six million. Six elderly survivors are called to the stage, among them survivors of Auschwitz, Bergen-Belsen, the Lodz Ghetto. They walk slowly, light the candles, then stand behind the candelabra. I suddenly feel again what this all means and am in awe. This woman was in Auschwitz. Imagine what she saw. That man was in Bergen-Belsen. Imagine what he lived through. Imagine what they all lost. Someone sings the *kadish*. I feel I'm about to cry.

I remind myself that survivors who suffered the experiences of the Holocaust should not be expected to be morally superior. Surviving Auschwitz does not make anyone an expert on anything, not even surviving Auschwitz. But also I must never forget the obvious: that survivors who are stubbornly wrong about Israel and its oppression of Palestinians are still survivors, Jewish men and women who suffered the experiences and losses of the Holocaust. The fact that they are not morally superior does not erase their suffering. Sometimes, in my passion, I am guilty of that erasure. I realize this as the survivors leave the stage. It is uppermost in my mind when I deliver my speech.

The Forty-fifth Anniversary of the Warsaw Ghetto Uprising: April 19, 1988

I was honored to be asked to speak on the anniversary of the Warsaw Ghetto Uprising, but I was also afraid. The anniversary has always been a painful day, reminding me of what my mother and I barely escaped and what my father, my aunts, cousins and grandparents did not survive. When I was a child, our early postwar memorials made vivid the horrors and atrocities, the deprivations that European Jews endured and they terrified me. I feared that memory would suddenly, perhaps the next day even, become a reality. I am no longer a child, but I still think a great deal about the relationship between the past and present and would like to talk about that now: its meaning to those who are survivors or children of survivors or American Jews deeply connected to our Jewish history.

Today, April 19th, is the forty-fifth anniversary of the Warsaw Ghetto Uprising, the act of resistance that has come to symbolize the period known in English as the Holocaust. During the initial postwar years, many of you were reluctant to speak about that period, while others were reluctant to listen. Since then there has been a major change, and the Holocaust has become the property of history, the object of historians, scholars, archivists, and filmmakers. And this is just, because the Holocaust must be known fully. It must remind us—Jews and non-Jews—of how far human beings can go in their dehumanization of themselves and in their attempts to dehumanize others who are different or alien. Jews especially must remember what was lost and must continue searching for ways of healing ourselves as a people.

But for those who are survivors, the Holocaust can never be transformed into history and will always remain simply der khurbn *(the destruction).*

Whatever the long-term effects on the descendants of European Jews, whatever the effect on Jewish history and the history of humankind, for survivors der khurbn will remain an individual, personal experience. It permanently changed and shaped our lives.

Perhaps this is obvious. And yet, I sometimes think that this most obvious fact is often forgotten in the whirl of rhetoric and research by political scientists and historians. Too frequently the Holocaust is spoken of in statistics, in analysis of power and powerlessness, too often evoked by photographs of lines of anonymous naked men and women or mass graves. Yet der khurbn that survivors experienced is not general but very specific. It is reflected in precious sepia photographs pasted into incomplete family albums. It consists of identifiable names, of familiar faces of family members, of named streets, stores and schools, teammates, friends, libraries, doctors, hospitals, lectures, marches, strikes, political allies and enemies—the people, places and institutions that make up the fabric of any human being's ordinary, everyday life. It is these specifics and the loss of that ordinary life that survivors remember and mourn. And not just today, but during all those frequent moments when memory of childhood or ghettos or camps is triggered by something in the present—an angle of someone's jaw, a special shade of color, a faint smell of certain food, a dream. During those daily moments when the fabric of our present life tears apart, survivors mourn and mourn again.

What we grieve for is not the loss of a grand vision, but rather the loss of common things, events and gestures. We do not grieve, for example, that Anne Frank had no opportunity to become a great writer, but rather that Anne Frank did not continue her schooling and learn more of the world about which she was so insatiably curious, that she did not spend more time with her friends and enjoy the normal process of growing up free to experiment, to experience the pleasures of success, the difficulties of failure. We mourn that Anne Frank was denied an ordinary, anonymous life. And looking at that lost experience, I have come to believe that ordinariness is the most precious thing we struggle for, what the Jews of the Warsaw Ghetto fought for. Not noble causes or abstract theories. But the right to go on living with a sense of purpose and a sense of self-worth—an ordinary life. It is this loss we mourn today.

But memorials are both for the living and the dead. Forty-five years after the Uprising of the Warsaw Ghetto, those of you who thought the ordinariness of life was lost forever—perhaps even felt that it would be immoral for it to be re-established—are reminded today that it was not. Our present life bears little resemblance to your life in 1939 or 1945, for it is grounded in different soil and society, expressed in a different language. Yet certain things, the building blocks of our life, are the same: ties to community and friends and commitment to a Jewish future are firmly rooted among us. We survived and somehow went on with the business of living. And the dead, if they could, would approve. I cannot imagine for one moment that my father or anyone of my family would have wanted anything else for my mother and me, just as I am sure that those who died during that period would have wished only the fullest of life to all survivors and their descendants. This new life was truly an unexpected, astonishing gift, particularly when you passed it on to us, the next generation. It was a major step toward securing Jewish survival.

Yet what seems even more astonishing is that the business of living after our tragedy and loss has turned out to be not all that different from what I imagine it must have been before the war. Miraculously, we were given opportunities for pleasure and joy, something that many of you perhaps thought might have vanished from your lives forever. On the other hand, if we imagined the war's agony would make us immune to future misfortune, we found out we were wrong. We were just as susceptible to failure and illness, to pain and suffering as we had been before the war. We found we were not shielded from having to make difficult political and moral decisions or from making mistakes. Der khurbn seemed to have balanced nothing out. It could be said that we were forced to face life once more as if this tragedy had not happened. Yet we know it did and it happened to us. We bear its physical and psychological scars; and though we have gone on living, we are not the people we were or might have been.

One difference is that we, a generation further removed from the actual experience of der khurbn, live with the knowledge of the war and the murder of six million. Like others, I ask myself what this knowledge and this anniversary mean to us and what they will mean to future generations. Our parents and friends, I know, had to use all their energies to come to value present life as much as the life before the war, to keep memories from overwhelming them and locking them into the past. We of a younger generation have a different task. Our energies must be directed toward holding on to the past in such a way that it is not an event apart from our everyday life, but rather is intertwined in the present and future.

Like many child survivors and children of survivors, I have not found it easy to do this. But I have concluded that one way to pay tribute to those we loved who struggled, resisted, and died is to hold on to their vision and their fierce outrage at the destruction of the ordinary life of their people. It is this outrage we need to keep alive in our daily life and apply to all situations, whether they involve Jews or non-Jews. It is this outrage we must use to fuel our actions and vision whenever we see any signs of the disruptions of common life: the hysteria of a mother grieving for the teenager who has been shot; a family *stunned in front of a vandalized or demolished home; a family separated, displaced; arbitrary and unjust laws that demand the closing or opening of shops and schools; humiliation of a people whose culture is alien and deemed inferior; a people left homeless, without citizenship; a people living under military rule. Because of our experience, we recognize these as evils, as obstacles to peace. At those moments of recognition, we remember the past, feel the outrage that inspired the Jews of the Warsaw Ghetto and allow it to guide us in present struggles.*

Like most of you, I consider April 19th a sacred day specially designated for mourning, a day for Jews to reflect on their history quietly and without distractions. But the present presses in on us, insists on our attention and we do not mourn in a vacuum. Forty-five years after the Warsaw Ghetto Uprising Jews all over the world are faced with serious moral and political issues. These are becoming more and more urgent and are very much on our minds. I know that the Israeli/Palestinian crisis is an explosive topic and I will not dwell on it. But I have referred to it not out of disrespect for this evening's memorial—this event is too important to me—but because of what the history of der khurbn and what many survivors taught me, taught all of us: silence about any form of injustice is wrong. Many of us are confused about what to do, what to say. We need inspiration and models, and I know of no better source on which to draw than the Warsaw Ghetto Uprising.

Today when we light candles in memory of the six million, we renew our commitment never to forget the grave moral lessons learned at a price no one should have to pay. These lessons we need to cherish and keep close to our hearts together with the family, friends, communities—all those we loved— who were not saved. On this forty-fifth anniversary when we have gained new strength, have recovered as much as could be expected from such trauma, we commemorate and honor our six million, express gratitude for the astonishing gift of the new life given to our people, and renew our dedication to preserving, for ourselves as well as for all others, that precious ordinary life that is everyone's right and of which we were once so brutally deprived.

* * *

Afterwards, backstage, many members of the chorus thank me. "Thank you for saying *that*," they say to me. "I'm so grateful." I go down into the auditorium. People ask me for copies of the speech. Survivors whom I know from Poland hug and kiss me. "It was good," they say.

"It was just right." "I'm proud of you." There are people who think bringing up the *intifada* was inappropriate, but they were not offended and I learn that later there was a lot of discussion. I am pleased. Discussion is what I had hoped for.

A friend who watches everyone's response says afterwards: "It's so clear they adore you." I don't think it's adoration, but deep love. I am, have always been, the child that survived. I suddenly realize that the depth of their love reflects the depth of their sorrow. I cannot make up for any of it, but I am proof to them that they have lived on. As a child, of course, I hated this, found it a burden. But this year on April 19th, I am moved beyond my anger at this community and feel again the meaning, the grief behind *der khurbn*. In my ardor on behalf of the Palestinians I want to make sure I don't lose touch with these feelings again.

Looking back I am also struck by how many of those present did actually feel relieved that I referred to the Palestinian struggle. Many of them want to take a moral stand, but are afraid or confused or frightened by history, much as I have been. There is more dissent than any of us working on this issue realize. It is not just among the fringes, as leaders of mainstream organizations would like us to believe. It is deep within the community. We need to learn how to bring it to the surface and how to break the taboos, the rules, without losing our credibility.

* * *

Progress is hard to measure at this level. A twenty-minute discussion that provokes thought rather than anger, that brings someone closer to thinking compassionately or realistically or morally about Palestinians and their need for a state of their own, is a victory. It is one of hundreds, perhaps thousands, of unrecorded events that form a chain reaction that ultimately will change history, will bring about a Palestinian state. I am particularly aware of these kinds of events and of their cumulative potential when I think about the vigils of the Jewish Women's Committee in relation to various women's groups that have been organized here in the United States and in Israel. For me, the Israeli women's groups are a critical link in this chain.

Women in Black began in Jerusalem shortly after the start of the *intifada* in December 1987. Ten women gathered opposite Shamir's house. They were dressed in mourning and stood silently, their only message on small posters: *Dai Lakibush!* (End the Occupation!). Today in May 1989, they still stand every Friday, but now number one hundred and fifty and have sister chapters protesting in Haifa, Beersheba, and Tel Aviv.[3] They do not argue politics with anyone, they do not answer insults. Though we sometimes have difficult moments at our protests at the Conference, these do not compare to what Women in Black must endure. They are spat upon and cursed as whores, as traitors. Rightwing Israelis constantly threaten them with violence, and force police to move in. The police themselves are not always sympathetic or cooperative. It takes great courage to stand there week after week taking the abuse and risking the violence. The photographs that I've seen of these vigils are inspiring.

Last summer and fall, a number of these Israeli women happened to be in the States visiting relatives. They would join us at the Monday night vigils and tell us of conditions in Israel and of the progress of their protest. I was moved by their appreciation of our work here, by their delight that *their* work was known and supported. They talked proudly of support groups in France and in Italy. We in turn told them of similar groups in Santa Cruz, Ann Arbor, Boston, Washington, D.C., Berkeley, and Los Angeles, and of plans in other American cities to organize Jewish women around this issue.

A number of these Israeli women were also members of other women's organizations. SHANI, the Israeli Women's Alliance, was also organized in response to the *intifada*; it has paid solidarity visits to Palestinians in hospitals and schools on the West Bank and is in dialogue with Palestinian women. Members of SHANI are simply ignoring official political obstacles separating Israelis and Palestinians. SHANI also organizes lectures and group discussions for Israeli women and tries to break down many of the same attitudes and fears discussed in this essay.

The Women's Organization for Women Political Prisoners, made up of Palestinian Israeli and Jewish women, is another group founded since the start of the *intifada*. Committed to improving the conditions in women's prisons, it brings to the forefront the suffering of Palestinian women illegally imprisoned under the military administrative detention regulations, many of whom are held in filthy conditions, without charges and without counsel. WOWPP is trying, through vigils, protest letters and telegrams, to alleviate the brutalities of imprisonment.

Among all these women are many Israeli Jewish lesbians who in the last few years have established an active lesbian organization, CLaF, Community of Lesbian Feminists. Based in Tel Aviv, it now has over a hundred and fifty members. As politically conscious Israelis concerned with the conditions of Israelis and Palestinians, CLaF members claim that one cause of the "sexist nature of Israel" is the "constant atmosphere of war and subsequent dominance of the military in the whole culture [and] a prevailing nationalism fueled in large part by the military occupation of the West Bank, Gaza Strip, and Golan Heights." Their statement goes on to say that Israeli lesbians are not optimistic about changing the sexism and the religious tyranny of the rabbinate in the future; "much of our energy goes into resisting the Israeli oppression of Palestinians." Because there is no way to be openly gay in Israel, these lesbians are politically active in other women's and mixed groups.[4]

It is evident that throughout Israel, women are protesting, organizing, resisting. Many of them, we are told, have never been politically active before, but all are sick of the violence, the human cost of this seemingly endless conflict. They are committed to organizing a powerful Israeli women's peace movement and bringing about a two-state solution. And their actions are, I believe, being paralleled here in the States. In both countries, Jewish and Palestinian feminists and lesbian/feminists are doing grass-roots work. This is very moving, for it is hard to be involved in this peace work without being conscious of the networking and bonding that are taking place among American Jewish and Palestinian women and Israeli Jewish and Palestinian women inside and outside the Green Line. This bonding is strengthening to Jewish women in our struggle against the Jewish mainstream, in both the United States and Israel, in breaking down our sense of isolation and fears of disloyalty. Increasingly we feel more confident in our challenges to the establishment and the work helps us create a supportive Jewish women's community of our own. Despite daily frustrations, there is more optimism among many Jewish women activists; it parallels the optimism resulting from the more positive recent developments among the Palestinians and the PLO.

The bonding among women activists has special significance, I believe, for American Jewish feminists and lesbians because we are furthest removed from the crisis. Our perception of Israelis and Palestinians and our evaluation of possible solutions are partly shaped by our distance, by our living in a gentile society that is not always sympathetic to our differences as Jews. As my Israeli friend Pearl once wrote me: "*We* in Israel must *live* with the consequences." And I thought, yes, the risk is the Israelis' both in war and in peace. It is Israeli Jews, not American Jews, who will suffer the consequences of a negotiated peace if it should fail. American Jewish women's increased contact with both Israeli Jewish and Palestinian women makes concrete the hardships and risks on both sides.

But it is also clear to me that Jewish fears of annihilation, of another Holocaust, cannot change the inevitable. A Palestinian state *will* be established. The Palestinians need and want independence and they will get it. The only question is how much more they will have to suffer for it. In our struggle to understand ourselves and other Jews, we must not forget that it is the Palestinians who are suffering grave injustices whose lifelong damage will not be undone even when a Palestinian state is finally established. I read in the paper that sixteen-year-old Madwan Abu Sabah was shot dead near Hebron. I know his friends and family will always mourn. I read that seventeen-year-old Ahmet Abu Mustafa from Khan Yunis died in an Israeli hospital and know his friends and family will always mourn. I learn that twenty-two-year-old Munira Daoud of Beita has been imprisoned because she threw a stone when her brother was shot by the Israeli settler guarding the teenagers. She was later arrested and her home bulldozed. I think of her parents, her husband, her children. They will never forget her brother, the pain of her imprisonment, the destruction of her home. It is easy to lose touch with the daily events that make up the Palestinian tragedy as we try to change Jewish attitudes, try to find the right road through the labyrinth of Jewish fears, defenses, and taboos. We must remember that every morning flesh and blood Palestinians wake up and face another bitter day's hardships: food and medicine shortages, the gaping emptiness created by the death of a daughter, son, cousin, friend, neighbor. Every morning Palestinians wake up and begin to try to adjust to the wounds that will remain with them for the rest of their lives.

Yes, Jews must learn to say without excuse, without equivocation:

despite our history and our powerlessness in the past, despite all the injustices that we have endured—today, now, the Palestinians are the victims of oppression, and their oppressors are the Israelis. The Palestinians must have Palestine and there must be peace between Palestine and Israel.

Notes

1. Other members of *Di vilde chayes* were Evelyn Beck, Nancy Bereano, Melanie Kaye/Kantrowitz, Bernice Mennis, and Adrienne Rich. Gloria Greenfield dropped out early in our work.

2. I am indebted for the idea of "the third way" to Raja Shehadeh, Palestinian attorney and activist, in his book *The Third Way*, reprinted under the title *Samed: A Journal of Life in the West Bank* (New York: Quartet Books, 1982).

3. As far as I know, the founding members of Women in Black were Israeli Jews. They were soon joined by Israeli Palestinian Israeli women who became members of the groups and active participants in the demonstrations. (In 1990 there are more than twenty-five such groups throughout Israel.)

4. Quotations attributed to CLaF are from its statement of purpose. Addresses for these organizations are as follows: CLaF, POB 22997, Tel Aviv 61228; SHANI, Israel Women's Alliance Against the Occupation, POB 9091, Jerusalem; Women's Organization for Women Political Prisoners, POB 8537, Jerusalem 91083; The Jewish Women's Committee to End the Occupation (JWCEO), Suite 1178, Room 1100, 64 Fulton Street, NY, NY 10038. JWCEO publishes the *Jewish Women's Peace Bulletin* (free/suggested donation $10) and has edited *Jewish Women's Call for Peace: A Handbook for Jewish Women on the Israeli/Palestinian Conflict* (Firebrand) available from JWCEO for $5.95.

IV

Secular Jewish Identity:
Yidishkayt in America

(1986)

> "The present generation stands in a shockingly new relation to Jewish history. It is we who have come after the cataclysm. We, and all the generations to follow are, and will continue to be into eternity, witness generations to the Jewish loss. What was lost in the European cataclysm was not only the Jewish past—the whole life of a civilization—but also a major share of the Jewish future.... It was not only the intellect of a people in its prime that was excised, but the treasure of a people in its potential."
> —Cynthia Ozick, "Notes Toward Finding the Right Question"

I. *Di yidishe svive* / The Yiddish Environment

All my life I have defined myself as a secular Jew. It is how I was raised and taught to think about myself in relation to Jewishness. I was taught that there is no God. I was taught that capitalism oppresses the working masses and all poor people, that it has to be smashed, and that we are to work toward building a classless society. I was taught that Jews have a right to be anywhere and everywhere, that they are not necessarily destined to return to their ancient homeland. And I was taught that Yiddish is *mame-loshn,* mother tongue, the language of the Jews, the medium through which Jewish culture and politics are to be transmitted. *Mame-loshn* was the language that gave all the tenets which I'd been taught form and substance. I internalized all this and fought fiercely with anyone who disputed these "facts."

My upbringing was not unusual if seen in its proper context. I was born to parents who were members of *der algemeyner yidisher arbeter bund,* the Jewish Labor Bund. Founded in 1897, the Bund was a socialist revolutionary *bavegung,* movement, whose primary influence was among the urban Jewish working class in Eastern Europe, particularly

Poland and Russia. *Di bavegung* swept those regions, becoming a kind of religion itself, claiming thousands upon thousands of adherents in less than twenty years. Many were from the religious community, and their "conversion" to socialism and the Bund often meant a painful break with family and tradition. My grandfather, Yakov Klepfisz, was among them.

On closer inspection, however, my upbringing was full of contradictions. Born in 1941 in occupied Poland, I came to the United States at the age of eight. I did not, therefore, learn about the Bund and its brand of *sotsyalizm* in the context and environment which shaped it and helped it flourish. I was learning a Jewish politics which was uprooted. That was the first contradiction, one which I never heard articulated. The second, also unarticulated, was that our presence in the U.S. testified to the fact that Jews did not have the right to be anywhere and everywhere. Poland had proven fatally hostile to us during and after the war and most Jews who survived left the country which for centuries had been their home and emigrated to the U.S. or Israel.[1] As frequently as I heard anti-Zionist* sentiments, I also heard that in the face of a common enemy, anti-Semitism had triumphed; Jews and Poles had fought almost entirely separate battles. Many *khaverim*, comrades, in fact, felt so strongly about the Poles' collaboration with the Germans that they vowed never to speak Polish again. And they kept that vow.

The third contradiction: Yiddish was not my *mame-loshn*. Because I was born during the war and my mother and I were passing as Poles, Polish became my first language. I began hearing Yiddish only later in Lodz, though in the first kindergarten I attended, I began to write Polish. In 1946, my mother and I emigrated to Sweden, where we lived for the next three years. I attended school and learned to read, write, and speak Swedish. At home, I continued speaking Polish though I heard and understood the Yiddish of the other DPs living in our communal house. And then we came to America. I began speaking English and ever so slowly, over the years, started to think, to dream in English. Eventually, English was the language I spoke with my mother.

My awareness (if I had any) of the contradictions must have been on the subconscious level, for as I grew up I continued articulating with-

---

*The Bund's anti-Zionism was formulated before the founding of the State of Israel and, indeed, long before World War II. A complex ideology, it opposed nationalism while maintaining that Jews were a distinct people and that socialism would eventually eradicate anti-Semitism. The Bund supported Yiddish as the language of Eastern European Jews in contrast to the Zionist adoption of Hebrew.

out hesitation the Bund's basic atheistic, anti-Zionist, socialist tenets, and accepted Yiddish as *mame-loshn*. In fact, in the fifties, from a child's perspective, the contradictions were very difficult, if not impossible, to perceive. A very large number of the *lebn geblibene*, survivors, lived in the same cooperative houses in which my mother and I lived, all within a few blocks of each other—a small, tight group in the midst of a Jewish, American-born, working-class neighborhood. For years, I thought every Yiddish-speaking adult was to be addressed as *khaver* or *khaverte* (male and female of comrade).[2] I simply did not know the Yiddish equivalent of a plain "Mr." or "Mrs." And if I wasn't fluent in Yiddish, it seemed everyone around me was. I heard Yiddish constantly—in our home, in the homes of other *khaverim* and Yiddishists, on the street, in the stores. *Der tog, Der forverts, Undzer tsayt* seemed to be flourishing. Yiddish books were everywhere. And besides, I was attending the *Arbeter ring shule,* the Workmen's Circle secular school, five afternoons a week, and later, its *mitl-shul,* high school, on weekends. I certainly knew more Yiddish than most of my American-born peers. I could read, write, and even speak—though very stiffly and self-consciously. Still, I loved the *lider un poezye,* songs and poetry, which I learned there, and today—thirty-five years later—still recite much of it by heart; poetry about poverty and the sweatshops; about the *khurbn* (destruction, i.e., Holocaust); songs and poetry about Purim, Hanukkah, and *pesakh*. We read the stories of Sholem Aleykhem—*Motl Peysi dem khazns* (Motl Peyse the Cantor's Son)—and I. L. Peretz—*Bontshe shvayg* (Bontshe the Silent); the poems of Avrom Reisen, Morris Rosenfeld; sang songs by Gebirtig, recited poems by Leivik and Itzik Manger. It was in the *yidishe svive*, Yiddish environment, that I developed a passion for literature.

Undzer svive was naturally focused on *"der khurbn."* The Yiddish word was important, for, unlike the term Holocaust, it resonated with *yidishe geshikhte,* Jewish history, linking the events of World War II with *der ershter un tsveyter khurbn*, the First and Second Destruction (of the Temple). Every April 19 (following the Christian calendar), my mother and I would attend *akademyes*, memorial meetings, commemorating the anniversary of the *varshever geto oyfshtand*, Warsaw Ghetto Uprising. *Di akademyes* emphasized the Bund's role in organized *vidershtand,* resistance, and the heroism of *poshete mentshn*, ordinary people. These were always very somber, painful events. When a speaker or singer finished, there would be total silence, no applause. People wept openly as they listened again to the details of the camps and ghettos.

As a child I naturally found *di akademyes* frightening and upsetting. At the same time, they instilled in me an enormous sense of pride in Jews, most of whom, under the worst circumstances, showed humaneness and heroism. *Poshete mentshn* were capable of extraordinary things. Repeatedly I heard Sutzkever's poem *"Di lererin mire,"* about the teacher Mira Bernstein from Vilna; Hirsh Glik's *"Shtil di nakht"* (Still the night), a song about the partisan Vitka Kempner (living now in Israel) and her heroism; and the song *"Papirosn,"* about a boy trying to sell cigarettes in the rain; and finally, *"Der partizaner him,"* the hymn of the partisans, *"Zog nit keyn mol"* (Never say), which taught me *"dos lid geshribn iz mit blut un nit mit blay"* (this song is written with blood and not with lead). All this seeped into my consciousness and left me with an unshakeable belief that Jews were not to blame, that they had not gone to the ovens and gas chambers like sheep. I have never in my life experienced a moment's doubt.

Di akademyes also provided me with a sense of peoplehood. It was there that I heard tributes to Arthur Zygielbaum, the Bundist leader sent to London and the Polish government-in-exile to mobilize help for the dying Jews of Poland. Unsuccessful in his mission, he committed suicide when he learned of the Warsaw Ghetto's final destruction. Selections from his suicide letters were frequently read at *di akademyes*:

> *Ikh ken nisht shvaygn—Ikh ken nisht lebn*—I cannot be silent—I cannot live—while the remnants of the Jewish people of Poland, of whom I am representative, are perishing. My comrades in the Warsaw Ghetto took weapons in their hands on the last heroic impulse. It was not my destiny to die there together with them, but I belong to them, and to their mass graves....
> I know how little human life is worth today, but as I was unable to do anything during my life, perhaps by my death I shall contribute to breaking down the indifference of those who may now—at the last moment—rescue the few Polish Jews still alive, from certain annihilation. My life belongs to the Jewish people of Poland and I therefore give it to them.[3]

Those words shaped my consciousness and helped me formulate my relationship to other Jews, made me conscious that a Jew didn't separate herself from her people—even when she could.

Though *di akademyes* and the constant contact with *lebn geblibene* emphasized what had been lost—political and cultural institutions, libraries, sports organizations, summer camps, schools, old age homes, unions, etc.—there was a way in which the loss was difficult to absorb. *Di svive* around me seemed to be thriving. Yiddish was alive. Chaim Grade, the poet and novelist, lived a few blocks away. He once visited us and on Purim presented me with a scroll of *megiles Ester* (the Book of Esther). Avrom Reisen visited my *shule*. Itzik Manger came to the *mitl-shul* which I attended for four years every Saturday and Sunday. He wore leather "arty" sandals and was probably the first bohemian I encountered. I was impressed. Yiddish was on the radio. I heard records by Dzigan and Shumakher, the comedians. One particular routine involved two Jewish soldiers in enemy armies facing each other during World War I. It was the first time that I became aware of the complexities of Jewish dispersion.

It wasn't even so much that Yiddish was alive. A small part of Poland seemed to be alive. Bolek and Anya. Vladka. Brukha and Monye. Rivka and Lolek. Khana. Bernard. Khevka and Lutek. All *lebn geblibene*. So for all the talk *vegn khurbn,* for all of my awareness of an absent father, aunts, and grandmothers, when I sat down at Brukha and Monye's *dritn seyder,* third seder, and heard the words *"ver es iz hungerik, zol kumen un esn; ver es neytikt zikh, zol haltn mit undz pesakh"* (whoever is hungry, let them come and eat; whoever is in need, let them celebrate *pesakh* with us) and looked around me and saw our whole community; or when I went to an *akademye* and saw an auditorium completely filled; or when I looked at a newsstand and saw the big, bold letters of *Der forverts*—it was hard for me to conceive that an entire world had been destroyed.

But more—my entire intellectual growth was bound up in this world and in Yiddish. It was only in this *yidishe svive* that I heard ideas discussed—the arguments between the *tsiyonistn, komunistn, un sotsyalistn*. It was in this *yidishe svive* that I puzzled and then agonized over the issue of *fargitigung*—it would be years before I learned the English word "restitution"—and whether Jews should accept restitution from Germany. Most of my political, ethical thinking was done here. *Di yidishe svive* seemed, was, very much alive.

A child, of course, assumes that her world is the whole world. To me *di yidishe velt,* the Jewish world, was all of Jewishness. I don't think I ever thought that a *lebn geblibene* and a *khaverte* might not be one and the same. Survivor and comrade. Wasn't everyone that?

Nothing around me ever supported my Jewish generalizations. The American world, as I saw it, was only a source of pain, a place where I was completely alienated, different, the greenhorn, the survivor. *Di yidishe velt* was where intellectual arguments took place, where I received a sense of identity, of history, of the struggles of the world. My early American education was never intellectually stimulating; the required readings were deadly and meaningless. I read "Evangeline" but remember nothing of it; and I had to memorize long sections of "Rime of the Ancient Mariner," whose language completely eluded me ("Eftsoons his hand droppeth he"—??).

In fact, for years I suffered over my inability to use English effectively and, throughout public school and most of high school, English remained my worst subject. I realize now that until the age of sixteen or seventeen, I really had no language in which I was completely rooted. Limited to our three-room apartment, my Polish did not develop and by my mid-teens was childish and ungrammatical. English seemed alien and lacked both intellectual and emotional resonance. And though Yiddish had the emotional and cultural substance, it simply didn't feel natural.

But eventually something changed. Toward the end of high school, I moved from reading mindless historical novels and romances to world literature—Dostoyevsky, Shakespeare, Hugo, Melville, McCullers. English words started to have some meaning. My English prose would remain problematic for years, but I began experimenting with poetry. And perhaps because it was private and had never been labeled with an "F" for grammar—writing poetry enabled me to discover possibilities in the English language, possibilities which were supported by my reading. It was an important breakthrough for me, but one which simultaneously seemed to doom the role of Yiddish in my life.

Like other children I tended to assume everything is forever, and took everything for granted. What appeared to me a very solid, self-sustaining world, *di yidishe velt,* was in reality extremely fragile, barely holding. Its fragility lay partly, I believe, in its isolation and its inability to establish a coherent attitude toward and connection to the American environment. Though the students in my public school were probably ninety-five percent Jewish, *not once* between the second and eighth grades do I remember a single teacher—Jew or gentile—discuss a Jewish topic or issue, holiday, leader. All things Jewish belonged outside the walls of P.S. 95. And with the parents' consent.

This also affected those students who came from religious homes. But the religious establishment in America was on a more solid footing, its institutions not dependent on a language or specific culture. For the secular Jew, the situation was more difficult. The Yiddish school, Yiddish books, theater, etc. were critical, and if these weren't maintained, the type of secular identity in which Yiddish played a central role was bound to become very precarious.

During my growing up years, there was no interaction between the American world and the *yidishe svive* and no demand that there should be. The 1950s were a period of severe reaction, of having to prove oneself a good American. I can understand that survivors, many with socialist and communist backgrounds, who had arrived four or six years earlier, might feel reluctant to challenge the school system when they were still threatened with deportation. The name of Ellis Island hung over us as a constant threat.

I did have one experience in which I was immersed in an ostensibly completely insulated *yidishe svive*. That experience proved, if anything, that this world was slowly losing ground. Established in the 1920s, Camp Boiberik was a Yiddish, essentially secular camp (it maintained a ritual for *shabes* and kept a kosher kitchen). Many parents who were already assimilated were sending their children to Boiberik to acquire the *yidishkayt* they could not provide for them at home. When I worked there in the summers of '58 and '59, however, Yiddish was no longer being used. What remained of Yiddish were phrases, individual words, and a great deal of heartfelt sentiment. Activities (*shvimen, shiflen*— swimming, boating), buildings (*der es tsimer*—the dining room), designations cf campers (*di eltste-eltste*—the seniors) were used by everyone and easily incorporated into English. And in addition to the usual "specialists," there was a Yiddish counselor who taught campers *dem alef-beys*, the alphabet, traditional stories and songs.

Actually, songs punctuated camp life and provided the strongest medium for passing on Yiddish. Every child knew the camp song "*In boyberik iz lebedik / In boyberik iz freylekh / Ver es kumt tsu boyberik / Lebt er vi a meylekh!*" [sic] (In Boiberik it's lively / In Boiberik it's joyous / Whoever comes to Boiberik / Lives like a king!) At night when the flag was lowered, we sang: "*Ven der tog vert mid, farmatert / Aylt zikh tsu zayn sof*" (When the day grows tired, weary / Hurries to its end). On Friday nights we dressed in white and lit *shabes* candles in the dining room and sang again. And the whole summer season culminated in a *felker yom tov*, a folk festival. Campers were grouped into countries and gave a grand performance in which each country danced and sang about *sholem un bridershaft* [sic], peace and brotherhood.

In other respects, the camp was like any other. There were regular sports activities, competitions with Camp Kindering, and performances of American plays. Though there were attempts to promote Yiddish and Yiddish culture as a norm, these inevitably were limited. I know of only one Yiddish performance, a dramatization of Sholem Aleykhem's *"Dos meserl"* (The knife). It was a unique event since most campers did not speak Yiddish.

But there was another part to Camp Boiberik, a "guest side," a modest summer colony of wooden bungalows. It was not all that inexpensive; on the other hand it wasn't Grossinger's either. The guest side also provided the usual summer activities—shuffleboard, boating, nature walks—but unlike the children's side, Yiddish was very much in use. Not that everyone spoke it. Still, Yiddish newspapers, magazines were always in view. And almost every day, there was an event *untern boym*, under the tree: *a referat, a diskusye, a retsitatsye*. Lectures, discussions, readings provided the basis for intellectual, political, and artistic arguments and were very popular.

In addition there was a small theater. A number of staff members in both parts of the camp were members of *Di folks bine*, the Yiddish theater, and performances were frequent. I was always eager to see them and felt quite disgruntled if I had to be on *vakh*, night watch. The most memorable performance that I saw there was one by the well-known actor Joseph Buloff. In Boiberik, Buloff's Yiddish material consisted of dramatic monologues, stories, and poems drawn from Yiddish and Russian writers. On that particular evening, Buloff transformed himself into a *tepele zup*, a pot of soup—a metaphor for life, for Jewish life and all its turbulence. Buloff was brilliant as he became and gave voice succeedingly to every piece of *marevke, kartofl, bubele*—carrot, potato, bean—which an unidentified but omnipotent hand dropped into the pot. As the story/poem progressed, Buloff's motions and speech became increasingly agitated as he tried to keep up with the pot's ever-growing chaos. But the soup just boiled more and more furiously and the chaos grew greater and greater.[4]

Though some of the adults were already themselves feeling deprived by assimilation, the difference between the two sides of the camp was quite clear. Few counselors came to the events on the "guest side." And certainly there was no attempt to bring material from the adults to the children. Though some Yiddish must have been understood by many children because they heard it at home, a rich, adult Yiddish would have been incomprehensible to the majority. The white wooden fence that marked the boundary between the two camps was also a boundary line that delineated two different cultural territories.

I must have been somewhat aware of these issues, though I don't ever remember discussing them. I was aware enough at least to try and build bridges between *di yidishe svive* and the American because I became involved in writing and directing a musical comedy about the Jews of Khelm. I felt proud because I perceived it as a purely Jewish (which to me in those days was synonymous with Yiddish) product, even though the Khelemites spoke pure English. Camp Director Leybush Lehrer, a staunch Yiddishist, felt otherwise and openly expressed his dissatisfaction. I would not admit to my own inadequacy, felt stung that my attempt to create "Yiddish" material was not appreciated and responded glibly, as only someone that age can: *"Di shprakh iz nit di gantse zakh!"* I told him. Indeed, language may not be everything, but I had yet to learn that it is a great deal.

At this time, I was already a student at City College (CCNY), a predominantly Jewish school with thousands of students from Eastern European backgrounds, most of whom I am sure had heard Yiddish spoken at home, many of whom probably even spoke it. Yet at the time there was no Yiddish course, no Jewish studies program of any sort.[5] Just as in public school, nothing encouraged us to look to our homes and backgrounds for cultural resources worthy of preservation. The message was just the opposite: we were to erase all traces of who we were and where we came from. Higher education continued the process of making us "become" something new.

Nothing symbolized this more than CCNY's four required semesters of speech which were in a large part devoted to divesting us of our working-class Jewish Bronx and Brooklyn accents. A speech test was required of all entering students and those who failed were placed in what amounts to remedial speech. In the regular classes we were taped and retaped in a desperate effort to get rid of our crude vowel distortions, glottal stops, etc. What were we supposed to think after such lessons when we returned to the Bronx and to our parents with their Yiddish intonations, heavy accents, misplaced adverbs and prepositions? Were we supposed to be proud?

But this "new" cultured individual whom we were becoming was also supposed to speak another language—and for my friends and me, that language was French, a real curiosity when you consider that so many of us were expecting to be teaching Puerto Rican children. But parents and school officials presented French as the language of a culture of the highest order, while Spanish was deemed far below, the lowliness of its condition reflected by its allegedly "easy" grammar.

There was, I know, real racism in this condescension toward Spanish cultures. But I don't think that's all it was about. I think, for example, that if most Jewish parents had valued Yiddish as a language, as a medium for a culture they wanted to preserve, had been able to envision it "in the world," they might have viewed Spanish somewhat differently. Certainly what the two had in common was that they were both immigrant languages. But immigrant languages were not valued in 1958. An Italian girl who studied Italian was usually characterized as looking for "easy" high grades. So why should a serious student study Spanish when Spanish-speaking children were being encouraged to forget Spanish as quickly as possible?

Despite this total indifference of the environment, sometime in my sophomore year I decided to study Yiddish literature. So a friend and I approached Professor Max Weinreich, who was teaching in the German Department. I was very lucky; Weinreich was perhaps the most distinguished living Yiddish linguist and historian and had been a founder of YIVO Institute for Jewish Research in Vilna in 1925. Just meeting him was a privilege, but I was unaware of it. He, of course, was delighted with our interest, took us to a Chinese lunch, and quickly agreed to make the necessary arrangements. We, in turn, rounded up a handful of students and the course became official.[6]

I cannot claim we were devoted students. The atmosphere was unpressured and completely unrelated to the rest of our more normal, but very anxiety-ridden academic lives. Certainly it was one of those "easy" three credits and we enjoyed the material and Weinreich, which I'm sure made the course academically suspect. Still, at the end of the semester, I wanted to do independent work and take honors in Yiddish.

I read the plays of H. Leivik (whom I legitimized to English-major friends as the Yiddish Shakespeare) and the poetry of Chaim Grade. I was particularly moved by Grade's writings about his mother, a poor, illiterate, pious woman who sold apples in the street while her son studied, oblivious to her struggle for survival. In one poem, Grade describes his mother's desperate effort to get everything done before sunset and ends with her blessing the candles while tears stream down her face because *zi hot farshpetikt dem shabes,* she was late for *shabes.* The irony, poverty, anger at religion's rigidity and his own youthful callousness made a deep impression on me. The power of that literature was enormous.

And yet—I didn't turn toward it. I had one struggle which represented my conflict. At the same time I was working in Honors Yiddish, I had been accepted into Honors English, an elaborate and long-established program—"the real thing." My struggle: Should I write my thesis on three American-Jewish writers—Bellow, Roth, Malamud—or on Herman Melville, whose work I loved? I was deeply interested in Jewish issues, but I was terrified of showing that publicly. This was not as contradictory with my studying Yiddish as it might seem. The Yiddish course was safe; after all, it was off to the side. Who knew what I was doing there? But in the framework of an English Department (even though that department had many Jewish teachers and students), to reveal interest in Jewish matters, to reveal that I *cared* about Jewish matters—seemed inappropriate. We were supposed to be above that. And so I chose Melville.

When I graduated from CCNY with Honors in Yiddish and English, Brukha and Monye Patt gave me a two-volume set of the complete works of H. Leivik. Inside they had written: *"Tsum shpits barg heyb oyf dayne oygn."* Lift your eyes to the mountain top. I paid no attention. I was looking straight ahead.

I realize now that I simply did not know how to be an active Jew in the world. Neither my American education nor my Jewish education had prepared me for it. If I had been shown a strong connection between the two worlds in which I lived, if they had been supportive of each other, if biculturalism and bilingualism had been encouraged in my American school, if English had not been perceived only as an enemy by the Yiddish world, then Yiddish would have lived on naturally in my life. As it was, the older and more independent I became and the further I moved into the American world, the more English took over my intellectual life, the more it seemed the two worlds I had been living in were mutually exclusive.

I never formulated any of this. I was not preoccupied with my identity. I took it for granted, much as I did the Yiddish world. Chaim Grade would always write. *Der forverts* would appear every day. So would *Di freie arbeiter shtime, Der tog.* Professor Weinreich would be there to answer questions. Camp Boiberik would be there for the next generation. So would my *shule. Di yidishe svive,* I assumed, would be waiting for me whenever I got home, whenever I needed it. At the age of twenty-one, it never occurred to me that *it* might need *my* support to ensure its survival. I never thought that as a secular Jew who defined herself through Yiddish culture, my sense of self was inextricably bound up in its existence, that when *it* was in jeopardy, *my own identity* was in jeopardy. I never realized that it was the mirror that made me visible to myself as a Jew.

II. The American Environment

Writing this essay in 1985, I take stock of the *yidishe svive* in which I grew up: Chaim Grade has died. Monye Patt is dead and the *driter seyder*, the third seder, which I always attended at his house, no longer takes place. *Der forverts* appears only once a week. *Der tog* and *Di freie arbeiter shtime* have stopped publishing altogether. Max Weinreich and his son Uriel, himself a great Yiddish linguist and scholar, have also died. So have many *khaverim*. Camp Boiberik is closed. So is Camp Hemshekh.[7] So is my former *shule* in the Bronx.

Generations pass. Institutions die. This is part of a natural evolution and cycle. But for a culture to survive, its losses must be replaced. And though there has been some replacement, I have become increasingly aware that in the Yiddish world each death, each closing of an institution represents a far greater loss than that of the individual. In 1985, I see that over the years *di svive* has become smaller and smaller and more precarious.

In the decade that followed my entering graduate school, a parallel process was occurring within me. It couldn't have been otherwise, since I took no care to protect against it. In 1963 I left for the University of Chicago and graduate work in English literature, and became completely immersed in an American environment. That is not to say I left my Jewishness behind me. The consciousness of Jewish history, the role of the *khurbn* in my life, and the politics which I had absorbed, I carried with me. *Sotsyalizm* was easily translated and I found no difficulty in applying everything I had been taught politically to the contemporary scene: the devastation created by urban "renewal" in Hyde Park, Chicago; the civil rights movement; or the war in Viet Nam.

But certain things resist translation. Bundist philosophy as I received it was not only socialism; rather it was a whole way of life in which Yiddish acted as the cement that bound the Jewish community together on a socialist foundation. What language we spoke was critical. It reflected our identity, our loyalty, our distinctness not only from the gentile environment, but from other Jews as well. The use of Yiddish was an expression not only of love of a language, but of pride in ourselves as a people; it was an acknowledgement of a historical and cultural *yerushe,* heritage, a link to generations of Jews who came before and to the political activists of Eastern Europe. Above all it was the symbol of resistance to assimilation, an insistence on remaining who we were.

Though I could share *sotsyalizm* with American-born Jews and gentiles, there was no way I could share Yiddish and all that it represented. As a result, the language and culture themselves became more and more isolated and apart in my life. A decrease in on-going contact and exchanges, a decrease in my facility with the language that had bound us together in an alien environment, that had acted as the borders which defined our cultural territory, that had defined us as a distinct Jewish group, inevitably loosened my ties to the *svive*. The less I was able to communicate with the *svive* in its own language and identify with its concerns over culture and survival, the more I became an outsider—the American Jew.

My awareness of how Yiddish and its role in my life had slipped came abruptly in 1975 when, almost by accident, I was plunged back into the *svive* and found myself teaching beginners Yiddish. I believe I was a good teacher. Still, in that class, over a period of three summers, I began to perceive what I had lost by not continuing studying, and even more painful, what I had lost from disuse. I was stunned at how much I had forgotten, not only of language, but of history and literature as well. As a result, the most difficult thing I had to face was that for all the intensity of my upbringing, for all of my love of *di kultur*, I had returned to a country which had grown frighteningly alien.

I also became acutely conscious of the extreme effort, the commitment required to keep a language and culture alive in an environment that, at best, is indifferent. I was particularly stung by the disrespect with which Yiddish is treated by Jews. Historically, of course, this was nothing new. I had always heard stories of the clashes, some of them violent, between the Bund and the *komunistn* who advocated "normalcy" and assimilation or with the *tsiyonistn* who pressed for a Jewish homeland and Hebrew as the national language. And in 1963, when I had visited Israel, I myself heard the scorn with which most Israelis regarded Yiddish. To them, Yiddish meant *shtetl,* and *shtetl* meant the Holocaust. Never again. We're a new breed here. A different kind of Jew. I consciously thought them anti-Semitic, felt enraged at their lack of understanding and caring. Israel was one place where Yiddish culture might have survived. (The Soviet Union was the other.) But Eastern European Zionists were determined to wipe out the past of all Jews who came to Israel—not unlike the melting pot philosophy in America—and eliminating Yiddish among Ashkenazi was one of the steps toward achieving that goal. The old antagonisms with which I had been raised in relation to Zionism seemed completely justified during that trip.

Here in the States, the story was not all that different, though until World War II there was a thriving Yiddish-American culture. At the turn of the century, German Jews considered Yiddish an embarrassment and couldn't wait to "clean up" and Americanize their Eastern European brothers and sisters who came after them. Philanthropic institutions like the Free Hebrew Schools and the Educational Alliance were vehemently against Yiddish; the philanthropist Jacob Schiff was purported to have given explicit orders that none of his contributions be used to support Yiddish culture.[8]

These early attitudes, the post–World War II push toward assimilation and American Jewry's increased involvement and identification with Israel, have made their mark on the present generation. When I would tell people that I was teaching Yiddish, most—especially Jews—were amused. Over and over again, I heard: "How cute!" I would counter that Yiddish is a language like any other. Generations of Jews in Western and Eastern Europe spoke it and wrote it, just like any other people in any other language. But here in America what had been *mame-loshn* to millions of Ashkenazi Jews, what had been a medium through which Jewish history, culture, politics, ethics were transmitted, had become a joke, a joke usually made by Jews, a joke now so Americanized it has become the property of the gentile mainstream. What is funnier than a Yiddish accent? And what is funnier than a Yiddish inflection? Yiddish is, after all, nothing more than a bunch of words like *kvetsh, shmate, shpil, mishigas, shnorer, shayster, shlep, yidene.* What's to teach? What's to learn?

Given these attitudes and the commonness with which certain Yiddish words and phrases are used in English, I have found it difficult to convince others that we, secular Yiddishists, are on the edge of tragedy. Because the view of Yiddish is so limited (really puny) and because there is basically no knowledge of Yiddish culture as it developed in Europe and in the States, I sense others think I am fabricating a drama when I draw attention to the crisis.

During this period in which I was developing a sharper awareness of the crisis surrounding *yidishe kultur* in my life, I was also becoming increasingly involved in a non-Jewish environment—the feminist and lesbian/feminist movement. (Needless to say, many of the feminists and lesbians I worked with were Jews; but our focus was never on Jewish issues.) The absorption of feminism into my politics, the recognition of gay oppression represented a major shift in my perspective, one that would permanently transform how I viewed the world. It was the first such shift in my political thinking since I had been taught socialism and *yidishkayt* as a child.

So toward the end of the 1970s, I found myself in much the same situation I had been in as a child. My life was once again split between two worlds, and I moved from one to the other without feeling any connection or ties. My Yiddish activities were barely noted by feminist and lesbian friends, or evoked only mild curiosity. And most Yiddishists with whom I had contact knew nothing of my life in the lesbian community; it was the late 1970s, and the subject of lesbians and gays remained virtually unspoken in the Jewish world.[9]

Unlike fifteen years earlier, the crisis I experienced over this split was conscious and my decision deliberate. I knew the kind of complete commitment continued involvement in Yiddish demands; I knew that by temperament I was not a scholar, but a poet; I knew that a complete commitment required a total immersion in the *yidishe svive*; and I knew I did not want to lead two separate lives. So I made a decision based on an "all-or-nothing" principle. Once again I left *di yidishe svive* and hoped that I could take with me and hold on to what remained.

The decision was excruciating. I did not want to feel alien in my own home. I did not want to be a stranger. But I saw no way out of the dilemma, no way to build bridges. I felt I had to choose, and did.

Because I was born during the war, I have always had a keen sense of how Jewish history has shaped my life. And at this time, history stepped in again; for just as I was withdrawing from the *yidishe svive*, the women's movement began to take notice of Jewish issues. Evelyn Torton Beck's *Nice Jewish Girls: A Lesbian Anthology*, published in April 1982, sold ten thousand copies over the next ten months and made an enormous impact on the women's community. And in June 1982, Israel invaded Lebanon, an event which forced many Jews—including lesbians and feminists—to examine their Jewishness and their relation to Israel. As a writer and publisher who had been very visible as a Jew, I became caught up in the turmoil and began leading workshops on anti-Semitism and Jewish identity.

It was the latter that ultimately absorbed me most because it was what I was struggling with myself. I began to see that whatever loss I was experiencing was but a fraction of what others felt. In workshops at various feminist and lesbian conferences, I met Jewish women whose last contact with Jewishness had been in early childhood with grandparents; women who had never been to a *seyder*; women who knew no Jewish history or culture. Still, they yearned: How can I be Jewish? Is being Jewish more than just *feeling* Jewish? What should I study? What should I do? Where should I go? Like me, many of them were not drawn to religion or ritual; they were looking for *secular* answers.

I was full of these questions when, in July, 1983—thirty-seven years after having left—I returned to Poland with my mother on the occasion of the fortieth anniversary of the *varshever geto oyfshtand*, Warsaw Ghetto Uprising. Though I had been raised in almost a *khurbn kultur*, a Holocaust culture, I was totally unprepared for the experience. In Poland I saw the *shadows* of Jewish-Polish culture and was able to infer from them the magnitude of what had taken place. It was like stepping into a negative rather than a photograph. I was overcome by the sudden realization of the scale of the loss.

A year before my return to Poland, I was finishing the manuscript of *Keeper of Accounts* and struggling with the last section of "Solitary Acts," the concluding poem. Rejecting dreams that can never be realized, I ended the poem with the following lines:

> This night   I want only
> to sleep   a dark   rich   dreamless sleep.
> to shelter   in me   what is left
> to strengthen myself   for what is needed.

Twelve months later, walking through the mammoth, overgrown, vandalized cemeteries of Warsaw and Lodz, standing in front of their crumbling and abandoned Jewish memorials, making my way among the hundreds of sculpted rocks that served as anonymous markers for those who died at Treblinka, I kept repeating the words *to shelter in me what is left, to shelter what is left, to shelter*. During those seven days, I knew that I would never take Yiddish culture for granted, never abandon it again.

III. *Di tsukunft* / The Future

In looking back, I wonder why something so basic as *di yidishe kultur*, so intimately connected to my life, has been so difficult to maintain, to be actively loyal to. Why have I experienced so many setbacks? The difficulty cannot simply stem from my own particular circumstances. Too many other Eastern European Jews of different orientation and ideology and focus have also found themselves distanced from that culture. The problem stems from American society, which does not tolerate cultures outside the mainstream and does everything, materially and psychologically, to weaken them. Whether to Spanish-speaking or Chinese-speaking or Yiddish-speaking children, the message is monotonously the same: Change your name. Americanize. Forget the past. Forget your people.

But to stop there is not to articulate the entire problem. We must also look to the Jewish community which seems to have taken two polarized views of itself. Some Jews express an intense ambivalence about our relationship to the American mainstream, an ambivalence manifested outwardly in a movement toward assimilation and internally in guilt and yearning for the very things it has given up. Other Jews verbalize an ideology for holding on to our culture, an ideology whose necessary fierceness has often hardened into a narrowness and a refusal to recognize any positive values outside of itself. These Jews ask us to sacrifice everything for Jewishness, and consider anyone who does not do so suspect.

What I have come to realize is that if I am to maintain a strong relationship to Yiddish culture I cannot afford the luxury of an "all-or-nothing" attitude. Nor can *di yidishe velt*. Such a purist attitude is destructive, alienating the vast majority of Jews of Eastern European backgrounds, diminishing our ranks, making *di yidishe kultur* available only to a few. This attitude turns Yiddish into a kind of *loshn-koydesh*, holy language; makes *yidishe kultur* a religion in which only *di groyse gelernte*, great scholars, can practice. "Do you know Yiddish?" someone asks my friend, a woman deeply committed to Jewish causes, to peace in the Middle East, a woman who is trying to educate herself about Jewish history, to teach herself the *alef-beys*. "No," she replies, ashamed. "*A goy*," she is told.

This is perhaps the worst side of *di yidishe velt*, the Yiddish world—

one which other Jewish communities share. We are all *goyim* to each other. In the *yidishe svive,* I have found provincialism, exclusivity, isolationism, a refusal to honor Jewish difference, a stubborn insistence that our *yidishe kultur* is *di gantse velt,* the whole Jewish world, a narrowness that has frequently looked down upon and denied the richness of Sephardic culture, that has mourned the destruction of Vilna, but forgotten that Salonika is also no more. A narrowness that dismisses the hard, sincere struggle of many American Jews to make up for what history and previous generations withheld from them. *Goyim*—anyone and everyone who is not completely immersed in *yidishe kultur* and/or fluent in the language. It is an attitude that drives many Jews away, that isolates Yiddish culture from the modern sphere, that keeps it from rejuvenating itself.

Yet Yiddish was never the exclusive property of *di groyse gelernte.* It was a language of a people of different ideologies, education, commitment, as much the language of gangsters and shopkeepers as that of poets and intellectuals. Never was it a private cult.

And for a language to remain alive it must be used. Yiddish is *mameloshn* to fewer and fewer secular Jews. But a passive knowledge of Yiddish is still quite strong and interest in Yiddish culture and Eastern European Jewry is on the rise. YIVO Institute for Jewish Research in New York City continues critical research and its general Yiddish studies and language programs draw Jewish scholars and students, many of them committed to Yiddish and Yiddish culture. Courses in Yiddish are now given at many universities, Y's, Hillels, community centers. Though most do not extend beyond the first year, they represent an interest and concern that should not be minimized.[10] And there is enormous interest in Jewish music. The sudden emergence and popularity of *klezmer* bands must reflect the hunger of American Jews for *yidishe kultur.*

Perhaps nothing better embodies the contradictory interpretations we could make concerning the present status of *yidishe kultur* than the growing prominence of the National Yiddish Book Center, a new institution in Amherst, Massachusetts, devoted to saving *yidishe bikher,* Yiddish books. In the past five years, the center has collected (sometimes from city dumpsters) over a quarter of a million *yidishe bikher* which would otherwise have been abandoned and destroyed. *Zol ikh veynen oder freyen zikh?* Should I weep or rejoice? And what about some of its *zamlers*, collectors, Jews who cannot read the alien alphabet of the very books they're committed to saving? Are they *goyim* or *tsadikim*, saints?

Neither. They represent a totally new phenomenon, Yiddishists without knowledge of Yiddish language but deeply committed to the survival of Yiddish culture. A paradox, but a reality that should not be dismissed or mocked. For if Yiddish culture is to survive, the Yiddish world must include those who care about the culture, whose property it is; it can no longer limit itself and define itself by language alone.

The survival of Yiddish and its culture does not rest on our ability to find the right term for "corn flakes" or "jet lag"; but rather on our ability to find a proper place for *yidishe kultur* in our lives, a place among other commitments; on our ability to infuse it with our contemporary values and politics learned outside of its boundaries. For example, feminism: women were co-creators and conveyors of Yiddish culture. This fact should be reflected in cultural history, as in contemporary Yiddish institutions and events. Contemporary Jewish feminists have much to contribute and their perspectives should be sought out. The Jews who would say "we don't need *them*" should think again about history, about the size of the Jewish community. I believe we need each other.

I know that some Yiddishists will perceive my call for greater inclusion as a dilution; will hear my own admission of other commitments as a reflection of my being a dilettante. I believe otherwise. I want my Yiddish involvement to be rooted in my life, in the present, want it to be infused with my contemporary politics and concerns, with the special quality of Jewish American experience. *Di yidishe svive* in the American environment. One world, not two. That's what will keep Yiddish alive for me.

To those outside the Yiddish world, my commitment to Yiddish will seem narrow. How can it compare to the "larger" struggles of the Middle East, Central America, South Africa, nuclear extinction—struggles to which I too am committed. Spiritual concerns are easily classified as secondary. Yet I am convinced, particularly because the world is such as it is, that the survival of cultures is critical and that the effort to save cultures is one of the healthiest signs of our desire to survive as a species. That as a Jew I have a personal stake in the survival of *yidishe kultur* is not something I am ashamed of. I want *yidishe kultur* to survive and I intend to contribute toward that end.

This commitment broadens my perspective, not narrows it. I believe that only when we ourselves are firmly rooted in our own cultural soil do we understand the commitment of others to their cultures, the binds of loyalty, the benefits of community. Furthermore, maintaining *yidishe kultur* supports Jewish diversity which feeds me, which continues to make life interesting. My recognition of Sephardic culture, for example, caused an expansion of my own perspective on people in general and specifically on the extraordinary breadth of Judaism and the Jewish experience.

I was conscious of this last summer when I did a reading with the Chicana poet Gloria Anzaldúa at Old Wives' Tales, a women's bookstore in San Francisco. I read my bilingual Yiddish/English poetry and translations from Yiddish women writers. Gloria, a Chicana from Texas, read her own material in Spanish and English. Our audience was a mix from our ethnic communities and from the general women's community. It was an experience that enlarged all of us, readers as well as listeners, offering both humor and pain, and breaking down the barrier that ignorance often creates. During the reading we bridged a number of worlds, Jewish and Chicana, lesbian and heterosexual, Yiddish and Spanish, Jews and gentiles. Diversity of commitments proved to be broadening, not limiting.

And as the Yiddish world needs to open to feminism, the feminist world needs to be open to Jewish cultures, including Yiddish. Women need to know of the powerful, brave, creative women from my culture, just as I and other Jewish women need this knowledge.

For example: the political activists, the Bundist women in Poland and Russia, *di yidishe froyen,* the Jewish women, who fought for workers' rights and human conditions, for Jewish respect in hostile environments; *di yidishe froyen* who led and participated in strikes, self-defense groups, workers' educational circles; *di yidishe froyen* who took endless risks for justice, for Jewish survival, for socialism, and who died for them. I linger over their photographs and brief captions in *Der Bund in bilder* (the Bund in pictures). Here are a few:

> Esther Lipshitz—Member of Lodz committee of Bund. Arrested March 14, 1903, tortured in Pitrokow prison. Died June 28, 1903.
> Anna Lipshitz—Active in Wilno, Lodz, Odessa, Copenhagen, Riga. Orator and writer. Famed for speeches deliv-

ered to revolutionary sailors during uprising on cruiser *Potiomkin* in Odessa.

Julia Abramowitch—Active in Warsaw, Siedletz, Kalish, Moscow, St. Petersburg, Caucasia. Wounded in both legs from a bomb splinter in Bialystok (1905). Spent long period in prisons of Siedletz and Kalish. Transported arms and illegal literature.

Nadia Kenigshatz-Grinfeld—Active in Kishinew, Odessa, Kiev, St. Petersburg, Paris. Was many times arrested and exiled. In 1905 belonged to Bundist Self-Defense Group in Odessa, was wounded by tsarist bullet. Early in 1918 Rumanian security police drowned her in Dniester while expelling her from the country.

Gina Klepfisz—Was active in work of snatching Jewish leaders out of railroad cars which were taking them to death in Treblinka.

Patti Kremer—Murdered September 1943 when German occupying power led last Jews out of Wilno. The seventy-seven-year-old woman gathered a group of women Bundists around her and said to them: "We will join hands and together sing the Bundist 'Oath' *(Shevueh)*, then death won't be so terrible."[11]

I turn to Fradel Schtok and know that another woman writer experienced similar conflicts over *mame-loshn*. I read her stories of the *shtetl* and America and see the two worlds between which she was caught. I turn to Kadia Molodowsky, predominantly known for her poetry, but whose stories minutely depict assimilation in America as she witnessed it in the 1940s and 1950s. All these Jewish women—Julia, Nadia, Patti, Gina, Fradel, Kadia—are my ancestors. They are *mayne bobes, mumes, shvester*, my grandmothers, aunts, sisters. *Mir darfn zikh bakenen.* We need to become acquainted.

But I do not want to live in the past. I need to move and build. I want to contribute toward a literature which is rooted in my experience, which reflects the special place Yiddish has had in my life. So I have begun experimenting to see if I could reflect in my writing the two linguistic and cultural worlds to which I am committed. So far I have finished only two poems in which Yiddish plays a major part.[12] Neither quite escapes from intellectual formulation into the active imaginative expression of poetic form. This can only happen with repeated experimentation and feeling more *heymish*, comfortable with the idea. I need time and patience.

I have no illusions. What I am using is not the *mame-loshn* I would have used had I been born into a different Poland. It is not even the anglicized Yiddish of American Jews. It is a somewhat schooled, timid, sometimes fragmented Yiddish, insecure and embarrassed by its formality, by its present starkness.

But history has frequently forced Jews to cope with fragments and, as a result, we have learned how to create new contexts, new structures, new wholes—this process, as in the case of Yiddish itself, sometimes taking centuries. It is, I think, part of our resilience, part of our great capacity to transform when we have the will.

And so perhaps this Yiddish of mine, this fragmentary language, this echo of a European era and culture in which I never lived and about which I have only heard secondhand like a family story, this *mameloshn* might prove worth salvaging and sheltering. I have no way of knowing what function, if any, it will have for me or for others. I do know that when I have presented my poems at readings, when I have formed the sounds, said the words out loud, those who had assumed Yiddish was a language of the past only, suddenly felt it had been revived. As my tongue, mouth, lips, throat, lungs, physically pushed Yiddish into the world—as I, a Jew, spoke a Jewish language to other Jews—Yiddish was very much alive. Not unlike a *lebn geblibene*, a survivor, of an overwhelming catastrophe, it seemed to be saying *'khbin nisht vos ikh bin amol geven*. I am not what I once was. *Ober 'khbin nisht geshtorbn. Ikh leb*. But I did not die. I live.

Notes

1. After Poland's liberation, some Poles staged pogroms against Jews who had survived camps and ghettos and were returning to their homes. The Many Jews who were considering staying in Poland left.
2. In Yiddish, *khaverte* is used for both married and unmarried women.
3. Aviva Ravel, *Faithful Unto Death: The Story of Arthur Zygielbaum* (Montreal: Workmen's Circle, 1980), pp. 178-79. Zygielbaum wrote two letters, in Polish to the Polish government and in Yiddish to the Bund. The passage cited is from the Polish letter; at the *akademyes*, I heard it in Yiddish.
4. Buloff was frequently typecast as a bungling Russian and is probably best known for his appearance in *Silk Stockings*.
5. Some courses on Jewish topics and Hebrew did exist, but only in standard departments such as history, religion, modern languages.
6. I have frequently wondered what Max Weinreich felt about CCNY. Surrounded by a vast, young Jewish population of Eastern European background, he taught only German and linguistics.
7. In 1959 the Bund opened Camp Hemshekh. It was Yiddish speaking and became a lifelong influence on those children who were lucky enough to attend it over the next twenty years.
8. Jacob Milner, "Yiddish and the Intellectuals," *Perspectives* (Winter 1964), p. 24.
9. It's a relief to see that the Jewish media has finally broken this silence. *The Jewish*

Week, The Reconstructionist, Jewish Currents, Moment, and The Book Peddler have all written about or made positive references to lesbians and gays. And organizations like New Jewish Agenda and the National Council of Jewish Women have included lesbians and gays in their programs and outreach.

10. Rakhmiel Peltz, "Who's Speaking Yiddish Today?" *Jewish Currents* (December 1985) p. 31.

11. J. S. Hertz, *Der Bund in Bilder/The Jewish Labor Bund: A Pictorial History 1897-1957* (New York: Farlag Unser Tsait, 1958), pp. 50, 154, 158.

12. "*Etlekhe verter.oyf mame-loshn*/A few words in the mother tongue" and "*Di rayze aheym*/The journey home".

Resources

Chagall, Bella. *First Encounter*. New York: Schocken, 1983.

Dubnow, Simon. *History of the Jews in Russia and Poland: From the Earliest Times Until the Present Day* (Philadelphia: Jewish Publication Society, 1916).

Dobroszycki, Lucjan and Kirshenblatt-Gimblett, Barbara. *Image Before My Eyes: A Photographic History of Jewish Life in Poland 1864-1939* (New York: Schocken and YIVO, 1977).

Hertz, J.S. *The Jewish Labor Bund: A Pictorial History 1897-1957* (New York: Farlag Unser Tsait, 1958).

Howe, Irving and Greenberg, Eliezer, eds. *A Treasury of Yiddish Poetry* (New York: Holt, Rinehart and Winston, 1969).

Mlotek, Eleanor Gordon. *The New Book of Yiddish Songs* (New York: Workmen's Circle, 1972).

Pratt, Norma Fain. "Culture and Radical Politics: Yiddish Women Writers 1890-1940." *American Jewish History*, LXX (1981), 68-90.

Rubin, Ruth. *Voices of a People: The Story of Yiddish Folksong* (Philadelphia: Jewish Publication Society, 1979).

Tobias, Henry J. *The Jewish Bund in Russia: From Its Origins to 1905* (Palo Alto, CA: Stanford University Press, 1972).

Weinberg, Sydney Stahl, *The World of Our Mothers: The Lives of Jewish Immigrant Women*.(Chapel Hill: University of North Carolina Press, 1988).

Weinreich, Uriel. *College Yiddish: An Introduction to the Yiddish Language and to Jewish Life and Culture* (New York: YIVO Institute, 1949).

Modern English-Yiddish Yiddish-English Dictionary (New York: YIVO, 1968).

Whitman, Ruth, ed. *An Anthology of Modern Yiddish Poetry* (New York: Workmen's Circle, 1979).

Institutions

The Association for the Promotion of Jewish Secularism, Inc., Room 601, 22 E. 17th St., New York, NY 10003. The English monthly, *Jewish Currents*, regularly includes articles on Yiddish culture and Jewish communities around the world.

Der forverts/Jewish Daily Forward, 45 E. 33rd St., New York, NY 10016. The original daily newspaper, currently bilingual and weekly.

National Yiddish Book Center, Old East Street Road, PO Box 969, Amherst, MA 01004. Publishes catalogue, sponsors Yiddish cultural events. Its quarterly English newsletter, *The Book Peddler*, includes translations.

The Jewish Labor Bund Archives, 25 E. 21st St., New York, NY 10010. Predominantly Yiddish material, but not all.

The Workmen's Circle, 45 E. 33rd St., New York, NY 10016. Has branches in major cities all over the United States. Publishes educational material for teaching Yiddish and Yiddish culture to children and adults. Lectures and courses. Catalogue of books, tapes, etc. available.

YIVO Institute for Jewish Research, 1048 Fifth Avenue, New York, NY 10028. Sponsors the Max Weinreich Center for Advanced Jewish Studies and the Uriel Weinreich Summer Program in Yiddish Language, Literature, and Culture (at Columbia University). Cultural events and lectures. Publishes scholarly work and a quarterly bilingual newsletter, *Yedies/News of the YIVO.*

Forging a Woman's Link in *di goldene keyt:*
Some Possibilities for Jewish American Poetry

(1988)

I began writing seriously in my teens. This was in the mid- and late fifties. I don't remember the content, but do remember writing poems in the voices of old men. I thought poetry should be wise and wisdom resided only in old men who walked down long roads. In the eighth grade I'd been forced to memorize the first ten stanzas of "The Rime of the Ancient Mariner," so perhaps I was imitating Coleridge.

This period is vague. I wrote a lot, but never showed it to anyone, though I did tell people I wanted to be a writer. Against all school counselors' advice and the prognoses of aptitude scores, I chose to be an English major in college. Everyone wanted me to be a science major, to study engineering like my father who'd been killed during the war. But I was drawn to literature, loved to read, loved to write, and persisted, despite undistinguished, sometimes poor, grades. I did eventually make it into the honors English program at City College and won third prize in a short story contest. My image of a poet was Dylan Thomas, dead drunk in a bar on the Upper West Side, talking about being "a windy boy."

I decided to go on to graduate school and ultimately received my M.A. and Ph.D. from the University of Chicago. This was during the sixties, a difficult period for me. Right after I graduated from college, a close friend, another child survivor four years my senior, committed suicide. Elza was in many ways my role model. She was brilliant in languages, translated Latin poetry, wrote her own poetry and fiction, had gone to Cornell and then graduate school. It was partly because of Elza that I wanted to write and distinguish myself. She too had admired Dylan Thomas and for my eighteenth birthday had given me a record of him reading his own work. When Elza died, I was left with a lot of questions and fears.

More than anything I wondered if our similar backgrounds, similar interests, and the very nature of being a poet indicated that I too would be a suicide. Was it a question of time? I wrote a great deal during those six years, almost exclusively about the Holocaust, about Elza. I wrote out of pain and terror. I abandoned the old man's voice and instead frequently wrote in Elza's voice—the dead poet, the child survivor, the woman incapable of being rescued. I wrote from within what I imagined to be her madness. It was an easy voice to take on. I reworked much of this poetry, but never had it completely under control. It just poured out—one depressing poem after another, one atrocity after another, death always the central motif. I suspect that it was solid therapy, that it saved me.

I am not sure how or why this changed. Either I was through with it or I learned something or both. I came to New York to teach and, in the early seventies, had contact for the first time with a young poet. He was neither obsessed with death nor planning an early demise. It suddenly occurred to me that writing poetry could actually be a way of living. At the same time, I was teaching in a department with a number of poets and they too, though all male, gave me a glimpse of possibilities, a way of being a poet in the world. I began rewriting in a different way. The act was no longer therapy; it was less concerned with releasing pain and more with shaping a poem. I developed a way of laying words out on a page and surrounding them with a lot of empty space—the poems were sparse, the words far from each other. They were as much about speaking as about silence. I was not aware of this, but silence had become and remains a central theme in my writing.

During this period when I was beginning to develop what I now recognize as an identifiable voice, I worried that the sole significant topic of my poetry was the Holocaust. I felt that my strongest poems were "death camp," "herr captain" and "about my father." I wondered how long I could keep writing about this and if I wanted to. I was very determined not to play into the commercialism with which the Holocaust was becoming increasingly surrounded. I wanted true poems, but was also drawn to write about other things. And it was during this period that I first became conscious of feminism and gay issues.

I had, of course, written poems about the present—responses to places and events, to people and lovers. I always felt, however, that these were dwarfed by my Holocaust poetry and had little significance.

But when I came out, I suddenly found myself confronted with material that was unacceptable and taboo. Feminist ideas, women's lives, lesbian love, the whole gay world—all were subjects that had few outlets. It was with this consciousness that I self-published in a cooperative venture with four other lesbian writers my first book of poetry, *periods of stress* (Out & Out Books, 1975). The book reflected the strict divisions between my Jewish and lesbian life. Soon after, in 1976, I helped co-found *Conditions* magazine. Open to all women and committed to women usually silenced and kept out of the mainstream, *Conditions* emphasized writing by lesbians. Helping to start a feminist press and a magazine made me begin to view writing and my present life in a more complex political and historical context.

But this sudden expansion had a surprisingly restrictive effect on me. As a lesbian, I felt alienated from the community of my roots. The original Jewish impulse behind my early poetry was still there, but it suddenly seemed out of place. I did not feel comfortable presenting my Holocaust poems in the lesbian community, and I felt to some degree unwelcome in the Jewish community. (Both communities have undergone significant changes in attitude since then.) It was a confusing time. The confusion and economic pressures and work on the magazine were not very conducive to creativity and I wrote little in this period. What I did write, like "From the Monkey House and Other Cages" was very Jewish—a direct outgrowth of my Holocaust poetry—but now the primary focus was women. My feminism led me also to write about office work. In 1973 I lost my teaching job as a result of economic circumstances that were to affect thousands of Ph.D.'s in this country. I was frequently forced to do office work to support myself. This work experience was predominantly a female one, a subject that I realized could be explored further in poetry. No doubt, my Jewish socialist background helped in my ability to understand this—so did feminist writers like Tillie Olsen and lesbian poets like Judy Grahn. So I wrote "Work Sonnets." Again the material was informed by my Jewish upbringing, but did not overtly deal with Jewish themes.

With "The Monkey House" and "Work Sonnets" I was also pushing boundaries of form and language. In the first I tried to deal with nonverbal beings expressing feelings through gestures; I pared down the language as much as possible. I did the opposite in "Work Sonnets" where I alternated between prose poems and lyrics. I stretched the sonnet to fifteen lines and explained in an epigraph I ultimately discarded: "Under these conditions don't expect the perfect form." I forced more prose into the poem by adding two sections after the sonnets themselves: "Notes" by the writer doing office work, and "A Monologue about a Dialogue" in which the "career" secretary reveals her perceptions of the feminist she works with. I knew the sections were not poetry, yet they clearly belonged with the sonnets. These experiments taught me that new content frequently demands new genres, definitions and boundaries.

It seemed, for a while anyway, that I had abandoned explicitly Jewish subjects. Ironically, it was activism within the lesbian and feminist movements that pushed me back to earlier themes. The publication of *Nice Jewish Girls: A Lesbian Anthology* in 1982, Israel's invasion of Lebanon, a more palpable anti-Semitism emerging outside and inside the women's movement—all contributed to my turning again directly to Jewish themes and the subject of the Holocaust. But this time the approach was not exclusively private or experiential. Now I tried to untangle both past and present issues as faced by a contemporary Jew in America. In addition, the Jewish content was informed by my feminism.

Three long poems—"Glimpses from the Outside," "*Bashert*," and "Solitary Acts"—focused on women in my family and other women in my life. I was using everything I had learned in the feminist movement and applying it to the Jewish experience. Thus, all the figures in the last section of *Keeper of Accounts*, "Inhospitable Soil," are women who struggled to survive in Europe, women who struggle to survive here. Without realizing it, I was beginning to think from a Jewish feminist perspective, helping make visible a woman's link in the chain of Jewish history.

For these poems I chose a variety of formats—prose poems, plain prose, ritual repetitions. I wanted to push the prose limits of poetry as far as possible. I did it to such a degree that I became afraid I would never be able to return to more rhythmical free verse. The result was "Solitary Acts," which by contrast is quite lyrical and formal. I also began to include in a more deliberate way non-English words. The central poem of that last section, "*Bashert*," uses some Yiddish (the word *bashert* means predestined or inevitable). I used the Yiddish word as the title because I realized there was no English equivalent to express a certain quality of Jewish experience.

Unlike my first book, *Keeper of Accounts* laid itself out almost chronologically and felt completely integrated. It seemed an accurate reflection of my expanding consciousness and is highly autobiographical. It reflects my internal development as a poet, a feminist and a Jew. It solidified for me certain aspects of writing, of the use of words in isolation and in large unwieldy clumps. I felt I had gained greater technical control over my material. With the completion of that book, I experienced a sense of closure, particularly with *"Bashert"* and "Solitary Acts."

I began looking around for new territory. Again my political activism pointed the way. Together with Melanie Kaye/Kantrowitz, I had been giving a lot of workshops on Jewish identity and for a number of years had worked with her on a Jewish women's anthology which would ultimately appear as *The Tribe of Dina* in 1986. I was thinking a great deal about assimilation, about the effect of the Holocaust (rather than the historical events themselves) on current and future generations. I was drawn to examine my own development and consciousness and began to realize the importance of *yidishkayt,* Yiddish culture, in my life. It had always been there. I'd been raised with it and had internalized it to such a degree, I was barely conscious of its great influence. Certainly I had never thought I had any active role to play in its preservation. But now I began to think more about Yiddish itself and how I might use it in my own writing. I began to think of how the Holocaust had robbed my generation of the language and culture which should have been our natural legacy. More than sixty years ago, Kadia Molodowsky, in the first poem of her series *"Froyen lider"* (Women poems) had lamented that *"mayn lebn [iz] an oysgeflikt blat fun a seyfer / un di shure di ershte farisn,"* her life as a woman was a torn page from a sacred book and the page's first line was illegible. I realized that for me and for many of my generation—as Jews and especially as Jewish women—*di sforim un di bikher,* the sacred and secular books, were lost altogether.

I was struck that as a poet, someone who is intensely involved in language and believes that the kind of language used should reflect what is being expressed, I had never thought about the discrepancy between *di yidishe iberleybungen,* the Jewish experiences I was trying to write about, and the language I was using. (The use of *"bashert"* was the beginning of that realization.) I was also struck by the fact that I had been intimately tied to Yiddish (I had attended Yiddish schools, studied it in college, had even taught it) and yet I had never considered incorporating Yiddish into my work. I began to try to conceive of ways of doing that. Chicana writer Gloria Anzaldúa, who mixes Spanish and English in her writing, was very influential in this process. And so I began experimenting with bilingual Yiddish/English poetry. *"Di rayze aheym*/The journey home" was one result, a poem in which I try to duplicate in language and form the thematic conflict in the poem itself—the loss of language and voice, the efforts to regain them. *"Etlekhe verter oyf mame-loshn*/ A few words in the mother tongue" is an attempt at total integration—to merge feminism, lesbianism and Yiddish language into one piece.

But I realized that being the only poet using Yiddish was not particularly gratifying, since such isolation defeats what I want the very use of Yiddish to represent. I wanted a context within which this poetry would grow *tsuzamen mit di lider fun andere froyen,* together with the poetry of other women, a context incorporating the present and the past. I wanted to search for *di bikher un sforim* from which Molodowsky's page might have been torn. I naturally felt a need to know more about Yiddish women writers, particularly immigrants, who faced some of the same issues I faced when I first came to the States. I was interested in how they dealt with assimilation, the language issue, and if they were conscious of feminism. But the Yiddish cultural legacy, *di goldene keyt*, which had been passed on to me was strictly male. As much as I loved such Yiddish writers as Morris Rosenfeld, Avrom Reisen, I. L. Peretz, H. Leivik, Sholem Aleykhem, and Chaim Grade, I was aware they were presenting male perspectives on Jewish life. I wanted to find out *vos di froyen hobn getrakht un geshribn,* what the women had thought and written. I was looking for a link to *yidishkayt* and to *yidishe froyen*. This could be in part done by establishing a dialogue *mit der yidisher fargangenhayt,* with the Yiddish/Jewish past, a dialogue that would have to include women. It would be presumptuous of any of us to act as if nothing came before us. And what I also realized was that I had to find the women myself—much as I did Fradel Schtok—pick them up through references in my readings, and in planned searches.

I knew that there were a lot of women writers, but aside from a handful of poems (and these mostly by Kadia Molodowsky) no women prose writers have been translated or are known to American Jews. So I began to look through the literature and the *Leksikon* as well as articles and anthologies. The work of Norma Fain Pratt was of particular use. Having become better acquainted with some—Rokhl Luria, Kadia Molodowsky, Fradel Schtok—I became committed to translating their work, and making them available to American Jewish women. (A couple of these translations appear in *The Tribe of Dina*.) One poem which resulted from my reading was "Fradel Schtok," a dramatic monologue in which I take on the voice of the writer as she expresses her confusion about adopting English and abandoning Yiddish. I hope to do more writing in this vein.

I am not completely satisfied with how I have used Yiddish in some of my poetry and am unclear how Yiddish will manifest itself in my future writing. My sense is that the bilingual mode is too artificial to maintain. I expect a strong Yiddish element will remain, however, because I feel deeply connected to that literary tradition and culture and this must inevitably find expression in my work. With all the talk about Yiddish being a dead language, I feel it is important to use whatever Yiddish is available to me, even if at times it is fragmentary. Currently I am using simple phrases in what are virtually exclusively English poems. Context usually explains the Yiddish and the Yiddish, I hope, seems appropriate because of what is being referred to. For example, in the poem "Warsaw, 1983: *Umschlagplatz*" about my trip to Poland and what I experienced there, it seemed natural to use Yiddish when referring to a plaque written partly in Yiddish. In addition, I used an epigraph from a poem by the Yiddish poet H. Leivik. The desire to use the epigraph, a phrase I had heard all my life—"*In Treblinke bin ikh nisht geven*" (I was never in Treblinka)—was but one small attempt to begin the dialogue.

Purists might ask: *Farvos shraybstu nisht bloyz oyf yidish?* But why not write only in Yiddish? I don't feel as in control of the language as I do of English. But there are other considerations. I want to remain accessible to as many people as possible and the fact is that using Yiddish exclusively would bypass the very audience which has appreciated and responded strongly to the presence of Yiddish in my work. The intensity and emotionalism of that response still takes me aback. Just a few Yiddish words, the very sound of the language evokes very strong feelings and memories. So I am determined that Yiddish will never be a barrier, as it has been for many Jews whose parents spoke it only *az di kinder zoln nisht farshteyn*, so the children won't understand. I realize I need to find ways in which I can use Yiddish, intertwine it with the English so that it is not directly translated, yet is intelligible. This can be done by repetition, inference, paraphrasing, etc. I'm beginning to consider more formal poems (such as the pantoum) which, because of their forced repetitions, would make integration of the two languages easier. I am still experimenting.

So the impulse for my writing at this stage is very different than it was when I wrote in my early twenties. I am more deliberate about choosing subjects and I find myself needing to read, research, and internalize what I learn. I frequently start with an idea, as in the case of the pantoum. Here the form is the idea. Often the content—a desire to create something about a certain subject—is the idea, as in "Fradel Schtok." Language, form, and content take on new meaning for me at this stage.

My perception of Jewish content has, I believe, broadened. I no longer view the Holocaust as dwarfing my new themes. The present and the more distant past seem significant subjects for poetry. And this includes everything in the present—whether cultural issues such as Yiddish and Yiddish literature, forms of secular identity, relationship to the past, assimilation, Israel and the Palestinian struggle for self-determination—all are fitting subjects for contemporary American Jewish poets. By turning to these, by framing them in the present context, by presenting them from a feminist perspective, we can create a viable American Jewish poetry and poetics, one that is linked to the past and contains a legacy for the future.

I often ask myself who I am writing for and who is interested in Jewish poetry and poetics with a feminist or lesbian perspective. I feel some confusion at this point about the different audiences for my work. I am deeply committed to the lesbian and feminist movements, to Yiddish and *yidishkayt,* to the Jewish community, to radical politics. How to reach all these audiences, through which journals and magazines, are questions I have not answered. I am working on the answers in the same way I am working on my poetry.

What I am certain of is that my political work—consciousness raising on feminist, gay and Jewish issues, building Jewish awareness of *yidishkayt,* teaching Yiddish, translating significant material, working towards a peaceful solution in the Middle East—has become as important to me as my writing. And this surprises me, given how I began writing in such complete isolation. But my commitment to these political causes has become very deep and I could never again think of poetry writing as the sole and central preoccupation of my life. I, of course, don't want to abandon entirely the personal, private inner life which was often the impulse behind my early work. But I have a keen sense of the present as historical, a turning point—Jews are shaping their future now. How we preserve and recast Yiddish culture and sensibility on American soil are questions I feel compelled to address both in my political activism and in my poetry.

The Lamp:
A Parable About Art and Class and the Function of Kishinev in the Jewish Imagination

(1989)

> *In 1903 a pogrom in Kishinev (Bessarabia) resulted in the death of forty-five Jews. News of the pogrom evoked mass protests in England and the U.S. and among prominent Russian intellectuals (including Leo Tolstoy).*

I have a lamp that two of my friends deem unbearable. It is tall and leans unforgivingly. The pole is loose in the plastic marble mooring. Its faded, dusty lampshade won't stay put because a screw is missing. It looks like a scarecrow that lost its arms and straw during a pogrom. And there it stands, right in my living room.

An artist friend of mine finds it repulsive. She, not surprisingly, is obsessed with aesthetics. It's a way of life. She's an artist always and finds the lamp intensely disturbing. She keeps asking me how I can bear to look at it all day. I laugh, never having given it a second thought. Once she stayed in my place while I was away. When I got back the lamp was missing. She'd shoved it into one of my closets. I immediately took it out and put it back in its place by the open window where I often sit and read.

Another friend hates my lamp because it reeks from poverty and what she thinks is indulgence—the yellow lampshade I refuse to clean up, the pole which I won't ground. To this friend, environment is self. She builds and rebuilds her apartment, paints her bookshelves then strips them, reviews her living room trying to find the one piece of furniture that could be dumped or replaced to make it all fall into place like a certain Cézanne painting she so admires. She wants to be able to sit in a room of her own creation and feel herself come together in a unified whole.

Such an attitude brings only disaster whenever she visits. She shudders at the rusted shower stall, at the misplaced furniture. Why isn't my desk at the window instead of in the darkest corner? Why is the bookcase free standing and not anchored to the wall? And that lamp! Why keep it? It looks like a scarecrow. This whole place, she tells me, looks like Kishinev after the pogrom.

But as I try to explain, the lamp is the least of my worries. I'm already middle aged and still unsettled. I still live alone with no illusions about finding a lover. I still have no steady work or profession. I'm not romantic about my poverty. I don't feel indulgent. My material circumstances feel terminal. *I* feel terminal. On the other hand, I think about the poor people living on the street or people living without heat or water in burnt out buildings, and I feel lucky. This time it's not me. My place's got heat, no leaks. I've managed to pay my bills. The electricity is on and so is the gas. It could be worse. It has been.

Besides, lately I feel like I'm a marathon runner heading full speed towards my cemetery plot in New Jersey. Time is going right past me or I'm rushing past it. Should I stop and shop around for a lamp? Maybe if I ran across one, just by accident, and it was real cheap, I might consider it. Maybe. It's not that I don't care for material things. There are many things I lust for. For example, pens, colored paper. I also covet books and am adept at switching labels when the price is way out of line and I grow indignant. So I'd much rather buy pens or paper or a used book than a lamp, especially a lamp which would only substitute for one that is working full well. And the lamp *is* working. The wiring is fine. Why *not* keep it?

As for the aesthetic argument…. Well, I'll confess, I have a weakness—let's just say I'm always more forgiving with artists. A wrong line to them is real grief. They can't help it. Who understands these things? I'm sure if this lamp were the only source of evening light, my artist friend wouldn't have shoved it in the closet. But it wasn't. So by hiding the lamp she was doing exactly what I do by keeping it out. It's a question of visions. She's a painter. And I—to my life's joy—am a poet.

Of course, there are other differences between us. She's not a Jew. And this too is important: we're at opposite ends of the spectrum when it comes to light. To me light is merely a means—to read a page from a book, to write a line of a poem. But it is in darkness that my poems come to me. It is in darkness my imagination finds comfort. Now, to my artist friend, light is essence. She clings to natural light, refusing to turn on any lamp until the last ray of sun has disappeared. Shade and color are all of life to her. I seek out dark corners and words to release me. Still, we understand each other. After all, we're both poor and that helps.

As for my other friend—we share five thousand years of history. Yet I can't make her understand that I'm getting closer and closer to New Jersey and there are certain things it would be stupid to stop for. Besides, it's all more than my grandmother had, more than my grandmother ever hoped for. With poems, it's more than enough. Perhaps it's the collective memory of Kishinev. I don't know. I do know it's been worse, much worse.

V

Jewish Progressives and the Jewish Community

(1988)

I do not accept the assumption that there exist two distinct Jewish worlds—progressive and mainstream (or traditional)—all of whose values and norms are always in conflict. My experience as a feminist and a lesbian is that the Jewish world we call progressive has been often as slow and reluctant to deal with feminist and gay issues as the mainstream Jewish world. Some advances have been made and many, though not all, Jewish progressives have reached the stage of paying obligatory lipservice and ensuring token representation at progressive events. But a clear-cut commitment to fighting sexism and homophobia and a dedication to gaining full rights for gays have not evoked the same passions which the struggles for rights of other minorities evoke. Most Jewish feminists and gays that I know remain angry and frustrated by Jewish progressives. Deeply committed to progressive causes, frequently in the vanguard of political action, Jewish feminists and gays find ourselves fighting for the rights of others without the secure knowledge that others will fight for us. Most of the time we fight sexist and heterosexist battles alone in both these worlds.

And because my expectations of these two worlds are different, my reactions to advances in them vary as well. For me the advances in feminism and gay rights in the mainstream Jewish community are more meaningful because they have required greater will than in the Jewish progressive community where I always expect validation and support. Thus, I find greater satisfaction in the fact that a lesbian support group exists at the New York Section of the National Council of Jewish Women than the fact that a lesbian and gay panel is sched-

---

This talk was delivered at the *Tikkun* Conference on Liberal/Progressive Jewish Intellectuals, December 18-20, 1988 in New York City.

uled at a progressive event, usually only after protests and at the last minute. In this instance, the National Council seems to have a higher consciousness and is acting more progressively than progressives themselves.

So from the viewpoint of a lesbian and a feminist, the two Jewish worlds—progressive and mainstream—do not differ that greatly and require the same energy in fighting these specific battles. Perhaps this experience as a lesbian and feminist is the reason I try to avoid the "us" and "them" division and try to find common ground in both worlds from which to launch various battles.

The "us" and "them" division—"us" meaning progressives and "them" being the mainstream—is too simple and veils a more complex reality. It also smacks of smugness and self-righteousness, which I find alienating. It assumes that the progressive world has everything to offer the mainstream and the mainstream's main activity is to unlearn its evil ways. This is neither useful nor accurate. I am, for example, often pained by the ignorance of many Jewish progressives in relation to Jewish history, culture, and religion and wish we would have more contact with the mainstream community and get our Jewishness on firmer ground. I am pained that we are often satisfied with so little, that we do not even feel our ignorance as a deficit, do not consider the struggle for evolving a solid religious or secular identity on our progressive agenda. I am as pained and frustrated with these Jews as I am with Jews who refuse to grant the most basic rights to Palestinians.

The "us" and "them" division ultimately reduces itself to politics being the defining element of the progressive community while Jewish content becomes the defining element of the mainstream. This is a dangerous division, for it forces unnecessary choices upon us, each of which leaves us incomplete. Clearly there needs to be greater communication between Jewish progressives and the Jewish mainstream, there needs to be an exchange, bartering if you will. If such exchanges do not take place we will still be progressives, but not Jewish progressives.

Let me give a brief example. At the National Women's Studies Association conference this past June, an Israeli friend of mine took on the difficult task of explaining the *intifada* to American Jewish women, many of whom were quite hostile to her political position. Among those participating was a woman rabbi who was definitely on the conservative end of this issue, but who later thanked my Israeli friend for her contributions and for giving her the opportunity to learn. My Israeli friend ended up feeling glad that this woman had come to the event and had participated. The rabbi, in turn, invited the Israeli to come to the *shabes* service she was conducting the next day. But my Israeli friend, who is nonobservant, did not attend. Afterwards she told me she felt she'd been wrong. If the woman rabbi had been willing to come to her event, to listen to her discussions, surely she, the Israeli woman, could have at least extended herself despite her misgivings and supported the woman rabbi in her struggle and interest, even though she did not fully share them. The Israeli woman said to me: "I expected this woman to come and listen to me, but felt no obligation to listen to what she had to offer. That is not right. I should support her efforts at her form of Jewishness if I expect her to support mine."

I agree with my Israeli friend. There needs to be among us a greater sense of an exchange between equals rather than between givers and receivers. If this sense of mutual respect does not exist, then we progressives will surely be forever seen as outsiders. I think the mainstream Jewish community is correct in its accusation that we do not care enough for what it considers Jewish issues: assimilation, identity, anti-Semitism, healing from the Holocaust. Certainly these are issues which we should share with the mainstream community and among which we could find common ground. It would assure the mainstream that we are concerned about the issues which it cares deeply about and would give Jewish progressives more credibility in the community.

I know, of course, not all progressives lack Jewish consciousness. But enough do that I think it is a real concern. As a feminist and lesbian, as a Yiddishist and a cultural Jew, I often feel alienated from Jewish progressives who do not share my cultural concerns, who do not worry about Jewish cultural survival. At those times, I feel closer to the mainstream community because I know I can turn to them for sources and resources and they will be appreciative of my efforts—and they always are. I have found, in fact, that my concerns about Jewish identity and culture often form the bridge to the mainstream Jewish community and enable me to get progressive issues such as women's and gay and lesbian rights a more sympathetic ear.

I have never heard of a tradition among Jews that encourages us to support each others' differences. Quite the contrary. What I've always been taught is that Jews forever see each other as bitter enemies whose differences are irreconcilable. We have many jokes about this—three Jews meet on a street corner and form five political parties, none of whom speak to each other. This is comic, but it also has its tragic side, as in the Warsaw Ghetto, where for a number of years the communists,

Zionists, and socialists could not get together to fight a common enemy. We have somehow got to learn to take the tolerance that we have for difference *outside* of the Jewish community and develop it for each other. For example, many of us are far more tolerant of Christians and other ethnic cultures than we are of Jewish sects and traditions. I know many Jewish progressives who will join hands with Catholic priests, but will not step into a synagogue. Ashkenazi Jews applaud the struggles of Hispanic people for biculturalism, but are often embarrassed by our own Yiddish tradition and give it no support as it struggles to maintain its footing in contemporary Jewish life. The degree to which this self-hatred is carried has been most evident in Israel in the last few years. We hate many of our own people and they in turn hate us. And what we see played out in Israel in the extreme is also true here in the States; the separation between Jewish progressives and the Jewish mainstream is just one manifestation of this intolerance. This separation must be bridged.

And the initiators of such bridging must, of course, be the progressives and radicals. It is they who need to develop the foresight, need to set the example. By incorporating the best of radical politics and Jewish tradition, they can serve as a role models and also as a draw to Jews in the mainstream. We Jews are living in a strange historical period in which our sense of history is often quite warped. For many American Jews, the Holocaust and Israel have reduced Jewish history to the years 1939-1945, or 1948 to the present. This extremely limited view of Jewish history naturally narrows the concept of Jewish identity and that narrowness is one which we as progressives ought to be countering. But the progressive elements are often, though not always, reluctant to take these issues on or are uninterested in them. And yet it seems to me that these are the very issues that the progressive world ought to be addressing with as much fervor as we do political questions. Progressives and radicals should not only offer a critique, but also serve as role models by showing how cultural identity can function in contemporary American society and how it can be intertwined with Jewish tradition and progressive ideals.

The sphere in which progressives have been most visible outside of the political arena is the religious one. There is much being done now by feminists—women and men—to transform the liturgy and religious concepts and to bring them in line with progressive ideals. But this movement does not touch a majority of us who remain intransigently secular and who need more substance, greater knowledge, and a stronger connection to Jewish history and culture. This is an area in which the mainstream is also foundering and one which can serve as common ground for both progressive and mainstream Jews. Let us not take the attitude that because of our politics we must remain pure and not mix with the Jewish rabble—the mainstream. Let us be as willing to meet with Jews in small community centers in our neighborhoods as we are to meet with Palestinians. The work to be done at these centers and synagogues is as critical as the work needed to resolve the Palestinian/Israeli conflict. The Jews at these centers and synagogues are our people, the people we need to reach and persuade to our way of thinking. And they have valuable cultural and historical gifts to offer in exchange—in Yiddish, Hebrew, Ladino. We need to work together and be mutually supportive in our struggle to make a reality of our political ideals, to maintain our Jewish identity and our sense of peoplehood.

Khaloymes/Dreams in Progress:
Culture, Politics, and Jewish Identity

(1990)

for Clare Kinberg

I. Setting Priorities

Like most activists and artists, I have difficulty establishing priorities. The tension between being active in the world and needing solitude is one all of us struggle with. I find myself discussing this tension with other Jews, particularly in regard to our activism on the Israeli/Palestinian conflict. Not an abstract discussion. A friend encourages me to return to Jewish art and to prioritize my previous focus, the strengthening of what seems to be a vanishing secular Jewish identity. She presses me to resume my translations of Yiddish women writers. I know she's right. Yet I constantly postpone this work, to which I have been committed for a long time. I have been totally absorbed by Middle East work and often feel out of control. I need to step back. I don't think it's healthy. But then I wonder: is that really true? What is the "healthy," "balanced" Jewish response to the current crisis in Israel and the Occupied Territories? And how does it relate to other aspects of Jewish life?

The Jewish artist in me feels displaced. I want to have time to write, to create literature which expands our notion of our Jewishness, which might in turn give us rest and inspire us to keep on with our peace work. But I don't make time for it. I remain focused on Israel and the Occupied Territories, where the situation is worsening. The Palestinians remain trapped in a life/death struggle. In Israel, activists still press on despite the grim reality of the strengthening of reactionary forces. Watching the evening news on May 3, I see Jewish settlers establish a *yeshiva* in the middle of Nablus while the Palestinian inhabitants are confined to their homes; the whole city is held under house arrest by the army. The camera focuses for a moment on a Palestinian woman at a window watching Jewish fundamentalists dancing around the Torah. A right-wing Knesset member tells the reporter: "Let *them* leave, go somewhere else. This is Israel." After such a spectacle, do we dare prioritize other Jewish concerns?

And yet we must. We respond to these kinds of events instantly, almost reflexively. I want to examine this response. I want to be able to define our responsibility and role in this crisis as American Jews—individually and as a community—and establish its relationship to other Jewish issues, especially Jewish identity. I want to understand why this crisis touches the core of my (our) Jewish identity—an identity that until now I've never doubted or questioned. I've written about the pride with which I was raised in regard to *yidishkayt un yidishe geshikhte,* Jewishness and Jewish history. This pride was always tempered by a clear-eyed perception of *yidishe mentshlekhkayt,* Jewish humanness[1] which included among our virtues such common, human flaws as greed and selfishness and indifference to others' welfare—Jewish and non-Jewish. My acceptance of *yidishe mentshlekhkayt* allowed for a complex understanding of *di yidishe yerushe,* the Jewish heritage (in my case, *yidishkayt*) which was passed on to me.

However, what this perspective never included—because until 1948 it had not existed—was Jews' collective capacity to abuse power in relationship to each other (religious laws imposed on all Jews, including those who are nonobservant) and to non-Jews (military laws imposed on Palestinians).[2] Because Israel has never been at the core of my identity, but rather more at the periphery of my Jewish consciousness, for years I did not focus on the issues of abuse of power by the Israeli government, either internally or externally.

But since Israel's 1982 invasion of Lebanon and the Sabra and Shatilla camps' massacres, I have experienced a slow disorientation around my Jewish identity. Israeli policies have caused me to question the adequacy of how I defined myself as a Jew. Like those Jews who until '82 were not focused on Israel, I felt discomfort and then rage about Israel's relationship to Palestinians and an increasing urgency about working to resolve the conflict. With great resistance, I have accepted that events in Israel and in the Occupied Territories—*no matter how I defined myself as a Jew*—affect my vision of myself as a Jew, my Jewish pride, my sense of how Jewish issues are to be prioritized.

I ask myself how this came about. How is it that Israel, which was "at the periphery of my Jewish consciousness" is now a central concern? One obvious answer: it's hard to ignore newspaper headlines. It's even harder to ignore inaccurate and anti-Semitic equations: Israeli = Jew, Israel = all Jews, and Israeli government policies = Nazi policies during the Holocaust. Such equations put most Jews on the defensive and I'm not particularly thick-skinned about them myself.

But on a deeper level, the process by which Israel became central to my consciousness is more complex. Over time, I have realized that events in Israel and the Occupied Territories are evoking the same questions that my Jewish upbringing, Jewish culture, secularism—in short, *yidishkayt*—had always challenged me to answer: what is the content of my Jewish identity? what parts of it do I want to pass on and how? what is the nature of the Jewish tradition which I want to preserve? what moral and political obligations do Jews have to their immediate Jewish community? to other Jewish communities? to non-Jewish communities? how do I define Jewish security and Jewish survival? In other words, what the crisis has brought to the forefront is that Israel's official actions and policies are offering answers which clash directly with those offered by my Yiddish secular upbringing. And as the *intifada* has continued, I have begun to understand that just as Israel made a profound mistake in not incorporating the answers that *yidishkayt* provided, so the *yidishkayt* that I inherited was mistaken in not incorporating the consequences of Israel's existence into its own answers.[3] Most U.S. Jews have not thought deeply about the consequences of the interconnection of Israeli and Diaspora Jews' identities. They have automatically professed to be Zionists and, until recently, have always assumed that such an enmeshment of identities was enriching. Since '82 and certainly since the *intifada,* they have continued in their ardent adherence to Zionism, but are beginning to feel uncomfortable with the responsibility for Israeli actions of which they disapprove, a responsibility which the enmeshment inherently implies. For the first time, many Jews are examining (often silently) their relationship to another Jewish community and to non-Jewish people.

My own consciousness of the connections and the consequences has sharpened. Today I view Sharon and Kahane and the *Gush Emunim* not simply as examples of the weaknesses of our *yidishe mentshlekhkayt,* Jewish humanness, but as a political evil. Some of my friends challenge this view as extreme. But I believe it. Kahane and Sharon are not concerned with Jewish values, Jewish security, Jewish survival. I don't believe that their policies are motivated by Jewish fears of annihilation. There are, I know, many Israeli Jews whose refusal to accept a Palestinian state is rooted in real fears, some of which I share. And because of this, I see their position differently, even though I strongly disagree with it. However, Kahane and his kind express blatant racism, chauvinism, a hunger for military power, a greed for territory, an insistence on religious and cultural supremacy. These can be easily analyzed as originating in feelings of inadequacy and insecurity and even fears of annihilation. Yet they are manifested in such hatred of Palestinians, such callous indifference to non-Jews and non-Jewish culture that I do not consider these "psychological roots" of fascism legitimate concerns.[4] And so I continue viewing Kahane and his politics as an evil that impinges on my Jewishness because they actively try to redefine and reshape it through the actions and policies of the Jewish State. Everything Jewish in me resists their efforts. Thus the despair I sometimes experience stems in part from my fear that I will not be able to resist effectively, that the Palestinians will continue living and dying under a brutal military rule; that right-wing Israeli policies will overwhelm and come to dominate Jewish identity; and that I will be unable to put my Jewish self together again and feel whole.

I know some will immediately argue that in light of what the Palestinians are experiencing, it is selfish (some will say obscene) to be even remotely concerned about my Jewish soul and my Jewish identity. But I am at core a Jew and motivated both by *menthshlekhkayt*, humanness, and a commitment to *yidishkayt* in which politics and Jewish identity are intimately connected. So, yes, I *am* concerned about the health of Jewishness and Jewish identity, and about the health of the Jewish people. I *am* concerned that Israel's democratic institutions are in jeopardy, that more Israelis seem to be tolerating greater internal restrictions, allowing for fewer democratic freedoms, fewer ways of being Jewish and of expressing political dissent. I am as concerned about this as I am about the violent conditions under which the Palestinians are living.

I am concerned not only about life in Israel, but also about life in the States in general and in the Jewish community specifically. When the Jewish Women's Committee to End the Occupation of the West Bank and Gaza held its vigils in midtown, I would get off at the 59th Street subway stop which contains an entrance to Bloomingdale's, one of New York's most posh department stores. Carrying my posters with the slogans *"Dai lakibush!"* (End the Occupation) and "Two Peoples, Two States, One Future," I would pass groups of the homeless who had set up cartons as shelters by the store's revolving doors. A few minutes later, I'd be distributing flyers and, on a couple of occasions, someone would ask: "What occupation?" and I'd reply: "The West Bank and Gaza." They in turn answered: "That's far away." And I'd think, yes, it is far away and I've just passed five people sleeping in the entrance to Bloomingdale's. Should I not be working for the homeless on New York City streets? Why is the Israeli/Palestinian conflict more important to me? Why don't I put my energy, for example, into abortion rights campaigns or race relations in the U.S.?

These are all urgent concerns, yet I and many Jews choose to make the Israeli/Palestinian conflict the political focus of our activism and, as others have expressed to me, our work consumes us to a degree that we ourselves do not totally understand. Though the Middle East is "far away," Israel, the West Bank, and Gaza remain close to our hearts, to our Jewish identity. We discuss the U.S. government's role in the region, the connections between defense spending and the homeless, between Third World people's solidarity with the Palestinians and the tensions between Jews and other racial and ethnic groups in the U.S. But these are not, I believe, at the core of our involvement. Israel retains a special place on our list of priorities because it is a Jewish state and we are Jews and cannot disengage ourselves from its fate. It pushes us psychologically, gnaws at our sense of personal responsibility. It keeps us constantly focused and conscious of our Jewish identity.

I also have to ask if the Israeli/Palestinian conflict is more important than Jewish issues rooted in our life here in the States. My own involvement with this issue over the past two years has suspended almost entirely all my other Jewish activities—creating Jewish art, addressing homophobia in the Jewish community, working on strengthening secular Jewish identity, translating Yiddish women writers whose fiction enriches our view of Eastern European Jewish culture and creates both a connection to the past and a context for feminist Jewish life in the present. My behavior could be interpreted to signify that unless the Israeli/Palestinian conflict is resolved, U.S. Jewish life cannot go on. Some Jewish activists have advocated such a position and I vehemently disagree with them. I believe Jewish life in the U.S. has been neglected for too long and is, therefore, in danger—a danger that the word "assimilation" does not even begin to convey in terms of urgency. For too long our preoccupation with Israel (either in the form of Zionism or fundraising for Israel as the primary content of our Jewish identity or in the form of political opposition to Israeli government actions) has prevented us from seeing and dealing with Jewish identity, and Jewish life in the U.S.[5] I have referred to this crisis in other writing, but in the past two years have barely addressed it. Paradoxically, I view it as becoming more acute, exacerbated by the Middle East conflict because the latter is intimately connected to the former. For many Jews, Israel has become the shortcut to dealing with the complex issue of Jewish identity in the Diaspora. For some, the symbolic gesture of unequivocally supporting Israel (morally and/or financially) has been the core and sole expression of Jewish identity. As they begin—with great resistance and probably in secrecy—to question that support, they find themselves unable to define their Jewishness, particularly if they are not observant. Other Jews, active for the first time on a "Jewish" issue by opposing Israeli government policies, are also struggling to define their Jewishness and explain their emotional involvement with a country which, until now, they never identified with. The "far away" crisis is triggering the recognition of an emptiness in the Jewish self.

When I write about the homeless, about abortion, or about race relations in the U.S., I feel on solid ground. I have confidence that these issues are perceived as important by Jews and non-Jews and deserving of as much attention as the Israeli/Palestinian conflict. Yet I grow self-conscious when I write about Israel's internal deterioration or Jewish identity questions. I know there are many—Jews included—who will scorn my notion of the importance of these issues and my daring to give them priority.

I am not only self-conscious, but also fearful. I fear some people will immediately accuse me of indifference to Palestinians, of weakening my commitment to their cause. I am also afraid those Jews already resistant to facing the realities of Israel's relations to Palestinians will use my concern for Jewish identity as an excuse to avoid the implications of the occupation. I am afraid of being quoted out of context—of my writing, of my life and of my activities. Also in the spring of 1990, I cannot possibly predict the political context in which this essay will be read in the future. Events in the Middle East are so unpredictable that any conclusion is almost instantly obsolete. I'm afraid of what future horrors might be perpetrated by the IDF or by the settlers or by the PLO which will set everyone back and place Israeli and Palestinian peace activists in seemingly untenable situations. Nevertheless, I truly believe that as U.S. Jews we must question the nature of our Jewish identity—specifically secular identity, since the majority of Jews are not observant—must start paying attention to what is happening to us *now* as a people in *this* country. This is not a diversion away from the Palestinian cause. Our neglect of identity issues has a direct bearing on our feelings and responses to Israeli government policies, and by addressing the former, we, in fact, clear our way through the tangled and confusing attitudes which have distorted our perception of the latter.

II. Defining Secularism

My work in the Jewish and women's communities has revealed many misconceptions about the nature of secular identity, the most common being that it is simply being nonobservant. Frequently it is confused with assimilation; almost always, both directly and indirectly, it is deemed illegitimate. For example, when *Moment* magazine publicizes a dialogue among different sectors of the Jewish community, what it really means is among those Jews affiliated with synagogues: orthodox, conservative, reform. The editors seem unaware—or perhaps do not care—that such a dialogue excludes the majority of U.S. Jews, who, in fact, have no connection or relationship to the synagogue.[6] The erasure of Jewish secularism as a legitimate expression of Jewish identity is best reflected by the fact that *The Encyclopaedia Judaica* does not even list the term. Such an omission is probably not intentional; it has historical roots in the European *haskalah*, enlightenment, movement of the eighteenth century.

It was the German *maskilim*, promoters of the *haskalah*, who first introduced "secular" ideas as a legitimate part of Jewish intellectual discourse.[7] At that time, the term "secular" characterized any study, language, custom, body of knowledge not encompassed by or derived from religious Jewish learning, *halakhah*, Jewish law and observance (science and mathematics, languages and literature of host countries—German, Russian, Polish, French, etc.). In the eighteenth century, to turn to secular matters meant to go *outside* of Jewish life, to relate to non-Jewish ideas and materials. However, early *maskilim* didn't reject religious observance. What they advocated was a necessary compatibility; they saw the need and possibility of Jews expanding their world view, of becoming active citizens in Western societies.

The possibility of becoming citizens of Western nations inevitably meant that "enlightened" Jews had to deny Jewish autonomy or nationhood. Supporting their belief that they were German or French citizens who practiced the Mosaic religion, they advocated relinquishing all those ties of language and custom which, in addition to their religion, had separated them from their Christian neighbors. Jewish observance did not escape "normalization" either. The *maskilim* encouraged the translation of religious texts and prayers into modern languages and incorporation of some of the trappings of the Church into the synagogue. Thus, secular languages and customs provided traditional Jewish observance with a more "normal" appearance and allowed Jews still to be "different," only now "less different." As a result, Jews could practice their religion, retain their Jewish identity and at the same time adopt non-Jewish national customs and traditions which supported their claim to full citizenship. Such a shift in perspective naturally expanded the sphere of Jewish life. However, it simultaneously reinforced the idea that observance alone defined Jewish identity.

One of the most paradoxical effects of the *haskalah* movement was the recognition and validation of a secular perspective and life that was Jewish, but entirely divorced from observance. It took time and development, but what ultimately emerged at the end of the nineteenth century was a very different notion of secularism—a secularism insisting on its Jewishness while denying Jewish observance and *halakhah* as the central elements of Jewish identity. This Jewish secularism accepted as reality Jewish life outside the synagogue. It was a Jewish secularism which rejected Torah as God's word, but accepted it as Jewish history and literature. It was a Jewish secularism which splintered into various ideologies, each of which recognized and defined Jewish nationhood and autonomy, promoted its own political tenets, values, and literature, and expressed these in Jewish languages. The content of this Jewish secularism was the diverse life of the Jewish people, their relations with their host countries, their place in the world.

In the West, in response to anti-Semitism (most notably the Dreyfus case), some Jews concluded that integration into European societies was impossible. Paralleling western nationalists, Jews began advocating for the creation of a Jewish state. Soon Zionists were entirely focused on Palestine and Hebrew as the national language of the Jewish people. In Eastern Europe, where full citizenship was not an option and diverse ethnic groups complicated national identity, many Jews became caught up in radical and revolutionary movements. Bundists (and in some cases other socialists, communists, and anarchists) promoted Jewish autonomy in the countries in which they lived by legitimizing the Yiddish language and Yiddish culture and supporting internationalism through class struggle.

Inherent in these forms of secularism was the acceptance of the Torah as a source of Jewish history and philosophy, and a sustained connection to those Jewish holidays like *hanukah, purim,* and *pesakh* not dependent on synagogue observance, but linked to historical and political Jewish events. Unlike those *maskilim* who "normalized" Judaism and/or entered the non-Jewish sphere, these secular Jews "Judaized" non-Jewish activities, philosophies, and ideas. Yiddish theater and film, Yiddish and Hebrew newspapers, journals, and literature (often imitating non-Jewish European models), Yiddish translations of *Das Kapital* and Hugo's *Les Miserables* became as much a part of the secular Jewish canon as the original Hebrew and Yiddish work of Bialik and Peretz.

Nothing better reflects the new character of this secularism than the two theoreticians of Zionism and Bundist socialism, Theodore Herzl and Vladimir Medem. Both came from assimilated backgrounds (Medem himself was baptized) and neither was fluent in the languages which their movements promoted. Yet both came to advocate Jewish autonomy and a radical concept of Jewish secularism which diverged completely from the eighteenth century *maskilim's* vision and intent: the possibility of being a committed, *unassimilated* Jew without being observant. And this concept had great power. At the turn of the twentieth century, Yiddish and Hebrew made Jewish secularism visible and legitimate to its adherents. With their linguistic and historic roots, they transformed whatever they touched—politics, theater, literature, education—into a Jewish expression of the life of our people. Even those secularists who seemed indifferent or apolitical served as preservers of Jewish identity and nationality by the very fact that they continued communicating in a Jewish language. Yiddish writers and artists who produced trashy novels and plays were as instrumental in maintaining and promoting Jewish identity as the writers and theoreticians who argued over Hebrew and Yiddish at the Czernowitz Conference in 1908.[8]

For the theoreticians, Jewish secularism had two distinct components: political and cultural. These are easily identifiable in the secular tradition of *yidishkayt* which was advocated by a diverse group of political parties at the turn of this century. This secularism was never associated with assimilation, but with a fierce determination to preserve Jewish identity through Yiddish and Yiddish culture. Committed to social justice and class struggle, all its proponents advocated *gerangl,* struggle, and radical change, many promoted *revolutsye,* revolution, and all integrated art and politics, introspection and activism, a concern for Jewish survival and for the survival of other peoples. *Yidishkayt* combined Yiddish with the ideas of an *arbeter bavegung, sotsyalizm, komunizm, un anarkhizm,* a worker's movement, socialism, communism, and anarchism, which resulted in its humanistic values and ethos. These political movements established the journals, magazines, and newspapers, organized the schools, libraries, cultural institutions which in turn taught, published, disseminated and popularized Yiddish literature, theater, music. They valued, preserved, and worked to expand Yiddish culture and to instill a sense of political and social responsibility among the Jewish masses. Zionists also had their own programs and politics, which differed drastically in their tenets and perspectives on relations with non-Jews. But they too promoted strong Jewish consciousness, learning, political commitment. And the great majority were secularists to the core, viewing Jewish identity as connected with a homeland and the Hebrew language, not to observance and the synagogue. There was little harmony among these secularists; rather, they existed in a continuous state of combativeness which kept each faction sharpening its politics, competing to convert the Jewish masses to its own brand of secularism through its literature, educational institutions and political agendas.

But observant and opposing secular Jews were not the only factions in the European Jewish community. There were also those who argued for assimilation—either from indifference or the self-interest of wanting to advance in the non-Jewish world or from political conviction. The latter, mainly communists, looked to a future when all differences between nationalities, cultures and religions would be erased.[9] These Jews found no value in the preservation either of Jewish identity or of Jews as a people. They rejected Judaism, Yiddish, and Hebrew, and all Jewish culture and advocated full assimilation into non-Jewish societies.[10] Active in radical and revolutionary movements, they viewed anti-Semitism as a by-product of capitalism and foresaw its disappearance if Jews abandoned their history and culture and merged with all oppressed people in the general struggle for a classless society. (Bundists and anarchists had a similar analysis, but many abandoned it after the pogroms at the turn of the century; their recognition of the special nature of anti-Semitism led them directly to accept and promote Jewish autonomy.) As the records of various political congresses at the turn of the century indicate, Jewish radical assimilationists vehemently opposed Jewish radical secularists who advocated Jewish cultural autonomy. Assimilation and Jewish secularism were clearly differentiated. Jews promoting one could never be confused with those promoting the other and there was great bitterness between them.

The heirs of the secular factions were active and still arguing in 1939. The complexity, refinements of their various positions, the splits and gradations within their individual parties provided a context and a richness to Jewish debate which we today can barely comprehend. Supported by a developed network of political, cultural and educational institutions, Jewish secularism was multi-faceted and offered specific answers and different options to Jews about how they could relate to the societies in which they lived. The sharpest conflict was between the Zionists and the Yiddish-promoting socialists, the latter rejecting the need for a Jewish state and insisting on the desirability and viability of maintaining Jewish national and cultural autonomy within the European societies in which they lived. It is a conflict that has re-emerged, in a very different form, for many of us as a result of the Israeli/Palestinian crisis.

III. Contemporary Secularism: Does It Exist?

The multitude of Jewish options that existed before World War II are ones which most nonobservant U.S. Ashkenazi Jews are hardly familiar with, much less recognize. The obvious causes for this are, of course, first, the Holocaust, which destroyed the masses and institutions which supported *yidishkayt* and Jewish secularism in Europe, and second, the establishment of the State of Israel, which permanently changed the meaning and form of Zionism.

But history is not solely responsible for our secular poverty. U.S. Jews themselves actively contributed to the undermining of Jewish secularism and *yidishkayt*. Before World War II many Yiddish-speaking European Jews were already rejecting observance and secularism. Eager to assimilate, they deliberately abandoned their Jewish language and culture. The well-known letters *(Bintl Brif)* of *Der forverts* (The Jewish Daily Forward), the thirties English stories of Anzia Yezierska, and the more modern forties and fifties Yiddish stories of Kadia Malodowsky describe this assimilation minutely.[11] The destruction during World

War II accelerated a process that was already evident in many Jewish communities. By cutting off the source of the sustaining culture of Eastern Europe, World War II created a vacuum that allowed the process to remain unchecked, and assimilation away from all forms of Jewish expression became a dominant trend in U.S. Jewish life.

As a result, the difference between secular and assimilated Jews is not even considered by most Jewish college students today. This became painfully clear to me recently after a number of informal meetings and lectures at university campuses. The word "secularism" is simply not part of this generation of Jewish students' vocabulary. With few exceptions, they define their Jewishness solely in relationship to Zionism (whose secular origins they don't even consider) and/or to the synagogue. Extremely conscious of the Holocaust, they commemorate *Yom Hashoah*, but are ignorant of Jewish European history before 1939. They've heard of Yiddish and know the word *shtetl* and are familiar with the names Sholem Aleykhem and I. B. Singer, but know nothing of the extensive cultural or political history associated with any of these. Born in the late 1960s and early 1970s, this next generation is, of course, the product of its upbringing, which almost never included Jewish secular culture and history. Raised in assimilated or semiobservant homes, educated till their *bar* or *bat mitsve* in Sunday Hebrew schools (which most of them disparage), contemporary Jewish college students are totally cut off from a Jewish heritage which was thriving just forty years ago.

A slightly older generation is not that better off. Over the past eight years, I have led and participated in Jewish identity workshops in the lesbian, women's, and progressive communities and have witnessed and experienced myself the difficulties in articulating the nature of a Jewish identity not connected to the synagogue. Until 1982, many of these Jews were comfortably active in their specific communities and did not think a great deal about either Jewish identity or about assimilation. But when Israel invaded Lebanon, they were taken off guard by the emergence of more blatant anti-Semitism and their own unexplained feelings of responsibility and guilt. For many, participation in such identity workshops was their first Jewish-focused activity in years. Many describe themselves as secularist in order to indicate they are nonobservant, proud of their Jewishness and do not want to be considered assimilated.[12] But the meaning of secularism eludes them. Nothing better exemplifies their helplessness and confusion than the two participants who isolated "warmth" and "matzoh balls" as the central components of their "secular" identity. Neither could point to anything else in herself or in Jewish culture and history.

The oldest Jewish generation, the one nurtured by Jewish secularism (primarily *yidishkayt* in its pre-Holocaust form) and rooted in its political and cultural tradition, does not provide us with clear answers either. Though some members of this generation—like those of the Association for the Preservation of Jewish Secularism and the League for Yiddish—have continued to promote Yiddish culture and literature, they represent a small minority. Isolated by a devotion to a language most Jews do not understand and have no desire to learn, they have not had a significant impact on the larger community.

The vast majority of self-defined Jewish progressive secularists are not part of this small Yiddish-based community. Though they have unequivocally maintained their identification as Jews and their commitment to political activism and social responsibility, they too abandoned the *yidishkayt* which originally shaped both their identity and politics. At a workshop organized specifically for such progressives, all found it difficult to particularize the secularism which they advocate for today. Some relied heavily on religious references for analogies and told of warm and positive experiences with grandparents whom they had accompanied to *shul*; at the same time, they strongly affirmed their present nonbelief, which, they confessed, differed markedly in its lack of hostility from their youthful rejection. Others simply emphasized they were nonobservant. Some spoke of a fondness for Yiddish, which they no longer use and which they had not passed on. Still others used their political work to define their secularism, maintaining that all or any political activism (on issues such as homelessness, Central America, etc.) is in itself an expression of Jewishness. Few seemed able to articulate the elements of a contemporary Jewish secularism which could be passed on to another generation. I was disappointed in the discussion, for it lacked the specificity, rootedness, and content that we need in order to remain strongly defined as secular Jews.

Overall, across all present Jewish generations, whether at progressive or college Hillel sponsored meetings, more and more Jews who for years were unconnected to organized Jewish communities and were indifferent to Jewish issues are suddenly becoming more conscious of their Jewishness. These Jews are angry about Israeli government policies and/or about anti-Semitic responses to those policies and now want to step forward as Jews to work for peace and/or to oppose anti-Semitism. Ignorant or forgetful of Jewish history in the States and

Europe or anywhere else, they often express themselves in tones which imply they are the first Jews to have ever acted politically. Pushed in part by anti-Semitism in the Left, by their own sense of justice, or by fear, and in part by something in them which whispers they must act as Jews, they return to the Jewish sphere experiencing contradictory feelings: a strong alienation from and anger at other Jews' "unreflective" Zionism and "empty" Jewish observance, and an equally strong desire to see themselves as Jews again—often as secular Jews—despite an inadequate grasp of their identity and a confusion about their roots.

This inability to define one's Jewishness combined with a lack of familiarity with Jewish history, culture, and politics is often a source of shame that is rarely articulated or acknowledged and that creates destructive feelings of insecurity and competitiveness over Jewish authenticity. (These, I believe, also exist in the organized Jewish community, though they are probably less obvious because of the validation inherent in membership in long-established institutions.) Sometimes these feelings are masked by an arrogance which defies other Jews to dare question our Jewish "credentials." Most often they are cloaked by a deep sense of inferiority, the kind that pervades a room when Jews come together for support for the first time, privately assess each others' backgrounds, and then feel inadequate, even illegitimate. Though U.S. Jews were quick to protest the Knesset's attempt to define "who is a Jew," it is a definition we are obsessed with. Beneath the opening pleasantries of meetings and workshops lies the very threatening question: Who is the *real* Jew in this room? The orthodox Jew? The Biblical scholar? The Holocaust survivor? The child of Holocaust survivors? The one who lived on a kibbutz for two years? The one who speaks Yiddish? Hebrew? Ladino? The one who knows the *shabes* prayer? The one who studied at a *yeshiva* for six months? The heterosexual? The Ashkenazi? The *sabra*? The one with the Jewish mother? The convert who learned what most born into Jewishness never bothered with? The answers buzz in our brains, shame us into silence. We don't dare ask questions about references or unfamiliar rituals. Some of us feel embarrassed, even terrified, that any minute we will be exposed as frauds. So we muster our courage, put on a brave face, and tough it out, trying to work towards familiarity and trust. But whatever pose we adopt externally, internally we remain lost and confused about what our "secular" identity consists of and what "Jewishness" is.[13]

IV. Resistance

Still many of us persist in wanting to satisfy our desire to define and strengthen our secular Jewish identity, though that desire is often mixed with contradictory feelings and fears. Raised to perceive all restrictions and boundaries implicit in any strong Jewish identity as reactionary and as a way of excluding other groups, we are reluctant to take decisive steps towards affirming our Jewishness. As we think more deeply about developing a clearer secular identity, we realize that it too—like observance—must take up time and energy. A true commitment to Jewish secularism inevitably means that we must make decisions—just like observant Jews—about how to structure our lives and our relations with Jews and non-Jews, how to incorporate the past (through songs, literature, holidays—traditional, contemporary, political, and historical), how to express, through contemporary fiction, theater, poetry, and political activism, our sense of ourselves as Jews as we interact with each other and with other peoples and their cultures. A true commitment to Jewish secularism inevitably also means a commitment to establishing and supporting secular Jewish institutions that provide us with a sense of community and common purpose.

Such commitment pushes us towards prioritizing our Jewish needs. Should we begin work on a Jewish secular calendar or work on helping the New York City homeless, whose numbers are growing and for whom no one has an answer? Should we begin organizing a secular Jewish institution which will address the needs of our secular identity, or help organize with NARAL and NOW in their pro-choice campaigns, or should we organize a Third World/Jewish cultural event or organize around AIDS-related issues? Or should we simply continue working on peace in the Middle East and focus our energy on influencing the Jewish community to accept negotiations with the PLO?

None of these issues or activities are, of course, mutually exclusive. But the reality is that individually no one person can work effectively on all of them. And it is in confronting these concrete choices individually that many of us become stuck. In setting our personal priorities, we judge ourselves and other Jews. Defining and setting Jewish boundaries, prioritizing Jewish concerns and Jewish needs (especially less concrete ones like identity building) are particularly difficult for those of us who have learned to value and respect other cultures and peoples. Committed to ethnic and racial diversity and integration, committed to fighting causes which do not affect us directly but which shape our society and which, therefore, inevitably affect our lives, most of us are muddled when asked to set boundaries for defining and establishing our Jewishness.

For example, during the workshop for secular Jewish progressives, many participants expressed confusion, conflict, sadness when speaking about their children—married to Jews, intermarried, gay, or single—who had little commitment to maintaining a Jewish identity. They were conscious that something has been lost, that their children's generation will never experience the kind of Jewish environment in which they were raised and which they took for granted. They realized that if we are to live Jewish lives, we must be connected, to a degree (some will argue, exclusively) to a Jewish community which embodies our consciousness of a Jewish peoplehood. They themselves never made this a central concern, for as progressives they were wary of placing such a high priority on Jewish self-definition which at moments may demand exclusion of those outside the tribe. In their inability to articulate a concrete contemporary secularism, in their regret over what had been lost, these progressives were facing the consequences of not prioritizing Jewish identity in their political lives. It was clear from what they said that they had raised a new generation of progressives, but not *Jewish* progressives.

Inner conflicts over boundaries are not limited to the older generation. For a number of years a Jewish feminist group in a northwestern city had organized seders open to the whole women's community. Though they were popular and well attended, the Jewish women ultimately felt the seders had become teach-ins or performances for non-Jews; the original intent had been lost—an event *for Jewish women* (though they were willing to share it) expressing their pleasure in Jewish celebration and connection to Jewish history and the Jewish people. Not knowing how to deal with exclusion or setting boundaries, the Jewish organizers suspended the seders all together. We seem unable to prioritize our own needs especially in a progressive context which teaches us—especially Jews—to be wary of selfishness and egocentricity.

Resistance to focusing on identity issues is also the result of deep, underlying suspicions that such a focus serves as an excuse for avoiding the more painful issue of Israeli oppression of Palestinians or of Jewish privilege in this country. Some of these suspicions are justified. As much as I don't like to admit it, I am convinced that some Jews want to use the *yidishkayt* of the first third of this century as an escape.[14] The tendency is towards a dangerous nostalgia which encourages us to identify with Jews who lived at a time when the occupation didn't exist and when Jews were the major target of non-Jewish hatred. To further emphasize the image of Jew as victim, some advocates of Yiddish culture simply erase its political component. They emphasize and make an icon out of a word like *shtetl* or a name like Tevye, Sholem-Aleykhem's ever-questioning, but ultimately ever-obedient, observant Jew. For these Jews it is more comfortable to think of Eastern European Jews not as defining history—and despite the pogroms, the anti-Semitism, the later purges, Jews did have influence on their own history and the history of others—but rather as "a vulnerable people who have lived on the outside of power for a thousand years."[15] But this is pure romance. It's an image of Jews and Jewish life that makes us feel better about ourselves after reading the day's news of Israel's actions against the Palestinians. Historically such a time never existed. Eastern and Western European Jews and struggling Jewish immigrants here in the States were neither completely passive nor pacifists in World War II or before that.

Before that—? Jewish men served in various European armies, sometimes willingly, sometimes by force. Jewish workers—men and women—staged strikes, often violent. Various Jewish political groups organized self-defense organizations. Political enemies fought each other with weapons which were not limited to words. To claim otherwise is to erase the historically documented active Jewish participation in European life as well as the less picturesque Jewish underworld of gangsters, alcoholism, prostitution, violence, wife and child abuse.[16] Emphasizing the seemingly more pious stories of Sholem Aleykhem and Peretz, stressing Jewish passivity over action, obedience to tradition over rebellion (and therefore upholding observance), many supporters of Yiddish and Yiddish culture have wrenched *yidishkayt* out of the active, political and radical context in which it flourished and thereby neutralized and depoliticized it. Institutions like YIVO (Institute for Jewish Research) and the National Yiddish Book Center—both of which remain underfunded and which deserve our unqualified support for their dedication in preserving archives and books which are the repositories of *yidishkayt*—unfortunately often foster the nostalgia in which Yiddish is becoming increasingly enveloped.

Proponents of Yiddish are not the only Jews caught up in nostalgia. U.S. Zionists too have done little to foster an atmosphere in which Jewish identity and the relations between the Diaspora and Israeli Jews can be examined. For many, Zionism was inherited at birth and they now think of it as synonymous with Jewishness. The threat of being labelled a traitor for questioning Israeli policies, and the allegation of self-hatred and anti-Semitism have inhibited an in-depth study of Zionism, its diverse political tenets, its history in relation to other Jews and to non-Jews and its role in defining Jewish identity in the States. They have promoted an automatic, unthinking rhetoric which, as the *intifada* continues, has become increasingly exposed as hollow. For many U.S. Zionists, contemporary Israeli society and life are completely obscured by nostalgic images and stories of struggle and survival of early Zionist settlers and of fighters in the War of Independence. This nostalgia associates the "settlements" on the West Bank (completely equipped Jewish towns containing modern housing, schools, stores, and public transportation) with the settlements of those who made *aliyah* in the 1920s under difficult, to say the least, physical conditions.[17] In reality, the Israel of 1990 is not the Palestine of the 1920s or 1930s—not physically, ideologically, or politically and U.S. Zionists have stubbornly refused to discard mythology and to examine history and the Israeli-inflicted abuses on Palestinians in the Occupied Territories—killings, administrative detentions, expulsions, home demolitions, collective punishment. Just as many contemporary Yiddishists romanticize and depoliticize the past, so do most contemporary Zionists romanticize and depoliticize the Israeli present.[18] Such nostalgia is rightfully condemned by those who want Jews to engage in the political present. But these critics erroneously conclude that any focus on their Jewish identity will inherently foster Jewish escapist tendencies.

One final Jewish concern which reinforces some progressives' resistance to dealing with Jewish identity (and this is the most difficult to address) is the Holocaust. In the last twenty years, memorializing the Holocaust, particularly in the U.S., has created a new but what I consider very distinct and destructive form of secularism. This form makes the Holocaust the core of Jewish identity. Even the most assimilated Jew knows something about the Holocaust and can claim some connection to Jewish history through it. As someone touched directly by the events of the war, I am committed to its memorialization, to understanding its implications historically and psychologically. But being conscious of the complex Jewish life before the Holocaust, I am disturbed to see U.S. Jews whose concept of Jewish history is limited to the years 1939-1945 and whose sense of Jewish authenticity derives solely from those years. These Jews place the Holocaust at the center of their

Jewishness, rely on their parents' experience to legitimize themselves, look to Jewish victimization and anti-Semites to define and shape their identity. To be born a child of survivors is to be a *real* Jew. One need not be or do anything else. A commitment to such a secular identification keeps us stuck in the past and is dangerous, for it distorts Jewish history, commits us to a lifetime of mourning, and prevents us from fulfilling obligations to engage with the present.[19] Only by placing the Holocaust in a larger framework, by insisting on moving toward a Jewish future that is informed, but not defined, by the Holocaust, can we develop a productive way of relating to each other and the rest of the world. Such an approach guarantees memory, without sacrificing the present or future.

The admission that the motives behind some Jews' advocacy of certain forms of Jewish identity or promotion of specific Jewish concerns are misguided or even deliberately manipulative does not invalidate all work towards defining and rebuilding Jewish identity. I have focused on these abuses because it's important to acknowledge their existence. I am always conscious, particularly as a result of reactions to my political peace work, that some Jews have grossly manipulated other Jews' feelings—fears of anti-Semitism, the desire to commemorate the Holocaust, the urgency of committed Yiddishists, the real fears of Jews for Israel's security—feelings which I myself experience. These misuses, however, should not deter us from the real issue: how we define our identity as Jews determines our politics and how we express them. As long as we allow either anti-Semitic and misinformed progressives to limit our concept of Jewish identity or reactionary Jewish promoters of nostalgia to limit the sphere of our political action, we will never extricate ourselves from the current identity-versus-politics tangle in which most progressive Jews find themselves. We must claim this area of concern for ourselves, on our own terms. By devoting ourselves to clarifying and establishing a secular identity as it was practiced before World War II we can, in fact, find the very answers which nostalgia and escapism currently block.

V. *Khaloymes*/Dreams in Progress

When pressed about a future secularism, I have no specific answer. The next generation's secularism is neither predefined nor predestined to be one way or another. Rather, it is something still to be invented after we have begun to shape and inform our lives by Jewish traditions, by Jewish history, by our commitment to having a Jewish future in this country. As in the past, the next generation's secularism will not be monolithic, but will express itself in a variety of forms, espousing different politics, different interpretations of Judaism, different conceptions of our relationship to other Jewish communities, including Israel.

This secularism will only develop, however, if we are able to pick up the threads of a heritage we are now only dimly aware of. We will guarantee another generation a Jewish future if we educate ourselves about the history of Jews, ancient and modern, about Jewish literature—probably in translation from Ladino, Yiddish, Hebrew and all the languages in which secular Jews and observant Jews wrote. We need to know how Jews were politically active in other societies, how they fought for the general as well as for their own good. This knowledge will help establish a secular Jewish calendar of Jewish traditional, historical, and cultural dates around which we can structure our lives and will become the content for the Jewish secularism we want to preserve. Once we have internalized this Jewish content, we can begin to describe our pleasure and rootedness in our culture and history through new poetry, theater, fiction, music, and other arts. And only then will our political commitments, including the two states—Jewish and Palestinian—have a context which allows us to struggle for the right of Palestinians without depleting ourselves, without giving into despair.

This secularism is not easily developed. Though it doesn't dictate the sequence and exact texts of our studies, though it doesn't tell us at what time of day we conduct them—it does demand a place in our lives. At some point those of us who are from assimilated backgrounds have to stop blaming history or our parents for denying us what was rightfully ours and take responsibility for shaping our own Jewish identity and future. And those of us who had rich Jewish backgrounds and are not assimilated, but who have been transformed by feminism, gay politics, and the politics of the Left, must stop longing for an irretrievable past, must give up expectations which cannot be met. Let's face it: we will never again experience the same emotions we felt when we attended *shul* with our grandparents; we will never again be present at the kind of seders we attended as children. We are in transition. Most of us are not trying to preserve traditions; rather, we are trying to discover and learn them and also to reinterpret them from a contemporary perspective. Because our Jewish events are shaped by our new consciousness, often what we attempt—gatherings, discussions, feminist or gay celebrations of traditional holidays—seem strange, awkward, even artificial. This does not mean they are not Jewish or valid or that nothing can come of them. It does mean they are new. We are experimenting, and in the process we're forging traditions for the future.

To help myself I often turn for parallels and models to the historical *yidishkayt* in which I was raised. It is not a tradition which we can or even should want to duplicate, but it serves as a fine example for combining culture, politics, Jewish concerns, and concern for others. The contemporary secularism I seek will do the same. Its proponents will be willing to use the Arabic word *intifada* and take the next logical and only possible step: public support of Israel and Palestine. Secularists will carry a banner at Gay Pride parades and give public support to gay and lesbian Jews. I have seen no better example of the intermingling of the old with the contemporary, the cultural and political, than Jewish gays identifying themselves as *"dos freylekhe folk"*—the happy (gay) people at the 1989 New York City Gay Pride March.[20] Like feminism, lesbian and gay rights will be incorporated into contemporary secularism openly, boldly, without hesitation. So the secularism I advocate does not take us out of the fray, but keeps us active as Jews in both the Jewish and non-Jewish worlds in which we live.

A major cause for Jews' alienation from Jewish institutions—secular and observant—is their refusal to be fully integrated. Established institutions are fragmented and compartmentalized and, as a result, the Jewishness they promote consists of a smattering of observance, loyalty statements to Israel, neutrality in controversies. Usually when a Jewish organization does take on one issue, it refuses to take on others. If it includes women and gays in its structure and concerns, it excludes Palestinians. If it promotes Yiddish, it refuses to take on the political nature of *yidishkayt*. There is little out there that integrates all our concerns, that helps deal with boundaries, that establishes the do's-and-don'ts of secularism, politically and culturally.[21]

So an institution willing to address multiple concerns—cultural and political—is a great need. Repeatedly that need is expressed by lesbians and heterosexual feminist mothers who are not drawn to Jewish observance even in its more contemporary and reformed formulations. They have children to whom they want to pass on a Jewish consciousness, a Jewish sense of self, of history. "What should we teach them?" they ask. Or another friend who teaches a Jewish class, talks about her concern that the curriculum does not get beyond Biblical stories and holidays.

"There's so much else to teach them. What should be the priority?" she asks. Or another woman discusses the possibility of establishing progressive secular Jewish schools and asks me what I think they should teach and I, in turn, ask: "Who is equipped to teach secularism? Where will the teachers come from?" Each discussion makes clear that there is no quick fix. Concrete material is needed and we'd better start researching it, writing it, developing a formal legacy, and creating the context in which it can be absorbed and passed on. Some secular Jews are talking about developing a secular curriculum for children as well as for adults. The curriculum would encompass a number of concerns and their interrelationships: identity questions, secular history and culture, and political responsibility.

Schools or institutions teaching such a curriculum would encourage debate, would risk offending, would risk unpopularity. They would provide us with an understanding of what it means to be a responsible Jew, what it means to be a Jew responsive to the world around her. The establishment of such institutions is critical, I believe, and cannot be put off, as some would argue, until the Israeli crisis is over. It must take place *now* as the peace work in the Middle East continues. Just as we must not allow our strong commitment to developing Jewish secularism to detract from the struggle in the Middle East, that conflict cannot be used to allow assimilation to take over our lives. It is true that the balance is hard to achieve. So we must provide ourselves with the supportive contexts that will enable us to find the balance. Only then will we understand what motivates our activism, what feeds our commitment and our sense of responsibility and caring about Israelis and Palestinians.

Epilogue

In her often-quoted poem *"Froyen lider"* (Women poems), Kadia Molodowsky wrote of Jewish women who appear in her dreams:

> *Es veln di froyen fun undzer mishpokhe*
> *bay nakht in khaloymes mir kumen un zogn...*
> (The women in our family will come to me in my dreams at night and say...)

Written in 1920, the words are stark and unambiguous: *"undzer mish-*

pokhe"—our family—the Jewish people, clear and simple, easily identified by the language they spoke—the Yiddish speakers of Europe, of the world. Kadia was rooted in her world and its history. Her writing echoes with the richness of the Yiddish culture which she loved, but which she was also conscious erased women and women's lives. As she herself says in this poem, she was a page torn from a book whose first line is illegible. Still, when Kadia dreamed, she knew and remembered who and what she dreamed of.

In 1990 my dreams as a Jew and a poet are murkier and not as easily remembered. My knowledge of *"undzer mishpokhe"* is more vague, more limited because of the Holocaust, and because much of my Jewish education was not active in the world and has faded. Though I too love Yiddish culture, I am more distant from it; I have yet to absorb its full richness. And my perspective as a Jew is vastly different because Jewish geography and consciousness have changed drastically since *"Froyen lider"* appeared. My vision of *di froyen fun undzer mishpokhe* includes Sephardim who speak Arabic and Ladino, proud lesbians, *sabras*, rabbis, single mothers, witches, elected government officials, and so many more. Some of them appear before me as individuals, others as shadows longing for daylight to disclose their identity. I am conscious of their presence, conscious that they are waiting for recognition as sisters: Jewish women of the past who cared passionately about the Jewish people and about other peoples, Jewish women today who continue the struggle. I want to learn more about them, for it is they who help me define who I am and show me how I can act as a Jew, a woman, a lesbian. They offer me the courage and confidence to move into the future.

Notes

1. *"Mentshklekhkayt"* in Yiddish means both "humanness" and "humaneness." Here I'm using only the first meaning.

2. I am aware of the religious power and the general sexism dominant in *shtetlekh* and cities, as illustrated in Chaim Grade's depiction of pre-war Vilna in *The Agunah*, *however*, Jews who wanted to break away from this religious tyranny could do so and were not restricted by laws they did not believe in, as they are in Israel.

3. Socialists, anarchists and other radicals and revolutionaries, of course, argued about the validity and implications of Zionist ideologies before 1939. After 1948 the Yiddishists whom I'm most familiar with, however, did not continue this debate. Most became Israel supporters, and I never heard a systematic analysis of the implications for socialist politics. This may be simply a limitation of my own experience.

4. This is the first time I have used the term "fascism" publicly in relation to certain

political elements in Israel. I believe it has become appropriate to do so, even though it feels dangerous. On the other hand, with persistent talk of massive transference of Palestinians from the Occupied Territories and possible increase in the number of settlements, it feels dangerous *not* to use it.

5. At the "Jewish Feminist Conference" of the (NYC) Jewish Women's Resource Center, December 3, 1989, Aviva Cantor spoke of the neglect by organized U.S. Jewish institutions of Jewish education, the elderly and poor, abuse and violence against women, feminist issues. She connected this neglect to our preoccupation with Israel and fundraising for Israeli institutions.

6. Nothing exemplifies this more starkly than *Jewish Possibilities: The Best of Moment Magazine,* ed. Leonard Fein (Northvale, NJ: Jason Aronson Inc., 1987). This anthology has virtually nothing on secular identity outside of Zionism (60 pages are devoted to a section on "Israel,"), but does devote 150 pages to "The Pursuit of Religious Meaning." The rest of the book, "The American Jewish Experience: Explorations in Identity" and "The American Jewish Experience: Threads and Themes" focuses primarily, under different titles, on experiences in relation to the synagogue. This is particularly strange since Leonard Fein identifies as a secular Jew in *Where Are We.* The assumption that Jewishness resides only in observance is also found in Susannah Heschel's *On Being a Jewish Feminist: A Reader* (New York: Schocken, 1983), which primarily addresses the implications of Jewish observance and Israeli laws for Jewish women, but makes no mention of Jewish secularism (outside of Zionism).

One exception is *Jewish Currents,* a magazine which continues to promote secularism and *yidishkayt.* Each monthly issue contains a balance of cultural and political material and keeps pointing back to Jewish history for sustenance and strength. Subscriptions are $15 and can be obtained from *Jewish Currents,* 22 East 17th Street, Suite 601, New York, NY 10003-3272.

7. The history that follows is necessarily quite general and simplified. I'm interested in providing a broad framework for various forms of secularism at the turn of the century rather than giving details about their different geographic origins (Eastern and Western Europe), political goals, and attitudes toward religion. Before the *haskalah* movement, Jews in Europe and in Spain were active in politics, arts, and science. They were assimilationists rather than secularists, though they held on to their Jewishness through marriage, which helped consolidation of family power.

8. The first Yiddish language conference ever organized, it aimed to legitimate a language that most considered "jargon." The Conference drew such famous Yiddish figures and activists as Nathan Birnbaum, I. L. Peretz, Sholem Asch, Avrom Reizen, H. D. Nomberg, and Chaim Zhitlovsky. There was enormous tension between those who promoted Yiddish and those who promoted Hebrew and some writers, who used both, felt cornered. A resolution to make Yiddish *the* national language of the Jewish people was passionately supported by Esther Frumkin, a Bundist and later communist; she walked out when it was agreed that Yiddish would be recognized as *a* national language. I am astonished to find that the newly published *Blackwell Companion to Jewish Culture* contains no entry for Czernowitz, nor is it mentioned in its section on Yiddish. Only entries about individual participants contain references to it. Standard writings about Yiddish by Irving Howe and Nora Levin have ample information about this historic event.

9. A small minority of communists did support Jewish cultural autonomy and promoted Yiddish language and culture.

10. Others tolerated Yiddish if it was used to support party policies.

11. See Molodowsky's collection *A shtub mit zibn fenster* (House with Seven Windows) (New York: *Farlag Matones,* 1952) in which she documents with irony and sometimes great sarcasm the decline of Yiddish and of Jewish knowledge and values. Typical is one of the opening stories, "*Shabes ru*" (Sabbath rest), in which the main characters go to the bank and play cards. Molodowsky's consciousness of assimilation away from Yiddish and Yiddish culture is also evident in the journal she edited, *Svive* (Environment), from 1960 till 1972, two years before her death.

12. Clare Kinberg first explained to me that the motive for using the term secular is the

desire to affirm Jewish identity and unequivocally to dissociate oneself from assimilationists.

13. For an explicit discussion of this sense of inadequacy, see Evelyn Torton Beck and Nina Rachel's "Mother and Daughter, Jewish and Lesbian," in *Nice Jewish Girls*, pp. 16-27.

14. A good example is Aaron Lansky's "*Yiddishkeit* [sic] and Jewish Renewal" in *Genesis 2* (Autumn, 1989) pp. 26-31. Part of this section of my essay is based on my response, "*Yidishkayt,* History and Politics: Another View," which never appeared because *Genesis 2* stopped publication.

15. For a discussion of Jewish power, see David Biale, *Jewish Power and Powerlessness in Jewish History* (New York: Schocken, 1986).

16. Bernard Goldstein's *Tsvontsik yor in varshever bund 1919-1939* (Twenty Years in the Warsaw Bund) and L. Berman's *In loyf fun yorn: zikhroynes fun a yidishn arbeter* (The Flow of Years: Memoirs of a Jewish Worker) describe an Eastern European Jewish life that is not readily acknowledged by many contemporary advocates of *yidishkayt*.

17. See Rachel Katsnelson Shazar, ed., *The Ploughwomen: Memories of the Pioneer Women of Palestine,* trans. Maurice Samuel (Herzl Press, 1975).

18. Rita Falbel was the one who stressed that nostalgia was prevalent in all Jewish political spheres.

19. As I write this essay, I find an article in *The New York Times Magazine* (April 22, 1990), "Holocaust Museum: A Troubled Start" by Judith Miller. The article describes the degree of preoccupation with the Holocaust and its big business aspects. The cost of the museum is estimated now at a million dollars. See also my essay, "Resisting and Surviving America" in this volume.

20. Students of Uriel Weinreich's *College Yiddish* will recognize the echo of translation exercises in which the word "gay" (happy) becomes "*freylekh*." For a photograph of the gay and lesbian Yiddishists at that march, see *Bridges,* Vol. 1, No. 1, (Spring 1990), p. 67.

21. Typical of such fragmentation is the Reconstructionist Rabbinical College, which advocates feminism and tolerates to some degree lesbians and gays. Yet in the early summer of 1989, it fired Arthur Waskow because of his statements on Israel. On the other hand, New Jewish Agenda is an organization that is trying to fulfill multiple needs. It recently adopted resolutions to implement its long-standing commitment to cultural and historical education.

About the Transliteration

IN THE TRANSLITERATION OF YIDDISH WORDS, THE AUTHOR HAS FOLLWED the rules established by YIVO Institute for Jewish Research and generally accepted by international linguistic organizations. The YIVO guidlines have also been followed for the transliteration of Hebrew words used in Yiddish. Well-known transliterations of the titles of books, poems, organizations and documents that do not follow the YIVO guidelines have been left as they are known.

About the Author

Irena Klepfisz was born in Warsaw, Poland in 1941 and emigrated to the United States in 1949. Educated in New York City public schools and Workmen's Circle Yiddish schools, she attended City College of New York and received her Ph.D. in English Literature from the University of Chicago. Over the past twenty years she has taught English, creative writing, Women's Studies, and Yiddish. An activist in the lesbian/feminist and Jewish communities, she was a founder of *Conditions*, a feminist magazine emphasizing the writing of lesbians, the co-editor of *A Tribe of Dina: A Jewish Woman's Anthology* and co-editor of *A Jewish Women's Call for Peace: A Handbook for Jewish Women on the Israeli/Palestinian Conflict*. She is the author of *A Few Words in the Mother Tongue, Poems Selected and New (1971-1990)* which was published in 1990 by The Eighth Mountain Press as a companion volume to this one.

About the Cover Artist

Marcia Barrentine did the artwork and designed the cover for *Dreams of an Insomniac: Jewish Feminist Essays, Speeches and Diatribes*. She is a graphic designer and artist who lives in Portland, Oregon. The cover art is loosely based on designs found on Eastern European Jewish documents and artifacts.

About the Book

The text typography was composed in Palatino. The cover typography was composed in Seagull . The book was printed and bound by Baker Johnson on acid-free paper. *Dreams of an Insomniac: Jewish Feminist Essays, Speeches and Diatribes* has been issued in a first edition of five thousand of which five hundred are clothbound.

The Eighth Mountain Press was formed to publish literary work of exceptional quality written by women. We began in 1982 with the publication of limited edition letterpress poetry broadsides and published our first trade paperback in 1985. For a complete catalog of books in print, send a 45¢ stamp along with your name and address to The Eighth Mountain Press, 624 Southeast 29th Avenue, Portland, Oregon 97214.

In 1988 we launched The Eighth Mountain Poetry Prize, an annual contest for a book-length manuscript. The winning poet receives an advance of one thousand dollars upon publication in the prize series. For full details about the contest, send SASE to The Eight Mountain Poetry Prize at the above address.